Visual Arts

for the IB Diploma

Heather McReynolds

Cambridge University Press's mission is to advance learning, knowledge and research worldwide.

Our IB Diploma resources aim to:

- encourage learners to explore concepts, ideas and topics that have local and global significance
- help students develop a positive attitude to learning in preparation for higher education
- assist students in approaching complex questions, applying critical-thinking skills and forming reasoned answers.

CAMBRIDGE
UNIVERSITY PRESS

University Printing House, Cambridge CB2 8BS, United Kingdom

One Liberty Plaza, 20th Floor, New York, NY 10006, USA

477 Williamstown Road, Port Melbourne, VIC 3207, Australia

314–321, 3rd Floor, Plot 3, Splendor Forum, Jasola District Centre, New Delhi – 110025, India

103 Penang Road, #05-06/07, Visioncrest Commercial, Singapore 238467

Cambridge University Press is part of the University of Cambridge.

It furthers the University's mission by disseminating knowledge in the pursuit of education, learning and research at the highest international levels of excellence.

www.cambridge.org
Information on this title: www.cambridge.org/9781009190701

First published 2017

20 19 18 17 16 15 14 13 12 11 10 9 8 7 6 5 4 3 2 1

Printed in Poland by Opolgraf

A catalogue record for this publication is available from the British Library

ISBN 978-1-009-19070-1 Paperback with Digital Access (2 Years)

Additional resources for this publication at www.cambridge.org

Contents

本书凡涉及Hong Kong, Taiwan, Macau (Macao), Tibet等地区的表述应为：Hong Kong, China; Taiwan, China; Macau (Macao), China; Tibet, China。

Contents

Introduction

0.1 Welcome

This student book is designed as a guide and companion to the International Baccalaureate (IB) Diploma Programme (DP) Visual Arts course (first examinations 2016). It will help you to understand the aims and objectives of the course, what is expected of you, and how to go about achieving it.

You will be introduced to the ideas and the language that underpin the course, and offered practical advice for navigating your way successfully through the requirements. The book will support and encourage you while you engage in your individual journey of inquiry, investigation, reflection and creative application in art.

Figure 0.01: ***Daydream*** **by student Sage Dever (mixed media collage on board). With freedom to explore a variety of art forms, ideas and different approaches, students can discover their own modes of visual expression.**

0.2 Who is this book for?

This book is for students taking the two-year Visual Arts course for the IB DP, part of Group 6, The Arts (first examinations 2016).

Although the IB Visual Arts course will appeal to students who wish to study visual arts in higher education, students with no previous experience will also benefit from it.

The course not only builds art-making skills and confidence but helps students to develop important analytical skills, divergent ways of thinking and creative problem-solving. Reflecting the IB emphasis on international-mindedness, students are encouraged to explore art from a wide range of contexts and practices, thus broadening their understanding and appreciation for the diversity of creative and aesthetic expression.

The study of art is much more than just a training of the eye. Through the study and practice of visual arts we are cultivating attention to the act of observing, and in doing so we learn to perceive the world differently, as well as art.

> Art is about paying attention.
> (Laurie Anderson)

Standard level or higher level

The course may be taken at standard level (SL) or higher level (HL). There are additional assessment requirements for HL: students explore art-making techniques in more depth and breadth and produce a larger, more considered body of work, with added awareness of the viewer's relationship. They also reflect more on how other artists have influenced their own work.

0.3 What is the IB Visual Arts course about?

The course revolves around three main aspects of art practice: theoretical practice, art-making practice and curatorial practice. As an IB Visual Arts student, you are all of these: a critic, a maker and a curator. Let's consider what these mean and what your learning objectives are for each one.

Theoretical practice (the critic)

Using investigative strategies, critical thinking, comparative analysis and reflection, you will examine various art forms and artists from different times, places and cultures. You will investigate different techniques and processes, enquiring into their contextual evolution. You will explore ways of communicating knowledge in both visual and written forms.

Art-making practice (the maker)

Through exploration and experimentation you will discover and apply a variety of artistic techniques. You will develop your own concepts throughout this explorative process and, with reflection and self-evaluation, produce a considered body of work.

Curatorial practice (the curator)

Through careful, informed viewing of artworks and exhibitions you will develop an ability to formulate your own considered response. You will begin to articulate your intentions for developing and displaying your own work. You will also consider the relationship between artist and audience and what it means to exhibit work; learn to select and present your own work effectively; and articulate your intentions and the connections between your artworks.

Figure 0.02: Seeing and experiencing art first-hand will help you to develop your own informed response. Whenever possible try to visit exhibitions, galleries and artists' studios to experience the work yourself. In Rudolf Stingel's *Untitled*, 2003, the artist invited viewers to interact with the aluminium foil covered walls by scratching, writing, pinning notes, or otherwise engaging in acts that would normally be considered vandalism of an artwork.

The visual arts journal

The visual arts journal is a central element of the course and you are required to maintain your journal throughout your study. The visual arts journal links together the three practices of theory, art-making and curating. You can use your journal to record your work on all aspects of the course – your critical investigations and reflections, your experiments with media and techniques, and your ideas, plans and intentions.

Your journal is not directly assessed but it contributes significantly to your comparative study (CS) and process portfolio (PP), which are externally assessed. Chapter 2 discusses the pivotal role of the visual arts journal in the course.

0.4 How is your work assessed?

You are required to submit your work on three major tasks for final assessment. The assessed components are as follows:

Part 1: Comparative study (externally assessed, 20%)

This is an independent critical and contextual investigation in which you explore artworks from differing cultural contexts. Both SL and HL students compare at least three different artworks, by at least two different artists, in a presentation (visual and written) over 10–15 screens. In addition, HL students reflect on how their own artwork and practices have been influenced by any of the art/artists examined (3–5 screens). (Chapter 7 looks in detail at the CS.)

Part 2: Process portfolio (externally assessed, 40%)

You are required to compile carefully selected materials, documenting your experimentation, exploration, manipulation and refinement of a range of visual arts activities during the two-year course. The presentation comprises 9–18 screens for SL students and 13–25 screens for HL students, and must demonstrate at least three different art-making forms. (Chapter 8 looks in detail at the PP.)

Part 3: Exhibition (internally assessed, 40%)

You are required to submit documentation (images or video) of a selection of resolved artworks from your exhibition. This is a coherent body of work, which shows evidence of technical skills, and that is thoughtfully considered, presented, and supported by a curatorial rationale. SL students submit 4–7 pieces, with exhibition texts and a curatorial rationale (max. 400 words). HL students submit 8–11 pieces with exhibition texts and a curatorial rationale (max. 700 words). (Chapter 9 looks in detail at the exhibition.)

(This is a brief summary. Chapter 10 explains the assessment procedures and includes tables that reference the assessment criteria.)

0.5 The learner profile

The IB believes that students today are responsible for shaping a better world tomorrow. The qualities set out in the IB learner profile are positive human characteristics that aspire to a model of international mindedness and to the creation of a more peaceful world.

The learner profile is reflected throughout the Visual Arts learning objectives, embracing a range of qualities that extend well beyond technical proficiency and academic learning.

As IB learners we strive to be:

- inquirers
- knowledgeable
- thinkers
- communicators
- principled
- open-minded

- caring
- risk-takers
- balanced
- reflective.

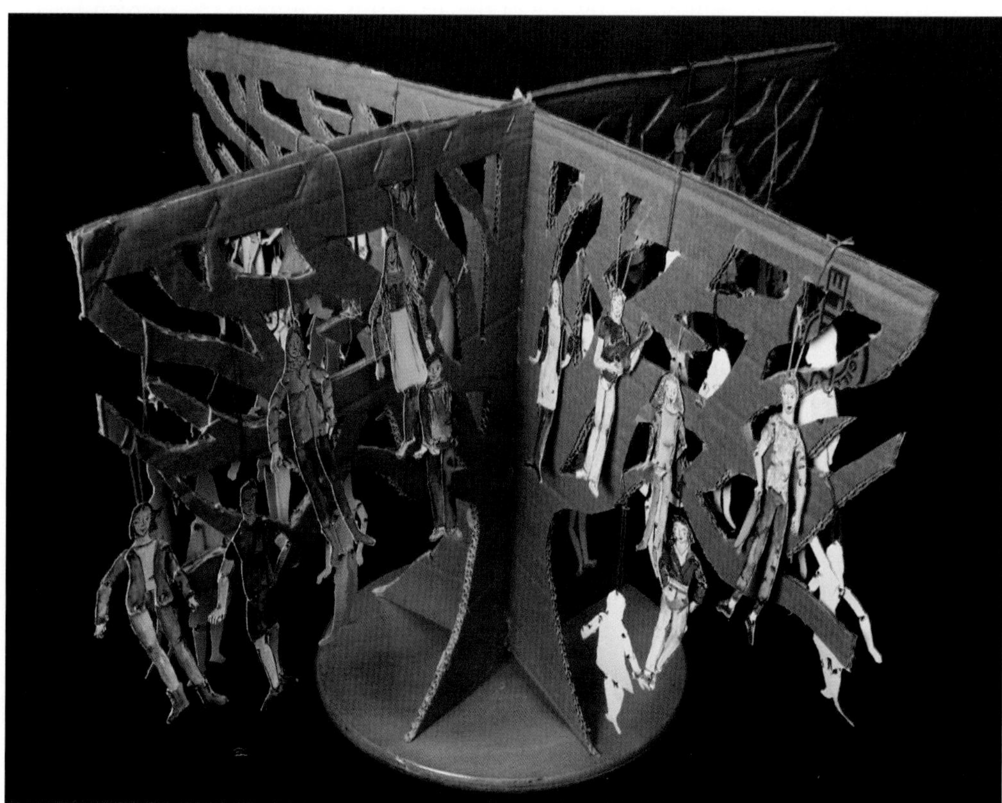

Figure 0.03: ***Tree of Life*** **by student by Julia Granillo Tostado (cardboard, paper and watercolour). Julia describes the piece as 'a tree of life, consisting of 50 movable puppets that are based on real people, experiences and conversations that surround me, helping me grow and develop'.**

0.6 The IB core

Supporting the IB learner profile are three other elements at the 'core' of the DP, which should all form part of your learning experience. These are: TOK, the extended essay, and creativity, action, service (CAS).

Theory of knowledge

In the TOK course you explore forms of knowledge through the natural sciences, the social sciences, ethics, history, mathematics, and religious and indigenous knowledge systems, as well as the arts. TOK also requires you to reflect on different ways of

knowing, including reason, emotion, sense perception, intuition, imagination, faith and memory, and to consider how knowledge is arrived at in the various disciplines.

TOK invites you to think critically and challenge your existing belief systems. For the art student it presents rich opportunities for asking questions that will inform your art-making investigation and practice.

Creativity, action, service

Many links can be made between the visual arts and CAS: exhibitions, workshops, productions, design, costumes, graphics, mentoring, murals and on-and-off campus projects. Put your creative skills to work, but remember, CAS activities must be distinct from the course requirements for any subject.

Extended essay

All DP students are required to write an essay (4000 words maximum) on a topic of their choice, based on independent research. For the art student with a particular area of interest to explore, visual arts may be an appealing subject area for this in-depth research paper. Visual arts topics may include fine art, design, architecture and aspects of contemporary visual culture. Students are strongly recommended to engage with primary sources, seeing and experiencing the work themselves whenever possible. (The extended essay is discussed further in Chapter 10.)

0.7 How to use this book

This book, like the Visual Arts curriculum, is meant to be approached as a whole rather than as distinctly separate units. The knowledge and skills that you need as a visual artist are explored in all the chapters. Each component of the course overlaps and influences the others, just as theory and practice inform and influence each other in art. The focus of each chapter is as follows:

- In Chapter 1, 'Start exploring', you will identify creative starting points for exploration using different visual and conceptual approaches.
- In Chapter 2, 'The visual arts journal' you will look at the visual arts journal and its pivotal role in the course.
- Chapter 3, 'Culture and place' contributes to your understanding of culture and context, and has significant links to the CS.
- Chapter 4, 'Materials and meaning' looks at different art-making forms and relates to both your PP and your work for the exhibition.
- Chapter 5, 'Developing focus' is about digging in deeper, developing and sustaining those initial explorations, and developing a body of work for your final exhibition.
- Chapter 6, 'Curating and presenting' will help you to develop your own curatorial practice and curate your own exhibition.

- Chapters 7, 8 and 9 are dedicated to the three assessed components (and supported by all the other chapters):
  - The CS (covered in Chapter 7)
  - The PP (Chapter 8)
  - The exhibition (Chapter 9).
- Chapter 10, 'Visual arts assessment' explains how the IB DP Visual Arts course is assessed and is your go-to point for assessment criteria tables and task requirements.

This coursebook therefore functions both as workbook and as a back-and-forth reference: you may follow the chapters sequentially, or move around the book as you take what you need at any given point in your progress.

The coursebook features

This coursebook contains several special features, which are designed to enhance your learning experience. They are outlined below.

ACTIVITIES

There is a wide range of activities in each chapter. Your teacher or tutor may set some as tasks, or you can use them as jumping-off points for your independent work. They are offered as seeds of inspiration for you to cultivate, as challenges to push you further, or simply to feed your desire for new experiences.

TOK and art

Throughout the book you will find a set of theory of knowledge (TOK) questions designed to provoke a conversation. TOK is a core aspect of the IB DP that encourages students to think **critically and curiously** (see also 'The IB core'). The study of Visual Arts offers many deeply provocative questions, from how we make value judgements to the meaning of originality. Hopefully some of these will lead you into unexplored territory, raise new questions, incite curiosity and bring insight into how you construct your own beliefs.

Your teacher may use these questions as discussion points or assign them as individual journal reflections. You may choose questions of particular interest or relevance to your own investigations and develop them as critical reflections.

STUDENT EXAMPLES

The examples of students' work shown throughout the book have been generously contributed by real IB art students from around the world. The work shown is of a generally high quality so as to be aspirational. Examples are not intended as prescriptive: they represent each student's individual approach, so please view them as examples, not prototypes. There are as many ways to make art as there are human beings in the world!

CASE STUDIES

The case studies are intended to provide a more in-depth view of one student's way of working on a particular task. These case studies are only a small sampling – they do not represent the student's entire body of work. Again, these examples are not intended as models but rather as insightful windows into how others approach the course work.

SPOTLIGHT ON THE STUDENT

This feature is an inside glimpse of a given student's areas of artistic interest, the topics and ideas they are looking at and thinking about, and the artists who have influenced their investigations and art-making practices.

Tip: This feature provides additional advice on how to meet the assessment objectives by highlighting key issues, including pitfalls to avoid, and suggesting time-saving strategies.

Key terms: This feature lists art terms mentioned in the text, with definitions.

0.8 Exploring unknown territory

IB Visual Arts is an enquiry-based and largely self-directed course. Although there are assessment objectives that serve as guidelines, the specific content of each of these is for you to decide, challenging your own creative and cultural expectations and boundaries. You will choose the artists that you want to investigate, the techniques you want to develop, and the ideas and concepts that you wish to explore. As you become more discerning you will be able to recognise your strengths and learn from your failures, discover the methods that work for you, and set your own personal goals and pursue them courageously. There is no specific set of questions (you come up with your own), and no right answers.

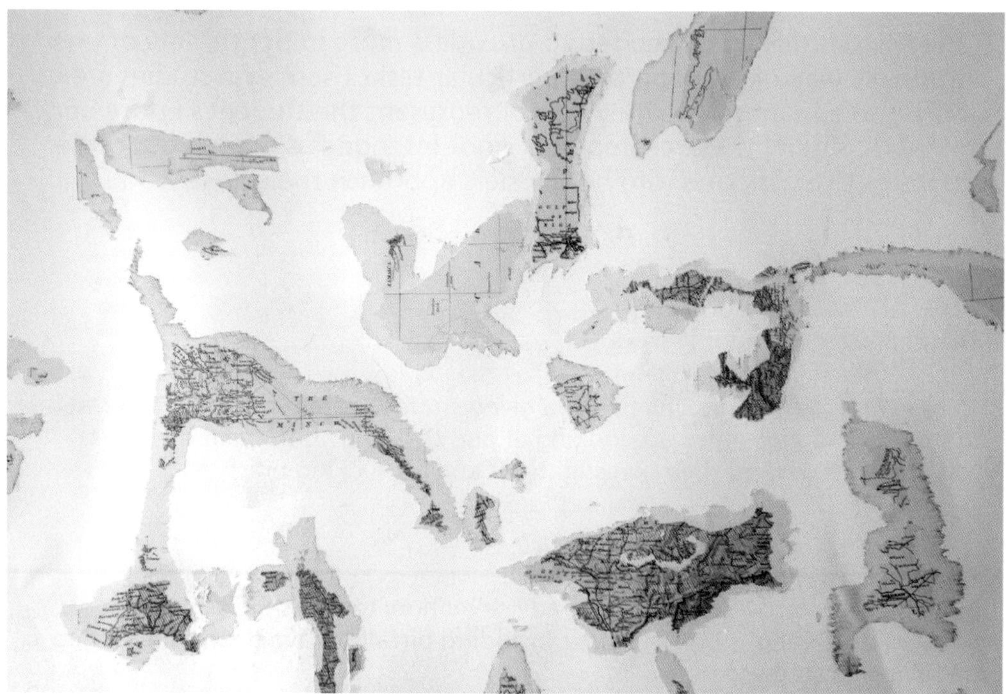

Figure 0.04: Detail of *Shift Happens*, by Heather McReynolds. This piece was made of maps torn from a world atlas and reconfigured into a new, unrecognisable map of the world.

This book can provide a sort of road map, with key features and main highways highlighted, but you are invited to chart your own path across this territory. As Georgia O'Keefe said:

> Whether you succeed or not is irrelevant – there is no such thing. Making your unknown known is the important thing – and keeping the unknown always beyond you.

Enjoy your journey!

Chapter 1

Start exploring

Introduction

This chapter examines how inquiry, exploration and reflection inform all of art-making. We will look at a range of strategies for getting started in the course with various activities for making discoveries, building confidence, considering different visual and conceptual approaches, playful exploration and self-reflection.

LEARNING OBJECTIVES

- Identify creative starting points for exploration.
- Experiment with ways of looking, thinking and making.
- Explore an idea using a variety of visual approaches.
- Engage in creative discovery through play.
- Explore how to transform failures.
- Through the above, develop higher-level thinking skills.

Figure 1.01: Art begins with exploration. Exploration is led by curiosity, fed by investigation and developed through intentional experimentation and reflection.

1.1 Starting strategies

Starting strategies are entry points, activities to get you looking, thinking and creating. While these are mainly suggestions for getting started, you can come back to them at any time during the course when you are stuck for ideas.

- Create a viewfinder (cut a rectangle from a piece of card) and use it to frame different **compositions** within the same view, then record it in your journal.
- Enlarge something tiny using a gridding system.
- Collect multiples of one thing: many different-shaped leaves, bus tickets, teabags. Create a method of display with labels. Photograph or draw this in your journal.
- Collect things in varying **hues** of the same colour. Arrange your collection into a composition. Document it. Give it a title.
- Look for found patterns, and record them with rubbings and drawings in your journal. Note where each pattern was found.
- Take something apart and put it back together in a completely different way that alters the form and the function.
- Make a 3D piece of work that fits in a matchbox.
- Choose a building or a landscape in your area, and draw it in chalk or charcoal at different times of day, observing the changing light, like Monet's paintings of Reims Cathedral.
- Select a small square section of the earth and meticulously record it, like Dürer's piece of turf.
- Design something to place on an altar. Explain why.
- Reinterpret an artwork in a completely different medium: for example, make a video of a drawing, or a construction of a painting.
- Make something ugly. Make something beautiful.

Composition: Composition in art refers to the arrangement of visual elements (shapes, lines, colours, forms) and their relationship to each other.

Hue: Hue refers to the gradation or intensity of a colour, such as 'the brilliant hues of autumn leaves'.

Start with something

Take an object. Do something to it. Do something else to it.
(Jasper Johns, 1964)

There are an infinite number of things you can do to an image, or to an object. In 1964, American **pop artist** Jasper Johns famously made this note in his sketchbook: 'Take an object. Do something to it. Do something else to it.' We might even say that making art is a series of decisions enacted on an image or an object, or an idea. Do something to it, then something else, and something else; through persistent visual exploration you can evolve and change even the most boring thing into something interesting – art? Maybe.

Pop art: Pop art was an art movement of the 1950s and 1960s in Britain and America. The artists of the pop art movement drew their imagery from popular culture, mass media, advertising and consumerism, often with an ironic or critical undertone.

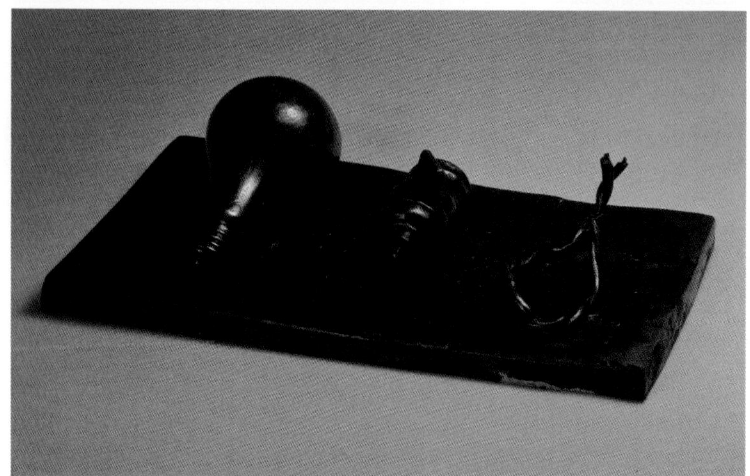

Figure 1.02: Jasper Johns, American pop artist, *Bronze, c. 1960-1*. Johns plays with the idea of low and high culture, taking a banal object from everyday life and elevating it to the status of 'fine art'.

In the 1960s, sculptor Richard Serra's interest in materials and the physical process of making sculpture led him to compile a list of action verbs: 'to roll, to crease, to curve', which he then carried out using the materials he had collected in his studio.

ACTIVITY 1.1: TAKE AN IMAGE. DO SOMETHING TO IT . . .

Make different-sized good-quality prints of a single image. Carry out the following actions by drawing, collage or a combination.

- Remove something.
- Expand or enlarge a portion.
- Fragment it.
- Simplify everything.

Continue to change it with your own actions.

> It struck me that instead of thinking what a sculpture is going to be and how you're going to do it compositionally, what if you just enacted those verbs in relation to a material, and didn't worry about the results? (Richard Serra)

ACTIVITY 1.2

Instead of an image, start with a piece of (choose one) rubber, fabric, wood, metal, plastic ... and so on.

'Enact these verbs' on your chosen material:

- Roll it.
- Bend it.
- Fold it.
- Rearrange it.
- Turn it upside down.
- Mirror it.
- Divide it.
- Compress it.
- Expand it.

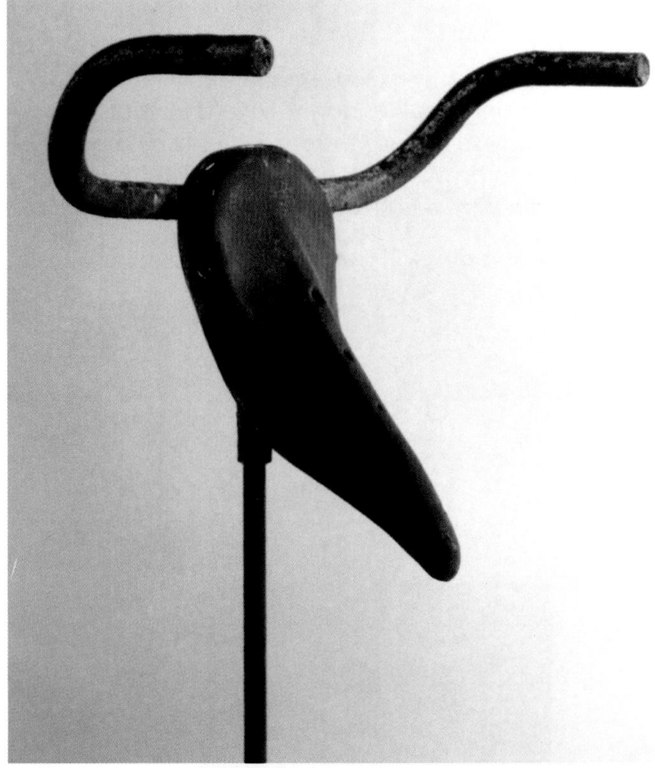

Figure 1.03: Pablo Picasso, *Bull's Head*, 1942. In this ready-made Picasso combines two objects, a bicycle seat and handlebars, and there you have it: a bull's head!

Ready-made: A 'ready-made' is a commonplace object or combination of objects selected and presented as an artwork. Marcel Duchamp created the first ready-made (*Bicycle Wheel*, 1913) by mounting a bike wheel on a stool. Duchamp and members of the Dada movement challenged the conventional notions of what is art and influenced much of the art that followed – including pop art, which took its subject matter from everyday objects of pop culture, and conceptual art, which values the artist's idea over the actual product.

ACTIVITY 1.3: READY-MADE AUCTION

Create your own ready-made from a found object or objects, give it a title and present it to the class. Be prepared to defend it as ART! Stage an auction of the works, just for fun. See which pieces are convincing enough to hold value.

Art lives from constraints and dies from freedom.
(Leonardo da Vinci)

What do you think Leonardo meant by this? How does having set limitations encourage creative thinking?

TOK and art: Language and art

- Does art need to be explained?
- Can an idea be more important than the physical artwork?
- How does a title influence our reading of an artwork?
- Can the ability to discuss and defend your ideas carry more weight than the actual piece itself?

1.2 Looking, thinking, making

This section offers the opportunity to carry out a comprehensive activity, the object study. The study shows you how to look at a single object in depth and breadth, considering its visual qualities, form and function, context and meaning. The activities in the object study will enable you to generate many valuable visual journal pages, which you could also use in your process portfolio. As the object study has many parts to it, you could develop your work on it over several weeks.

ACTIVITY 1.4: OBJECT STUDY

a) **Choose an object** that interests you for both its visual qualities and its symbolic value, preferably something small enough to hold in your hand. This will be your object of study so choose thoughtfully. It helps if the object has an interesting shape to draw, and lends itself to multiple meanings (for example, an apple, an egg, a lightbulb or even a teacup!).

b) **Draw your object from different viewpoints.** Try unusual points of view, distortion, changing scale.

Figure 1.04: Page from student Ewa Nizalowska's visual arts journal. Ewa takes a simple object (a common drinking glass) and using different drawing media, contour lines, shading and reflections, she observes it from different points of view.

Figure 1.05: Ewa practises observational drawing of a glass, using cross-hatching to create subtle variations in tone. She has written 'This is not a glass' boldly across the top of the page, referring to René Magritte's famous painting *The Treachery of Images*. With the addition of this text, she is introducing a conceptual way of thinking about the object and representation in general.

Figure 1.06 *The Treachery of Images*, 1929, by Belgian Surrealist René Magritte, is a painting of a pipe with the words 'Ceci n'est pas une pipe' (This is not a pipe) painted underneath. The painting depicts an image of a pipe but it is a painting, not a pipe, making the point that an image is a representation of a thing, not the thing itself.

c) Place in different contexts and draw. Alter the surroundings, the composition, colour and/or juxtaposition (place it next to something else). How does this affect the meaning of the object?

d) Use different materials to interpret your object, such as pencil, paint, clay, words, fur, print, photo, film, cardboard, wax . . .

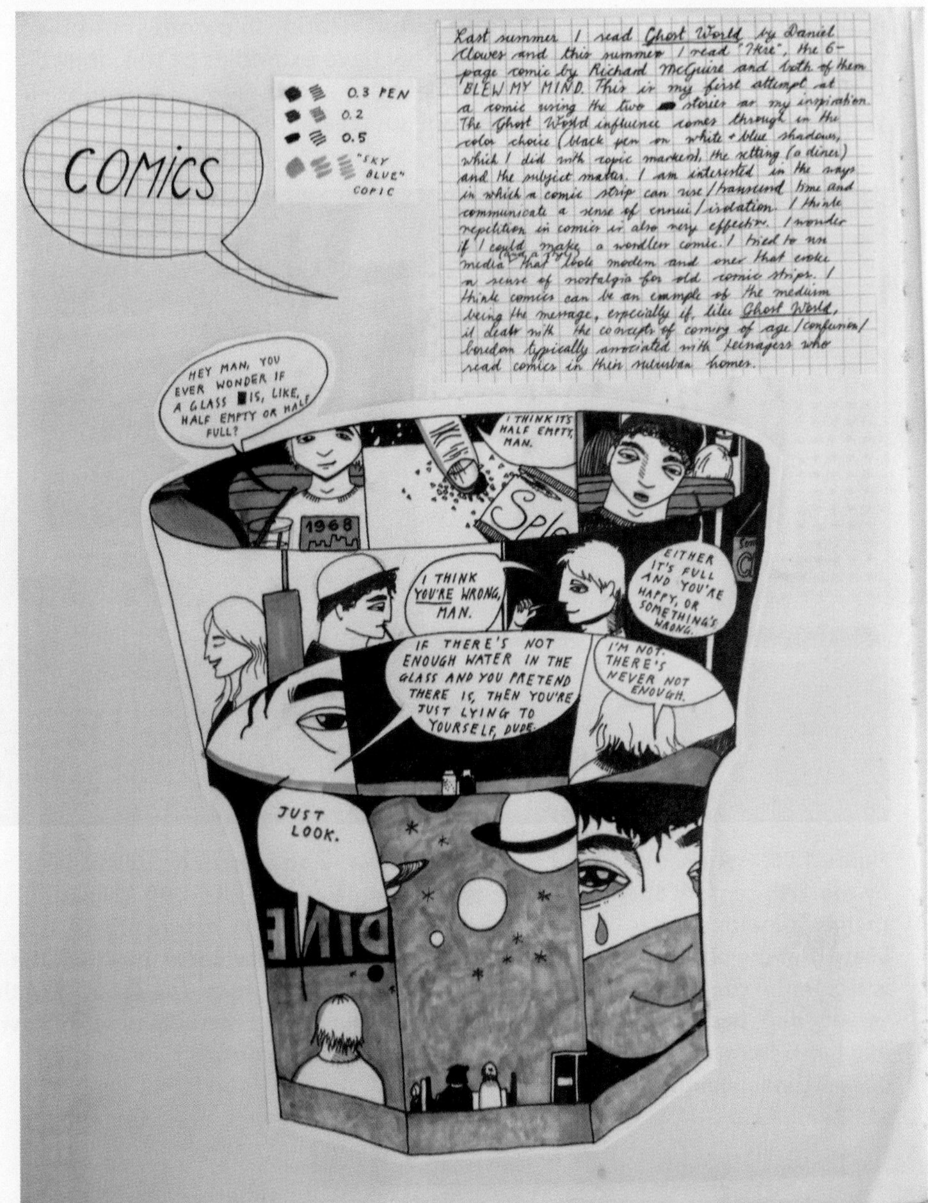

Figure 1.07: In this drawing, Ewa has turned her glass into a cartoon in which the characters discuss the notion of 'the glass half empty or half full', in a humorously philosophical take on teenagers in suburban homes.

Iconography: The use of a symbol or specified image associated with a subject or theme in art.

Vanitas: A still-life painting genre of the 16th and 17th centuries, mostly Dutch, that references the transient nature of life through the use of symbols of death and decay: for example, skulls, hourglass, jewels, fading blossoms, rotting fruit. Vanitas is the Latin term for vanity, the vanity of wealth and clinging to earthly existence. These pictures were intended to remind people of their mortality and the passing nature of all things. Ironically they became desirable worldly possessions themselves.

e) **Consider possible meanings and symbols.** What is the significance of your object: inherent, attributed and invented?

f) **Consider the historical and cultural context.** How has this object evolved in time? Consider the design: how was the object used in the past? What is its cultural **iconography**, its role in technology and its social significance?

g) **Make connections to other artworks.** What relationship does your object have to art history and other artists? How have examples of this object been addressed by others? Make connections and use visual examples in your journal (remembering to cite your sources).

Figure 1.08: Francisco de Zurbarán, *A Cup of Water and a Rose*. A rare still life by the 17th-century Spanish painter, who often painted works with religious themes, or with *vanitas* (works that reference the transitory nature of life). It is likely that the objects depicted here also have a religious symbolic function: the water in the cup signifies purity and the flower a 'mystic' rose. The contrast of the velvety dark background and the luminous objects evokes the duality of shadow and light, form and emptiness, life and death. It is also a delightful example of observational painting.

ACTIVITY 1.5: MIXED MESSAGES

- Read the caption to Meret Oppenheim's *Object*. What messages do the materials in this artwork communicate?
- What do you think is meant by the phrase 'Art . . . has to do with spirit, not with decoration'?
- Now combine two unlikely materials to create a new message of your own.

Spirit, not decoration

The materials an artist uses may have their own inherent significance already, and when materials are combined in unusual ways they can create new meaning altogether. (Chapter 4 takes a closer look at this topic.)

> Art [. . .] has to do with spirit, not with decoration, Meret Oppenheim.

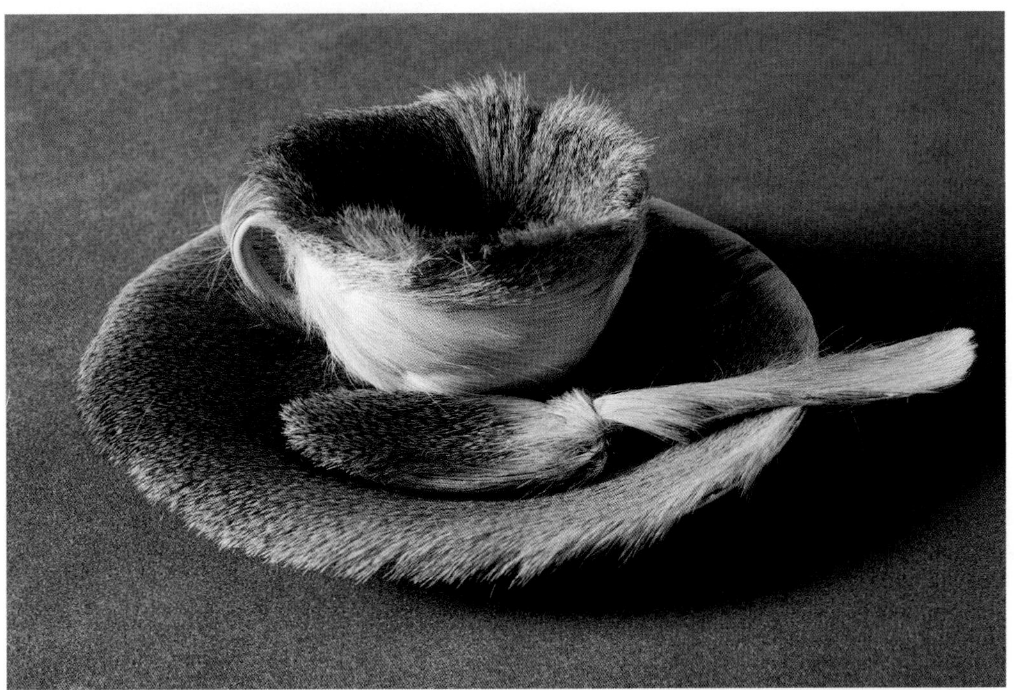

Figure 1.09: Meret Oppenheim, *Object*, 1936. This piece (also known as *Breakfast in Fur*) began as a joke. The artist took a porcelain teacup, covered it in fur and gave it the title *Object*. '... a work as small and economical as Object has such outsized spirit because fur combined with a teacup evokes such a surprising mix of messages and associations. The fur may remind viewers of wild animals and nature, while the teacup could suggest manners and civilisation. With its pelt, the teacup becomes soft, rounded, and highly tactile. It seems attractive to the touch, if not, on the other hand, to the taste: imagine drinking from it, and the physical sensation of wet fur filling the mouth. This humorous juxtaposition of unlikely materials and their connotations earned Oppenheim a reputation as a Surrealist artist'. (http://www.moma.org/learn/moma_learning/meret-oppenheim-object-paris-1936)

Surrealist: Historically, the Surrealists were a group of artists, writers and intellectuals in Europe between First and Second World Wars who responded to postwar society's rigid order by creating works that intentionally challenged rational ways of thinking. Led by the poet André Breton, the Surrealists made work that arose from the unconscious, from dreams and the imagination. When we say an artwork is Surrealist we mean that it is not bound by the rules of the conscious, rational mind.

1.3 Fun and games

On those days when inspiration is elusive, or your inner critic is being particularly harsh, you could try a more playful approach. When we are free from the expectations of perfection we are able to experiment and make mistakes without fear of failure. A playful approach can introduce a sense of lightness into the serious business of making art. You might even find that through play and accident you make some discoveries worth pursuing (seriously).

Juxtapose: To juxtapose is to place things next to each other in contrasting relationship. The Surrealists used juxtaposition by rearranging everyday things in ways to create new meaning, challenge reason and open the doors to the freedom of the subconscious mind.

Figure 1.10: "There's some wonderful things in the world" a playful piece of sculpture by artist Maurice Citron using a cable drum and exercise balls. Maurice says *I love making things that end up surprising me.*

ACTIVITY 1.6: (DE)FACING THE BLANK PAGE

That crisp white page or canvas can be pretty scary sometimes. Here are a few ways of getting over the fear of making the first mark:

- Spill a cup of tea on your paper and begin a drawing from the stain.
- Walk on your paper, making footprints.
- Rub the page all over with charcoal and buff it off so you have a nice atmospheric surface to work on.
- Erase an old drawing you don't like, almost all the way – now start drawing on top of this ghostly image.

Figure 1.11: Joan Miró, *The Beautiful Bird Revealing the Unknown to a Pair of Lovers* (from the *Constellation* series), 1941 (gouache, oil wash, and charcoal on paper). Miró recalled how he began these small works on paper: 'I dipped my brushes in solvent and wiped them on the white sheets of paper with no preconceived ideas.' Then he drew animals, stars and other whimsical figures on the already marred surface.

ACTIVITY 1.7: DRAWING WARM-UPS

These warm-up drawing exercises require you to focus completely on looking at your subject; they also help you to loosen up and let go of expectations . . . You might even be pleasantly surprised by the results!

- Draw with the 'wrong' hand.
- Draw blindfolded or without looking at the paper.
- Draw an object you can feel but can't see, held under the table.
- Draw with chalk taped to a very long stick.
- Draw symmetrically, with a pencil in both hands.
- Draw, with a continuous line, a figure who is moving around the room.
- Try a collaborative drawing (see Activity 1.8).

Figure 1.12: Blind drawings by student Polina Zakharova. Polina drew her classmates without ever looking down at the paper. Drawing like this forces you to relinquish control of the outcome and surrender to the act of looking.

In the 20th century, the Surrealist artists brought a sense of play into art-making, favouring approaches that involved elements of unpredictability, chance, unseen elements and group collaboration – all to disrupt the waking mind's desire for order. They would play a collaborative, chance-based game, typically involving four players, called 'cadavre exquis' (exquisite corpse). This was originally a game based on words, resulting in nonsensical phrases, but it developed into one using drawing, resulting in absurd combinations of drawings.

ACTIVITY 1.8: CADAVRE EXQUIS

All you need is three or four people, paper and pencil, but collage works well for this too. Each person begins by making a 'head' on a piece of paper then passes it to the next person who makes a 'body', and so on. The work has no individual ownership; it is truly collaborative. Warning: this activity may generate ideas that are absurd, whimsical and wild!

ACTIVITY 1.9: TAKE A COLOUR WALK

Pick a colour and follow it wherever it appears, down the street, through a museum, wherever it leads you. Notice the variety of **hues** within a colour range. Can you find an interesting way to document your colour walk?

Figure 1.13: This 'exquisite corpse' collage from 1938 is by the Surrealist artists André Breton, Jacqueline Lamba and Yves Tanguy. It depicts a body that is part human, part mechanical and part mannequin.

1.4 Failures and transformation

Sometimes things don't work out as we would like them to. In fact, the number of successful art works produced by most artists is probably far fewer than the number of unsuccessful ones. One solution might be just to make lot of work to increase the likelihood of getting a good one!

Of course we have to be able to define what we mean by 'successful' and 'unsuccessful' work. Discernment is an important part of IB DP Visual Arts. You need to learn to recognise your stronger work and, just as importantly, to see what is weak or unresolved, and reflect on this constructively.

Your less-successful works are as much a part of your learning process as the successful works; one cannot exist without the other. It is the so-called 'failed' pieces that point the way to something else – sometimes by knowing what we **don't** want to do we understand what we **do** want to do. When confronting a disappointing piece, you might ask yourself what you could do differently. Then forgive yourself: you are not defined by your 'failures'.

> The seed for your next artwork lies embedded in the imperfections of your current piece. Such imperfections (or mistakes, if you are feeling particularly depressed about them today) are your guides – valuable, reliable, objective, non judgemental guides – to matters you need to reconsider or develop further. It is precisely this interaction between the ideal and the real that locks your art into the real world and gives meaning to both. (From *Art and Fear: Observations on the perils (and rewards) of art making,* David Bayles and Ted Orland.)

> Everything I needed to know about creativity I learned by making mistakes. (Tanner Christensen, product designer)

Artist Susan Hiller deals with failed paintings in a different way: In *Painting Books and Painting Blocks* she reconfigures old unwanted paintings on canvas as books, or sewn together as blocks. The paintings are given a new chance at life as a different art object.

Tip: Record your critical reflections on your successes and failures to include in your process portfolio (covered in Chapter 8) as part of the progression and development of your work.

Figure 1.14: Susan Hiller, *Painting Books and Painting Blocks*, 1972–84, two series of previously exhibited paintings, reconfigured in sculptural formats. (Top, open: *Big Blue*, 1976. Bottom: *Three Painting Blocks*, dated with size of originating works.)

> Artists have a vested interest in our believing in the flash of revelation, the so-called inspiration . . . shining down from heavens as a ray of grace. In reality, the imagination of the good artist or thinker produces continuously good, mediocre or bad things, but his judgement, trained and sharpened to a fine point, rejects, selects, connects . . . All great artists and thinkers are great workers, indefatigable not only in inventing, but also in rejecting, sifting, transforming, ordering.
> (Friedrich Nietzsche, in *All Too Human*, 1878)

Inspiration: where does it come from?

To inspire literally means to breathe in. Inspiration is simply whatever we take in from outside us. Each one of us creates our own opportunities for inspiration – it doesn't just descend from above (or very rarely).

ACTIVITY 1.10: TRANSFORMING FAILURES

Give an unsatisfactory piece of work a new life. Deconstruct it and put it back together in a different way, making it into something else altogether.

Figure 1.15: *Detonate* (ceramic and glaze) by student Eleanor Wells. Eleanor reflects on how her piece *Detonate* was the result of an accident: 'I was looking at the work of Cornelia Parker, whose work is inspired by destruction and often incorporates broken fragments. When one of my ceramic pieces exploded in the kiln, I decided to create a new artwork, with glazed pieces piled on top of one another. These form a volcano structure ready to explode – a volcano made of pieces that are the result of an explosion!'

However, if you look for inspiration, it is everywhere – it's a matter of paying attention and being curious. If you give something your full attention – a human face, a humble leaf, a maths problem – you may be surprised to find there are infinite possibilities for creative exploration. Making art is 99% perspiration and 1% inspiration . . . so don't wait for inspiration to visit you – go look for it, and sweat it out!

Summary

This chapter is designed to help you enter into the spirit of art-making with curiosity, seeding ideas for you to build upon throughout the course. The starting strategies in this chapter have launched you into a playful exploration of ideas for making art. You have experimented with a range of activities using different visual and conceptual approaches. You have seen how this kind of exploration can help you start thinking about and making art. Now you are ready to follow those ideas, developing your own lines of inquiry, deepening your knowledge of artists and techniques.

(Chapter 5 looks at cultivating individual areas of focus in your art-making and developing a coherent body of work.)

Chapter 2

The IB visual arts journal

Introduction

This chapter looks at the pivotal role of the visual arts journal in your course. All students are required to make a visual arts journal. The journal brings together many aspects of your learning process, including research, analysis, reflection, experimentation and personal response. There are many ways to work in your journal: this chapter shows some examples of the sorts of work you could include.

Figure 2.01: The IB visual arts journal is a place to record your first-hand observations, personal reflections and experiments with media, along with your ideas and their development, and your responses to the world around you and to the art and artists you encounter.

LEARNING OBJECTIVES

- Consider how artists use sketchbooks and journals.
- Use the visual journal to develop your skills and techniques.
- Use the visual journal to develop your ideas and intentions.
- Develop good research skills.
- Reflect on artists, artworks and on your own developing work.

2.1 Artists' sketchbooks and journals

> I should recommend . . . keeping . . . only a small memorandum-book in the breast-pocket, with its well-cut sheathed pencil, ready for notes on passing opportunities: but never being without this. (John Ruskin, *The Elements of Drawing*, 1857)

For an art student, artists' diaries both past and present provide valuable insights into the sometimes mysterious creative process. People often keep journals as a record of observations and reflections on life: an artist's journal is also the record and observation of the artistic process. These depositories of the inner life and evidence of the artists' way of thinking can be a great source of information when researching an artist for the comparative study (CS).

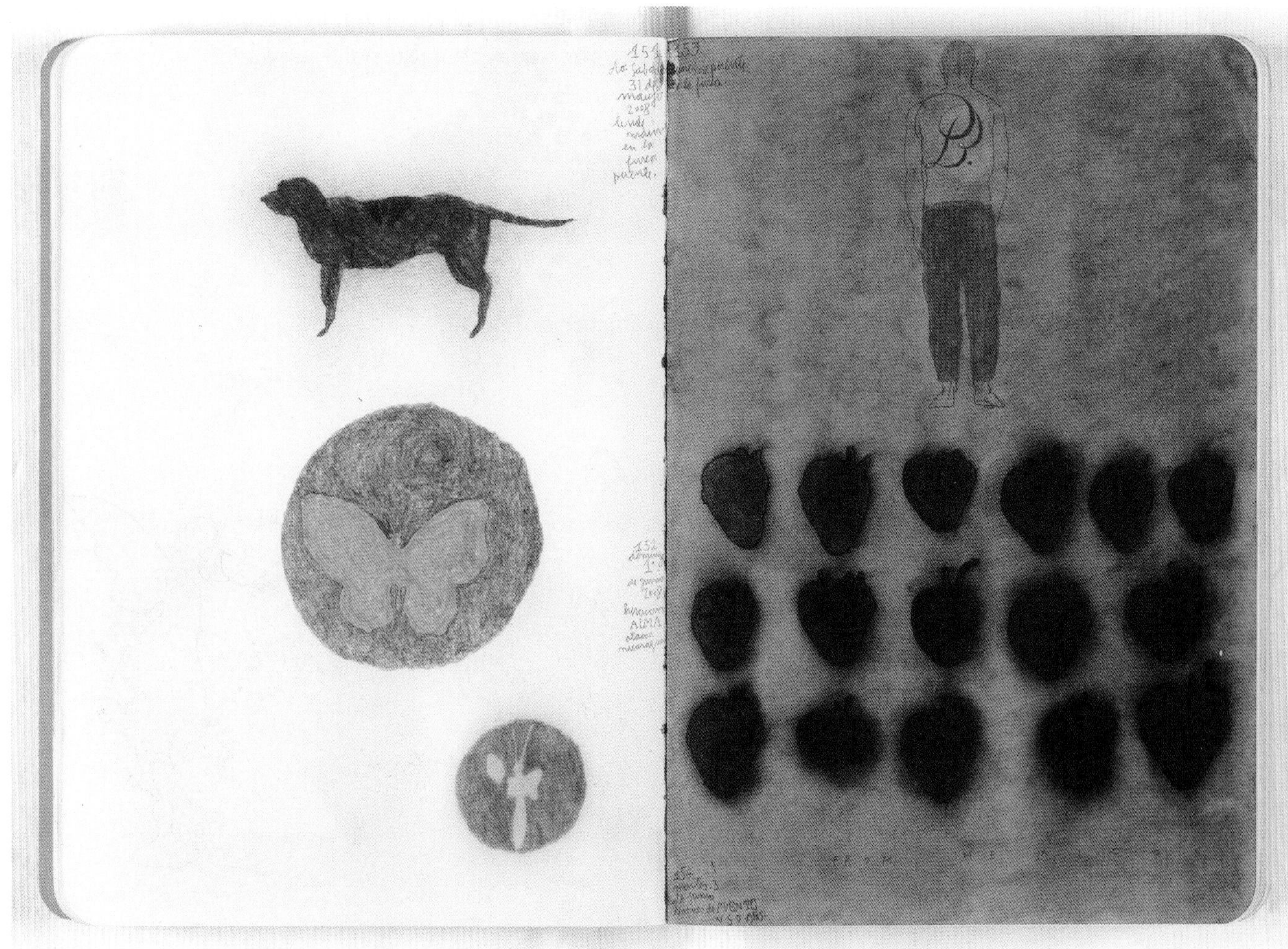

Figure 2.02: Colombian artist José Antonio Suárez Londoño's notebooks, which he refers to as 'yearbooks', are an ongoing project in which he creates a drawing a day in a small sketchbook. These drawings are based on a particular book or a series of books he is reading over the course of a year.

The IB visual arts journal

Not every artist keeps a journal, and those that do have many different approaches: Degas's sketchbooks are primarily observational, Frida Kahlo's diary is an expressive outpouring, Paul Klee's diaries teach, Eva Hesse makes diagrammatic drawings, Leonardo da Vinci works things out, Suárez Londoño keeps a 'yearbook' with a drawing a day. Most artists' journals are a combination of notes and images, but graffiti artist Keith Haring's journals contain more words than images, and sculptor Henry Moore's sketchbooks are surprisingly full of drawings of woolly sheep! What you are aiming for in your IB visual arts journal (your artist's journal) is a balance of both visual and written content, in your own unique style.

ACTIVITY 2.1: LOOK INSIDE THE BOOK

Find out about an artist by studying their sketchbook and journals.

- **What is the relationship between the journal and the work the artist makes?**
- **What are the connections between your work and this artist's work?**
- **Record your reflections in your own visual journal.**

ARTIST'S SKETCHBOOKS AND JOURNALS

Leonardo da Vinci's notebooks

Keith Haring Journals

The Diaries of Paul Klee

Gerhard Richter, *The Daily Practice of Painting*

Frida Kahlo's diary

Louise Bourgeois's diaries

Suárez Londoño, *The Yearbooks*

The sketchbooks of Degas, Delacroix, Giacometti, Eva Hesse, Henry Moore, Frank Lloyd Wright

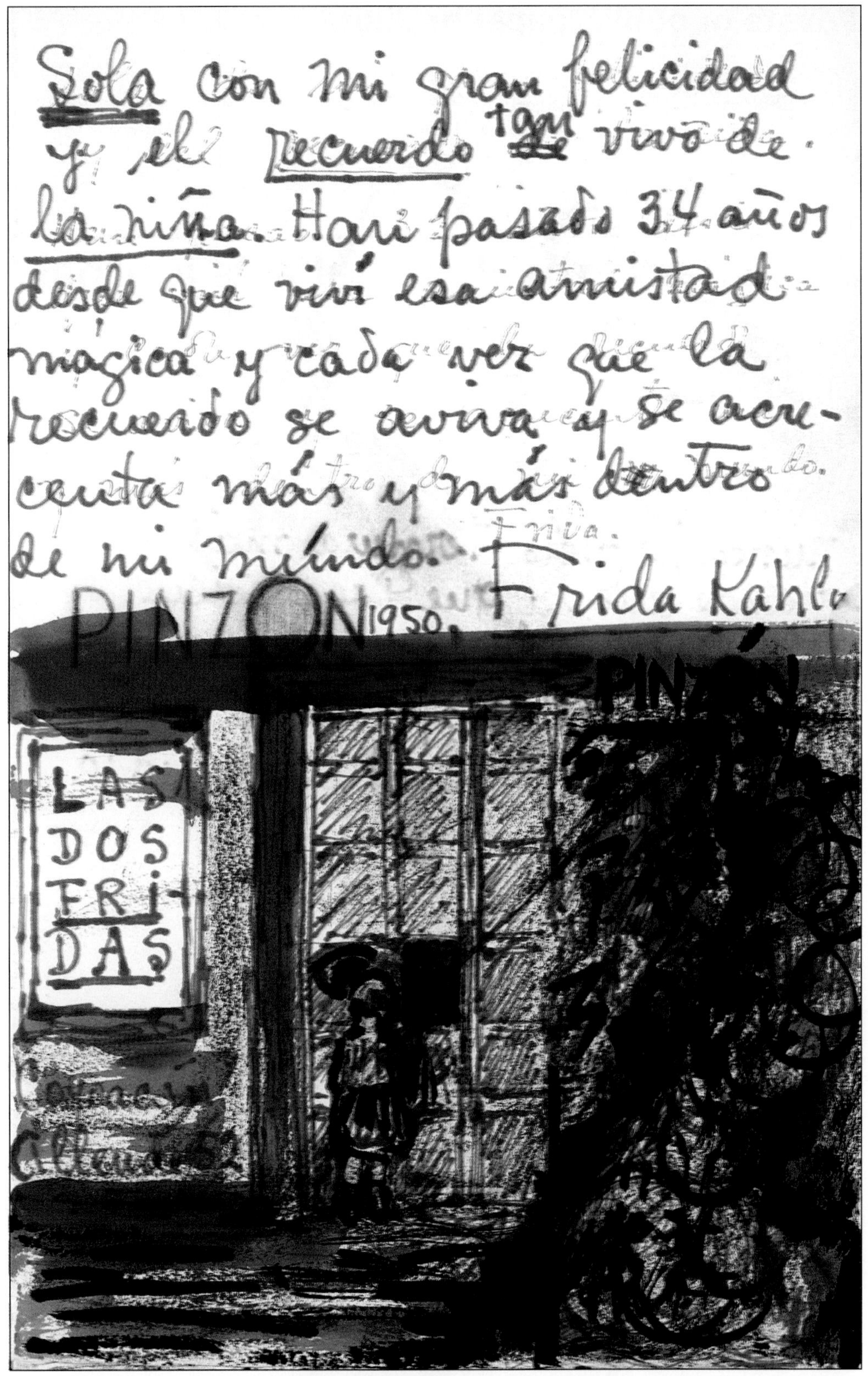

Sola con mi gran felicidad
y el recuerdo tan vivo de
la niña. Han pasado 34 años
desde que viví esa amistad
mágica y cada vez que la
recuerdo se aviva y se acre-
centa más y más dentro
de mi mundo.
PINZON 1950. Frida Kahlo
PINZON
LAS DOS FRIDAS

Figure 2.03: Frida Kahlo's colourful journal is half intimate personal diary, half artist's sketchbook, just what you might expect from an artist whose work is so emotionally driven.

Private or public, paper or digital?

Today, many artists use social media: websites, blogs, Facebook, Tumblr and Instagram. These online 'journals' are often open to the public. Ideas about privacy are shifting. The formats may be changing, but are the contents? How is an online diary different from a diary in book form? What other forms might a diary take?

Tip: Make working in your journal a regular habit, documenting your process as you go along. You can also make notes of useful feedback from teachers and peers as well as your own reflections on your development. Include investigations and detailed analysis of artists, art works and exhibitions you have seen. Record your responses to the world: collect ideas as well as images, things you have seen or read that could be a starting point for investigation.

2.2 What is the IB visual arts journal?

All art students are required to have a visual arts journal as their own record of the course. The journal is intended to support the development of your skills and nurture the elaboration of your ideas. The visual journal is much more than a sketchbook; in some cases it might not even take the form of a sketchbook!

A rich and varied visual journal in which you continually record your work is invaluable as a record of your artistic journey and as the source from which you can extract material for the three assessed components: the CS (discussed in Chapter 7), the process portfolio (PP; Chapter 8) and the exhibition (Chapter 9). The journal itself is not handed in for final assessment but any of the materials that you submit may be compiled from your journal pages.

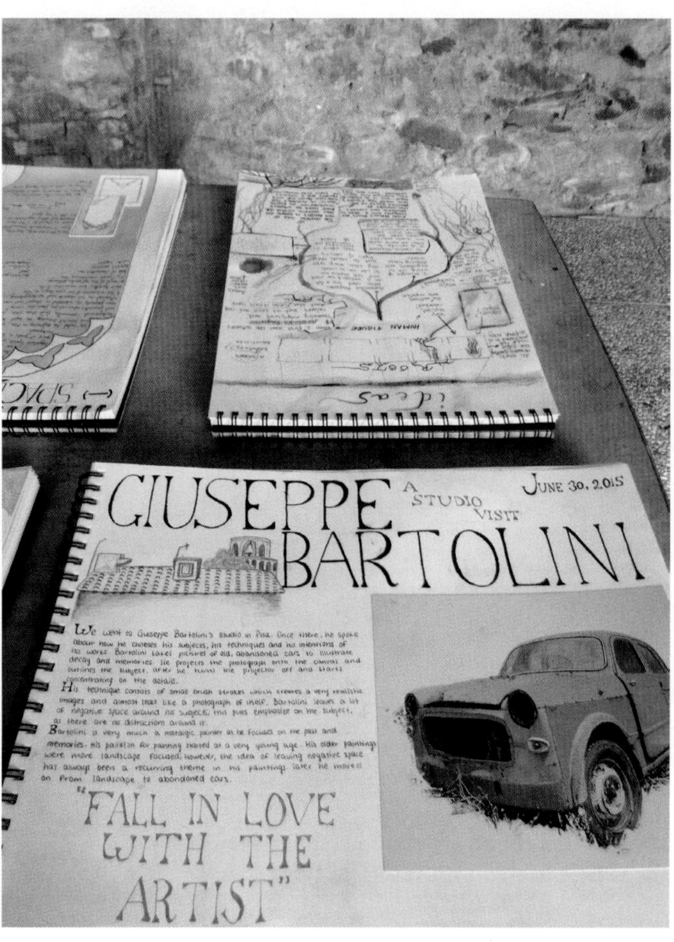

Figure 2.04: Student journals at La Vigna Art Studios, Pisa, in Italy. These large-format A3 journals have plenty of room for writing and images. A horizontal (landscape) format makes it easy to scan a journal page into a process portfolio screen.

The format of your visual arts journal and what to include

The IB visual arts journal does not have a prescribed format: it can be a sketchbook or several sketchbooks of varying sizes, a folder, a container or a digital document, depending on what is most appropriate to your way of working.

Your visual arts journal is a work in progress and as such should be a place of freedom and **experimentation**. Don't censor yourself; there will be time for editing and revising portions of the journal later when you choose extracts to hand in for the assessed components.

Your journal is a place to explore and develop your ideas. You can show the trajectory of an idea through various stages of development, including reflecting and reviewing, by:

- mind-mapping ideas and themes for exploration
- reworking an idea or image using different techniques
- reflecting on how meaning is communicated through your choices of imagery and materials.

Experimentation: Experimentation is when you try something new or different, not necessarily knowing what the result will be, for example experimenting with materials, media and technologies, and developing skills and techniques through trial and error.

In your journal, you can . . . draw, analyse, explore, observe, discover, design, doodle, document, dissect, develop, invent, compare, collect, compile, experiment, evaluate, record, respond, rework, reflect.

Figure 2.05: Visual arts journal page by student Daryl Baclig. On this page Daryl experiments by mixing sand and petroleum jelly with ink, trying out different papers (tracing paper, newsprint) and recording how the materials react on the different surfaces. Daryl says: 'I wanted to look at different options for creating depth and texture in my contaminated ocean piece. I observed my tests with different pastes made from sand and ink and realised they looked like coral reefs.'

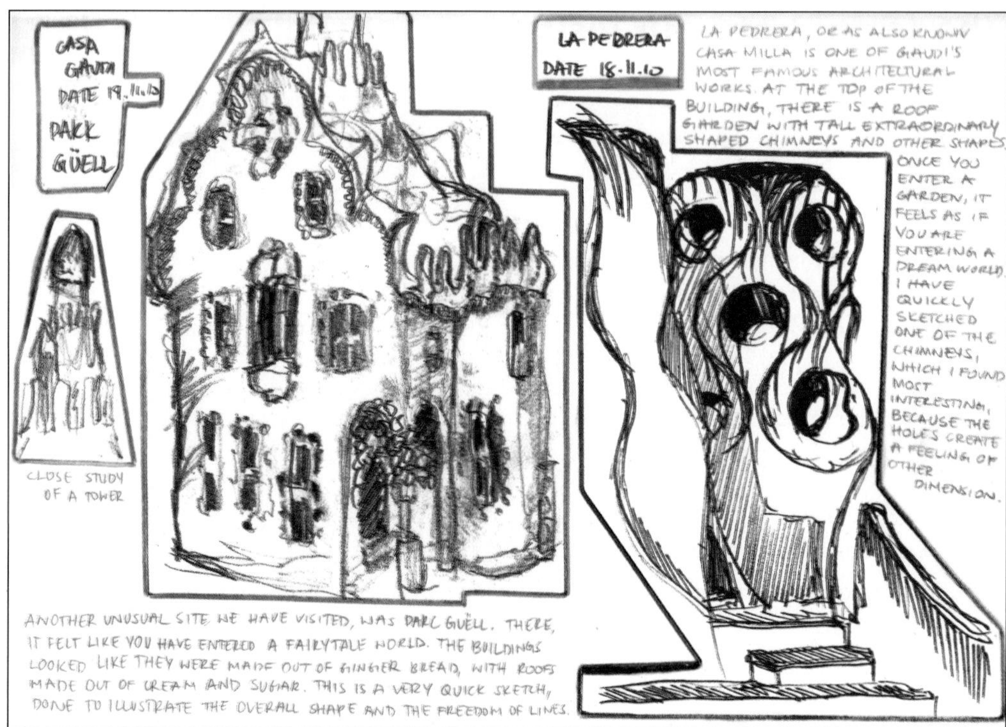

Figure 2.06: This journal page by student Anastasia Leonovich shows quick sketches made during a visit to Barcelona to observe the work of architect Antonio Gaudí. Anastasia writes of visiting La Pedrera: 'There is a roof garden with tall, extraordinarily shaped chimneys . . . it feels as if you are entering a dream world. I quickly sketched the chimneys, which I found most interesting because the holes create a feeling of another dimension.'

Observation: Observation means looking around you and recording your experience, both visual and written, including first-hand observations, drawing on site, written and visual responses to artworks you encounter.

Record your encounters with artworks and artists, including:

- reflections on gallery and museum visits
- making connections between an artist and your own work
- detailed evaluations of artworks and critical analysis.

Your journal should also include reflections on your progress, including the challenges you met along the way. (See also Figure 2.11, Beverly Chew's work.)

Tip: Bring a small sketchbook along whenever you go on a trip to capture the immediacy of your experience. You can cut and paste these smaller sketches and transfer your notes to your visual journal or PP later.

Documenting your process

You can record your process in many different ways, depending on the techniques and materials you are using. You might try including several of these approaches in your journal:

- notes and steps of art-making processes
- mind-maps
- preliminary studies and plans
- compositional sketches
- photos of your work in progress at various stages
- photographic contact sheets and test prints
- computer screenshots.

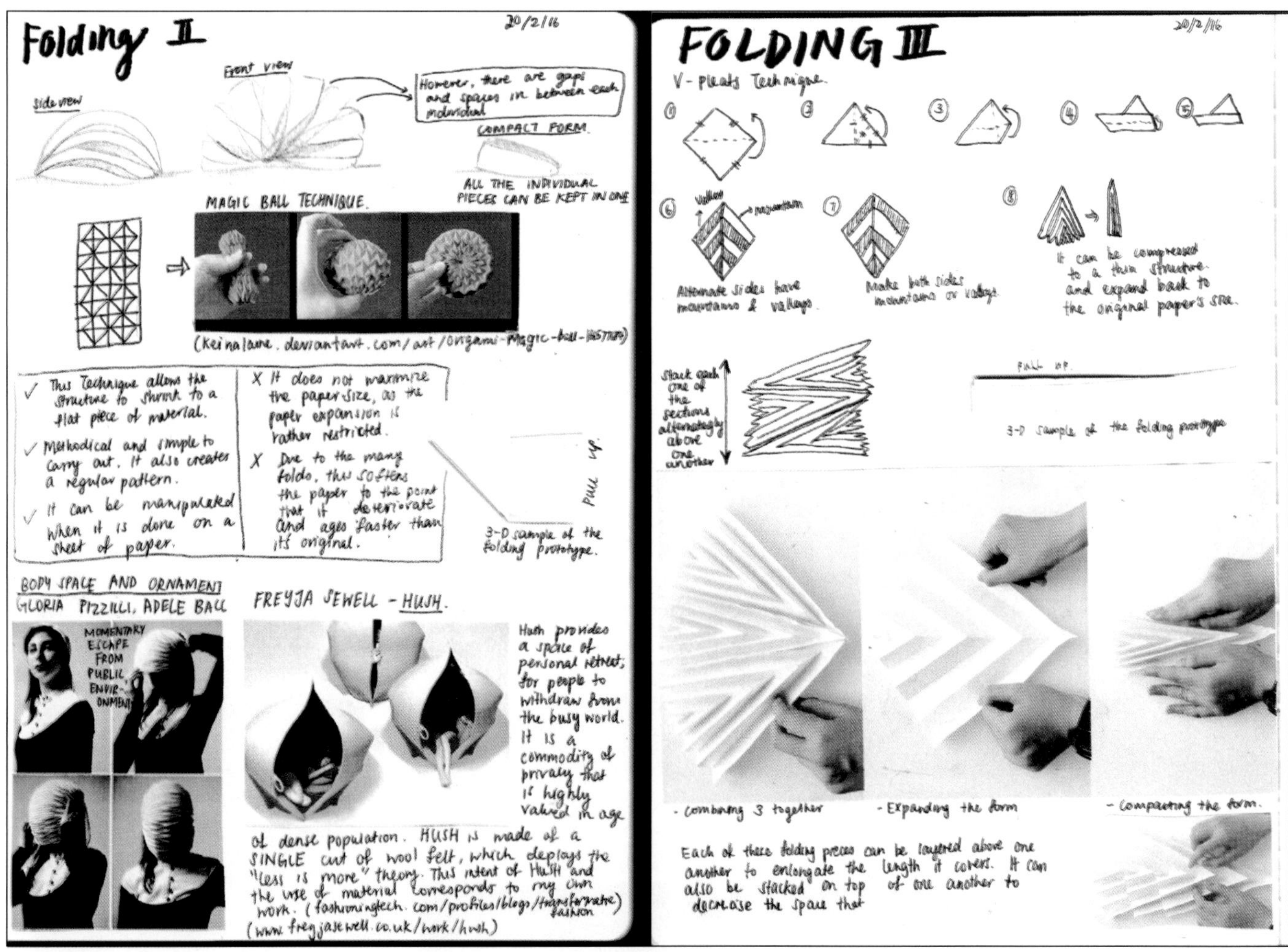

Figure 2.07: Visual journal pages by student Anabel Poh. She documents her process both visually and in written form, using a mixture of drawings, diagrams, photographic documentation and annotation, showing the steps involved in her exploration of folding paper into forms.

2.3 The role of your visual arts journal in the course

As well as assisting and recording your learning process on the course, your visual arts journal is a source of raw material that you can use when compiling work for the assessed components of the course: the CS, the PP and the exhibition. Analysis and comparison of artworks for the CS may come from notes in the journal. Entire pages or portions of pages may be used for the PP screens. Reflections on resolved artworks and planning for the exhibition in the journal may be useful when writing your curatorial rationale and your exhibition texts. All of these elements and more may be adapted from your journal.

Figure 2.08: Student journal page by Elisabeth Lauer. This page looks at the influence of traditional Japanese Ukiyo-e printmaking on contemporary graphics and illustration, comparing Suzuki Harunubu's *Mitate No Kinko*, 1765, to Yuko Shimizu's 2007 design for a CD cover. The student engages in detailed visual analysis, looks at symbols and meaning, and makes numerous connections between the works. Elisabeth says: 'Mitate-e is one of the most common and important genres in Ukiyo-e printmaking. Many layers of meaning are layered on top of each other, often to humorous effect. Historical or fictional events or personages or ideas are embedded into these images.'

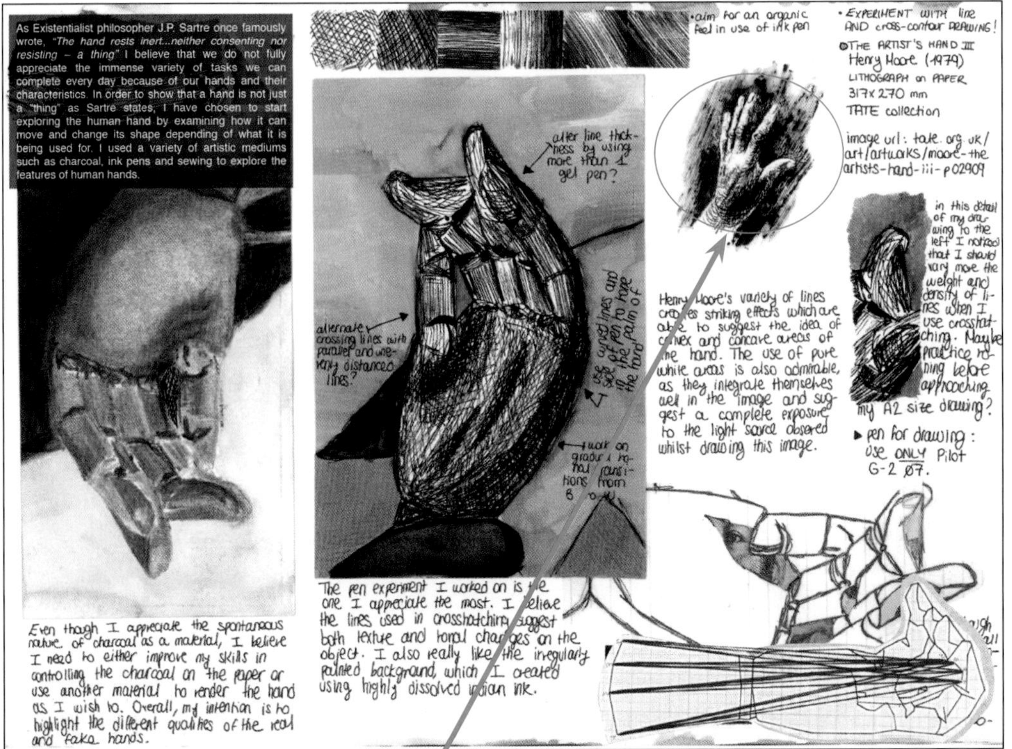

Figure 2.09: Journal page by student Enrico Giori. In these hand studies, Enrico experiments with drawing media (charcoal, pen and ink) and with variations on technique (cross-hatching and *sfumato* shading) to find the solution most appropriate to his creative intentions. Enrico says: 'Henry Moore's variety of lines creates striking effects which suggest the idea of concave and convex areas of the hand. The use of pure white areas is also admirable as they . . . suggest an exposure to a light source observed while drawing the image.'

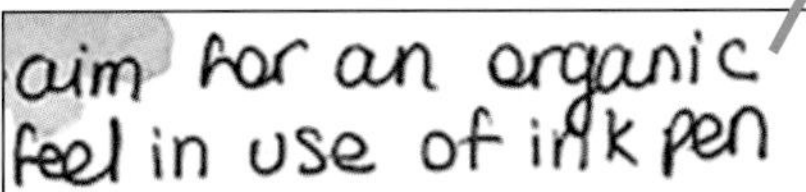

Figure 2.10: In this detail of Figure 2.9, Enrico makes a note of the artist, date and source of the image by Henry Moore that he includes in his journal.

Cross-hatching: Shading forms by using overlapping parallel lines.

***Sfumato* (Italian):** Shading forms by using subtle and soft gradation of tone (literally, 'smoky').

The visual arts journal → comparative study

You can use your journal to document your exhibition visits and investigations of artists' work, and to interpret any art works that you see first-hand or reproduced. You can practise visual analysis of one artwork and compare two or more works in your journal. When compiling your CS you may select and adapt passages from these journal pages where relevant.

Tip: Research skills
Develop good research skills now, to save you time later. Keep track of artists' names and the websites where you found images and information. Copy and paste URLs, including dates accessed, into a document that you can copy from later when assembling your PP. Get in the habit of citing works as you encounter them, so you don't have to search for the source again. See the example in Figure 2.10.

The visual arts journal → process portfolio

In your journal, try out different techniques, record your process and document your experiments with media and technology. Reflect on your decision-making, your artistic intentions and your discoveries. This content can be selected, adapted and presented in your PP screens.

The visual arts journal → exhibition

Periodic reflections in the journal on the development, refinement and review of your own work will be useful references when writing your curatorial rationale for your exhibition. You can use the journal to reflect on the intention for each of your resolved art works and refer to this text when your are assembling your exhibition submission and writing the exhibition texts.

Use the journal when planning your exhibition: design the layout, and create a thumbnail map considering relationships between works and the overall viewer experience. (Chapter 9 includes an example of planning the exhibition in the visual journal.)

2.4 Reflection in the visual arts journal

Reflection in your visual arts course requires thoughtful consideration, of the artists and the artworks you encounter, of the techniques and ideas you explore, and of your own development as an artist. Reflection is an essential part of the course that takes place throughout your entire developmental working process.

Your journal gives you an opportunity to reflect on your progress, your strengths and your challenges by recording your processes (including those that were not successful or resolved), the difficulties you faced and the obstacles you overcame.

Include your reflections on:

- artists' work
- gallery and museum visits
- curatorial practice
- techniques and processes
- materials and meaning
- mind-mapping and ideas
- your personal areas of interest
- feedback from teachers and peers
- the difficulties, challenges and obstacles your encountered and how you dealt with them
- your personal development and achievements.

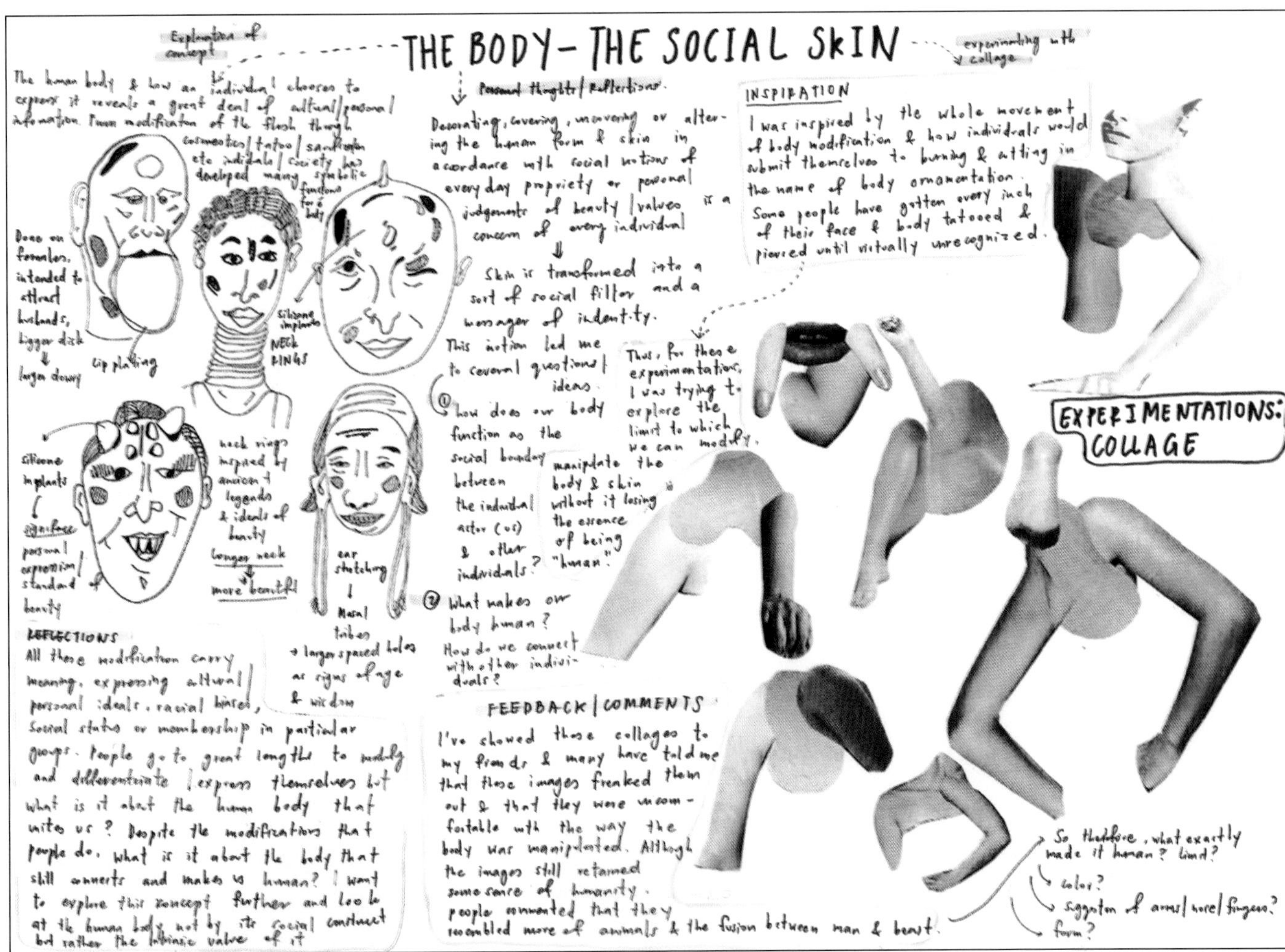

Figure 2.11: In this journal page student Beverly Chew reflects on the development of her work around the idea of the body as a 'social skin'. She writes that she is interested in cultural ideas of status and membership through bodily manipulation and how the skin is a sort of social filter and 'messenger of identity'. She poses the question 'How far can we modify and manipulate the body without it losing the essence of being human?' She includes records of valuable feedback from peers and teachers, recording that people found them 'freaky' and that the images resembled animals more than humans or a fusion of man and beast.

CASE STUDY: EDUARDO MODENESE

This case study shows a series of journal pages by student Eduardo Modenese that explore a topic of his choice with thorough visual and written analysis. This engaging visual journal strikes a balance between visual and written content. In these pages the student explores a topic (the tie or knot) in depth and breadth. He uses various graphic approaches in several different media (pencil drawing, collage, pen and ink). These visual studies are supported by analysis and informed by his contextual investigation of artists. A content-rich and visually exciting journal like this can be easily adapted into PP screens. (An example of how to do this is discussed in Chapter 8.)

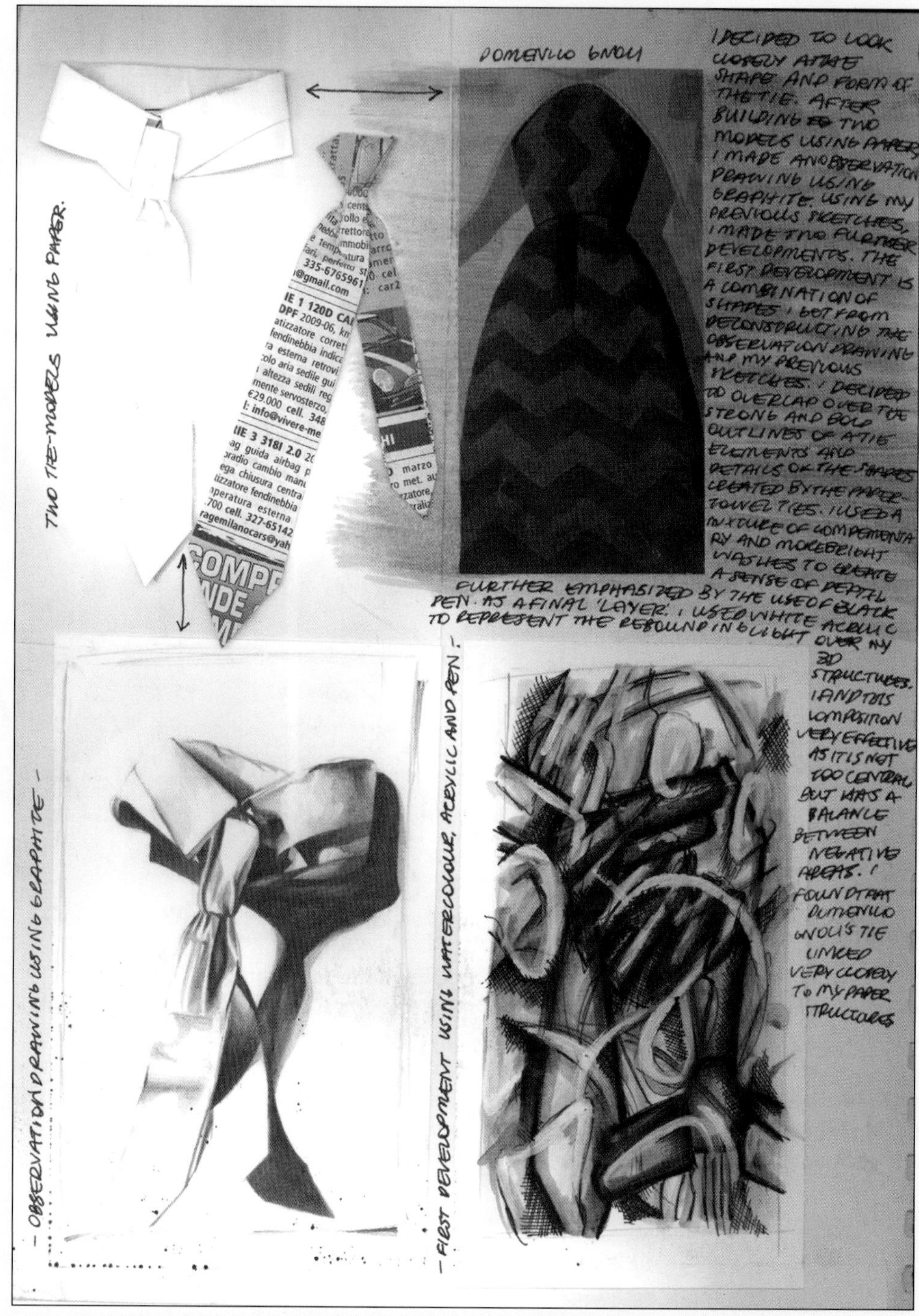

Figure 2.12: Eduardo constructed ties out of paper, one in white paper, the other in newspaper. He then made an observational drawing of his white paper tie (below left). The coloured drawing (below right) is a deconstruction of this. He says: 'It is a combination of shapes I got from deconstructing my observational drawing. I decided to overlap the strong and bold outlines of the tie elements and used a mixture of complementary colour washes to create spatial depth further emphasised with black pen crosshatching.'

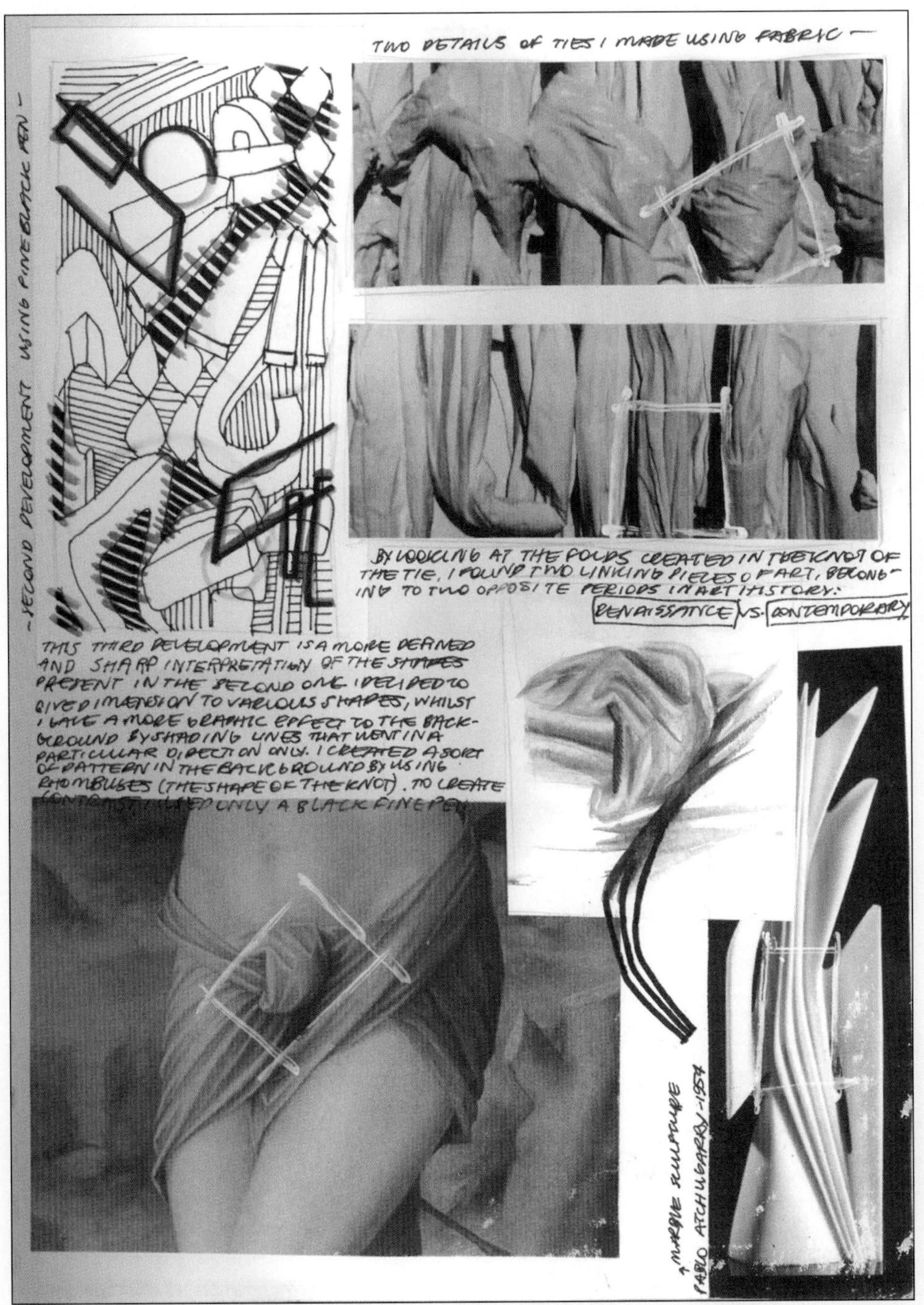

Figure 2.13: Eduardo made ties out of fabric and dipped them in paint and began to explore the shape of the knot and look for links with other artists. He says: 'By looking at the folds created in the knot of the tie I found linking pieces from two opposite periods in art history, Renaissance and Contemporary.'

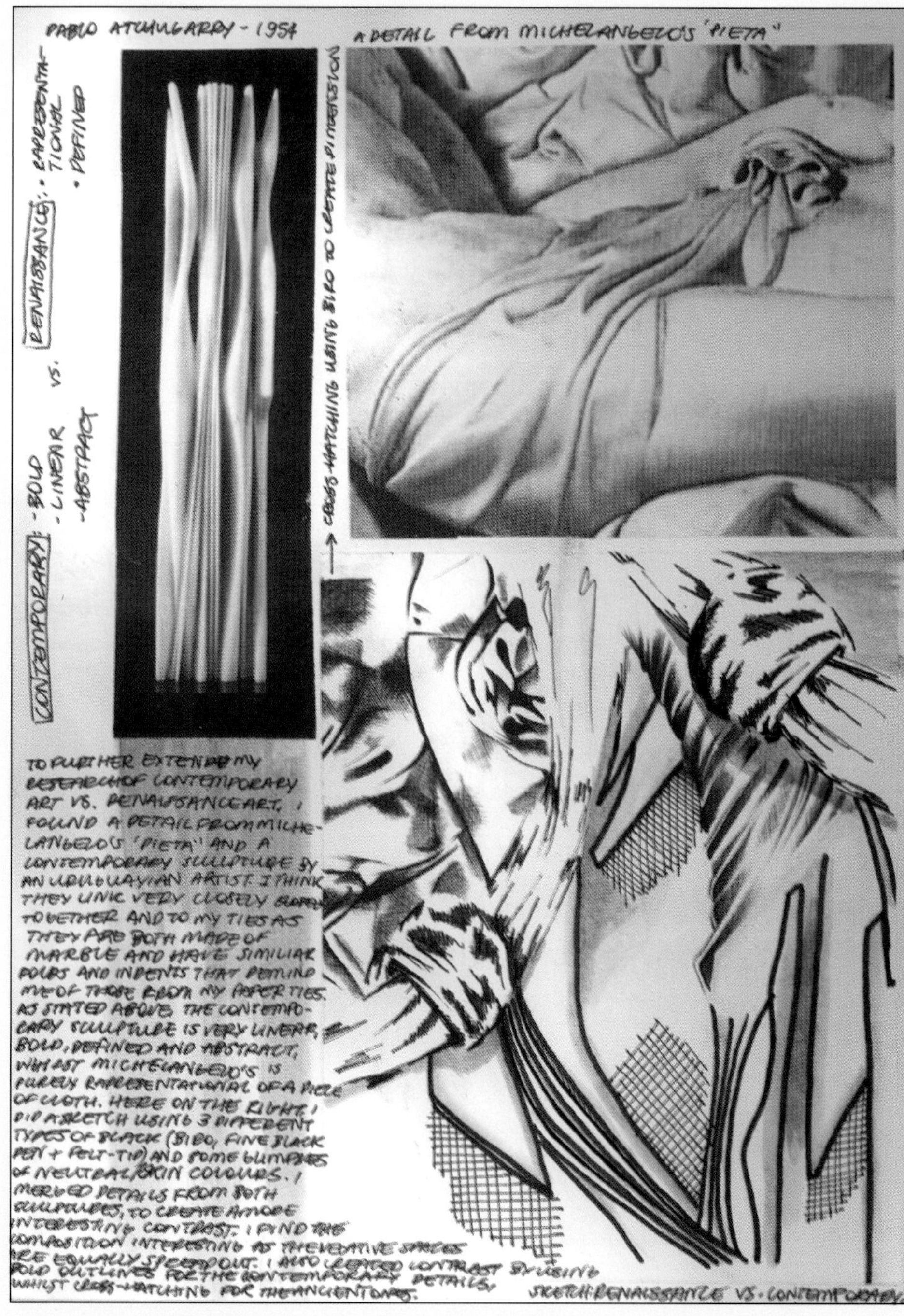

Figure 2.14: Eduardo says: 'I found this detail of Michelangelo's *Pietà*, and a contemporary sculpture by Uruguayan artist Pablo Atchugarry . . . both made of marble with similar folds and indents. The Atchugarry sculpture is very linear, bold, defined and abstract, whilst Michelangelo's is a pure representation of cloth in marble. I made a sketch using three different types of black pen (biro, fine tip and felt tip) and some glimpses of neutral skin tones, merging details from both sculptures but trying to create more contrast and a composition of my own.'

What makes this visual journal a fine example?

Eduardo's visual journal pages already include many of the qualities that are desirable when assembling the PP:

- skilful application of several techniques
- experimental and analytical approaches
- comparisons of artists and art styles
- exploration of how ideas develop
- clearly articulated content
- legible writing
- visually pleasing layout and design.

Summary

In this chapter we have introduced the visual arts journal, explored its content and format and looked at how other artists use sketchbooks and journals. Your visual arts journal informs and enriches all of the assessed components. It can be used to record exhibition visits and the investigation of artists for the CS. It can be used for developing skills and experimenting with techniques and processes, which will be very helpful when compiling your PP. It is also a place for you to reflect on the development of your work and how you wish to present it, including planning your final exhibition. In these ways, your journal supports and underpins the entire visual arts course.

Chapter 3 Culture and place

Introduction

Cultural awareness and understanding are at the heart of the IB educational philosophy. It is through being open minded and interested in other cultures that we gain knowledge and understanding of the world and its people. We can then look at the meaning of culture in a broader sense and value the role of place, home, ancestry and tradition, both yours and those of other cultures.

In this chapter we see how place and culture can play an important role in shaping your artwork. Where you live can be a great starting point for making art, and your cultural background is a rich source to draw on. There are many activities here to help you explore your surroundings and your culture, including observational drawing, photography, collecting, collaging, mapping, and making installations and site-specific work in response to a particular place.

Sgraffito: A form of wall decoration in which a surface layer of paint is scratched into to reveal the colour beneath. The wall is prepared with lime plaster using the same materials and techniques as fresco painting.

Figure 3.01: A student photographing a detail of the façade of the Scuola Normale in Pisa, Italy, decorated with grey and white *sgraffito* designs. Recording your surroundings through photography or drawing helps you to observe more closely.

LEARNING OBJECTIVES

- Gain a broader, richer understanding of different cultural perspectives.
- Explore your own background and cultural traditions.
- Consider the historical, cultural, social, aesthetic contexts from which art can evolve.
- Respond to your surroundings through various media and techniques.
- Make connections between ideas, materials, artists and environment.
- Investigate site-specific and installation art in your environment.

3.1 Defining culture

Culture is a complex concept and can be quite hard to define. It encompasses human intellectual achievement as well as popular customs and beliefs. However, for our purposes in this course 'culture' is broadly defined as follows:

- **Culture is global.** It exists on many levels: international, national, regional, local and personal.
- **Culture is a framework.** It is constructed from human thoughts, emotions, behaviours and beliefs. It is what humans create, organise and express in their daily lives.
- **Culture is dynamic.** It is fluid and always changing, continually influenced by historical, geographical, social and technological conditions.

ACTIVITY 3.1: CULTURAL PERSPECTIVES

Spend a few minutes thinking about how you view the art of other cultures. Use the following questions to help you.

- When looking at unfamiliar art from other cultures, do you consider it the same way you do art from your own familiar culture?
- What sort of 'lens' or viewpoint do you use for looking at it?
- Does the unfamiliarity of the other culture distance you from the work?
- Do you try to relate it to your own culture or do you use a different set of criteria to understand it?
- Do you consider art from other cultures for its aesthetic value, or its social and historical context, or both?

ACTIVITY 3.2: FAMILIAR AND UNFAMILIAR

Refer to the images in Figures 3.2 and 3.3, or find your own familiar and unfamiliar artworks or artefacts that share common qualities. What you choose as familiar will depend on your individual cultural background. Compare the two pieces using the questions in Activity 3.1, 'Cultural perspectives'.

Figure 3.02: The Hindu deity Ganesha is one of India's most beloved gods. He is a remover of obstacles and a bearer of good fortune.

Figure 3.03: The Winged Victory of Samothrace (Greece 200–190 BCE) is a monumental marble sculpture of the goddess Nike. It is an iconic image in western art history, depicting both the divine and the triumphant spirit.

> People of different religions and cultures live side by side in almost every part of the world, and most of us have overlapping identities which unite us with very different groups. We can love what we are, without hating what – and who – we are not. We can thrive in our own tradition, even as we learn from others, and come to respect their teachings. (Kofi Annan, former Secretary-General of the United Nations)

3.2 Your own cultural traditions

Culture is not only about the **other**; by investigating your own roots you can broaden your scope of appreciation and understanding when encountering the art of cultures you are less familiar with.

Many artists make powerful work that is based around belief systems, religion, ritual, history, stories and memory. The culture you come from, your family history, and your ancestry and its traditions can be a very rich area of investigation.

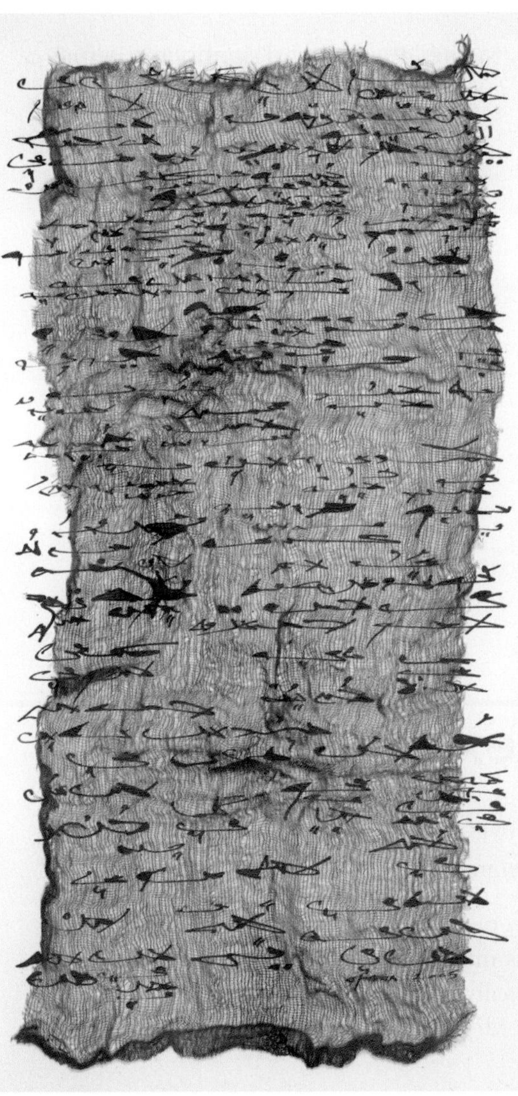

Figure 3.04: Maliheh Afnan (Iran–UK), *Veiled Threats*, 2006 (ink on paper overlaid with gauze). In this piece, the artist has laid a gauzy black fabric over a delicate ink pattern that looks like writing. The calligraphic forms resemble letters but are actually patterns, inspired by ancient Middle Eastern scripts. The sheer fabric evokes the idea of the veil and makes the mystery of the hidden message more pronounced. The title of the work gives us a clue as to the work's meaning, without telling us what the threats are.

TOK and art: What's your viewpoint?

- Is all art an expression of its particular time and place?
- Can art be considered a documentation of a society or era?
- What understanding of art can we realise from looking at its cultural context?
- Does art lose or gain value over time?
- Is art from other cultures better appreciated by looking at its cultural differences or its universal qualities?
- Does art eventually become outdated?

Depending on your culture, some topics are sensitive or controversial and censorship often exists around such subject matter. Many artists prefer to work with meaning in a subtle or indirect manner, as Maliheh Afnan does (Figure 3.04), especially when the subject matter is potentially inflammatory. Rather than address the topic directly, they work with hidden content, making the mystery part of the art.

> I think of art as a glue, a cultural and social glue. It's one of the means that has served to show us the things we believe in and the things we celebrate; it has served to reinforce our relationship to each other. (Eric Fischl)

ACTIVITY 3.3: VEILED CONTENT

a) Decide on a topic that is sensitive in your culture and think about how you might represent your ideas on it without being explicit or confrontational. (If you can't think of a topic, choose one from those listed.)

Instead of representing your idea with an image that makes an overt statement, choose materials, symbols and allusions that give a feeling for what you would like to say.

b) Consider your piece. Can the visual, tactile, physical and symbolic qualities of the work allow it to speak for itself? Make the mystery a part of the work.

TOPICS TO EXPLORE IN THE CONTEXT OF YOUR OWN CULTURAL BACKGROUND:

- belief systems
- religion
- ritual
- conflict
- money
- gender
- taboo subjects.

> If all the world were clear, art would not exist. (Albert Camus)

3.3 Historical context

All the art that is being made today has its origins in the art that was made in the past. Many artists make work that deliberately references art that came before.

Every artwork that we encounter carries its own story that has been shaped not only by its creator but by the era in which it was made. What was happening at that time historically, politically, socially and intellectually? What wars were being fought, what books were being written, what music played?

Figure 3.05: Seated female musicians, Tang dynasty, late 7th-century China. These small clay figures playing traditional musical instruments are *mingqi* or 'spirit utensils', burial objects that serve as bridges between the living and the dead.

GUIDING QUESTIONS

- Why does something made long ago, in a far-away era, still have the power to speak to us today?
- What makes the art of today different from that of 100 years ago?
- How have media and techniques developed and changed over time?
- What do you think are the biggest influences on art in your lifetime?

ACTIVITY 3.4: VISUAL JOURNAL REFLECTION ON HISTORICAL CONTEXT

Choose an artwork from an art historical movement or from a period in non-western art history, preferably a work that interests you for its content or style. Write your thoughts in your journal, including visual examples with citations. Use the questions to help you:

- What was happening in the world at that time and how might this have affected the artist?
- Were other artists working in a similar way?
- Was this artist part of an art movement and, if so, was this a reaction to the times?

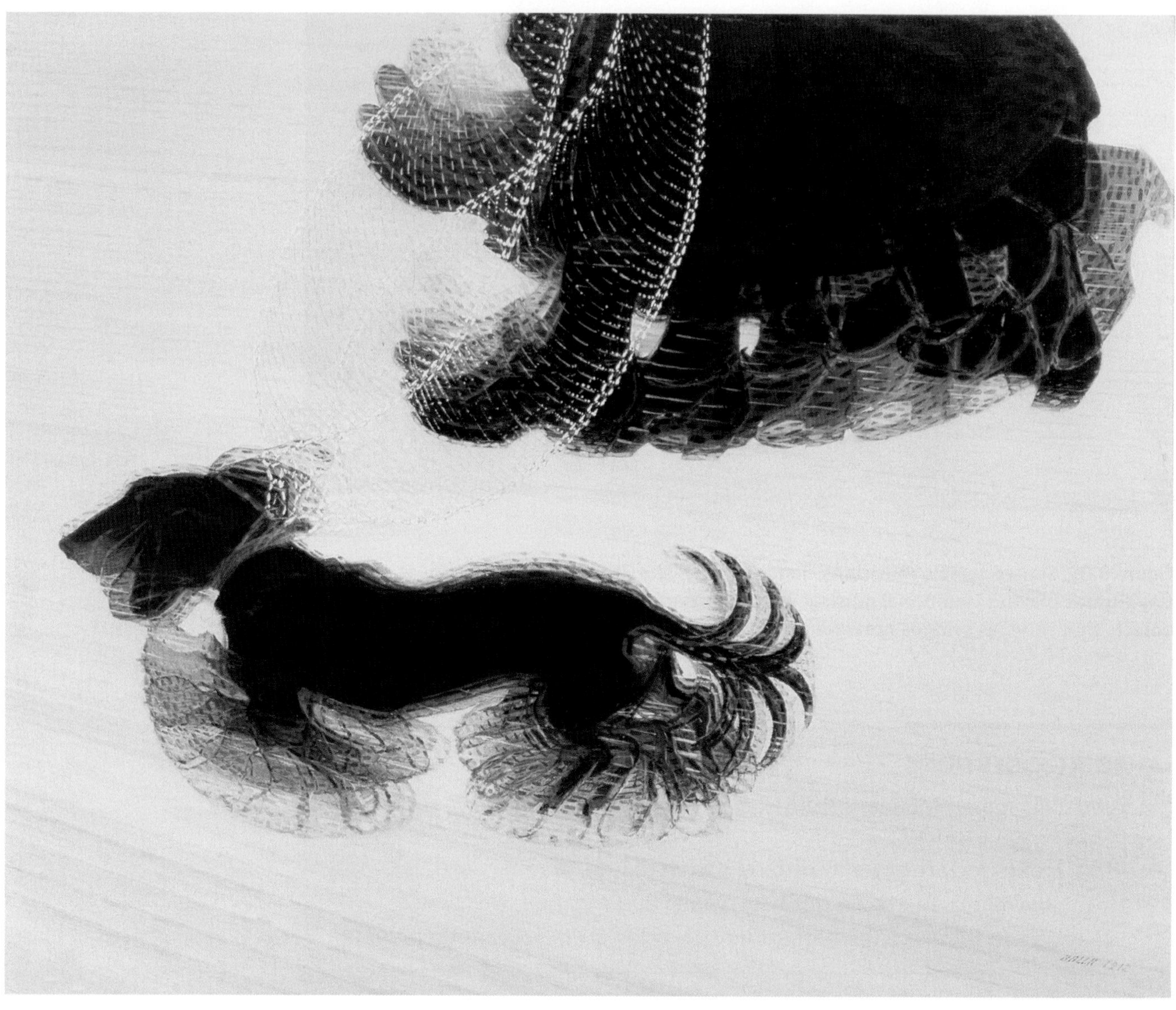

Figure 3.06: Giacomo Balla, *Dynamism of a Dog on a Leash*, 1912. Balla was part of the Italian Futurist group. Futurism was an early 20th-century artistic and social movement that exalted the power of speed, machines and technology. The Futurists rejected the past and celebrated the future, glorifying war and patriotism. Like many modern art movements, Futurism can best be understood by looking at the historical context from which it arose.

Notice how Giacomo Balla depicted motion in this painting and remember that this was made in 1912. What kind of work do you think a Futurist artist would make now?

Modern art: Art from about 1880 (Impressionism) through to the 1970s.

Changing materials and technology

The availability of materials and technology play a significant role in how artists approach ideas. A significant example is photography: when it was invented in the 1800s, the role of painting changed forever. And in turn, digital technology has completely transformed photography.

Figure 3.07: Malekeh Nayiny (Iran–France), *Misajour* from the series *Updating a Family Album*. The artist uses old family photos in black and white and reworks them in Photoshop, adding colour and overlaying patterns. She addresses her personal family history through the lens of changing photo technology.

ACTIVITY 3.5: UPDATING FAMILY PHOTOS

Take an old (pre-digital-era) family photograph if you have one. If you prefer, you can use a **found** photo. Your objective is to change something about the photo in a way that gives it a new meaning and brings it from the past into a **contemporary** context.

- Scan the photo into your computer and, using image-manipulation software, alter the background or the clothing, or introduce objects or text.
- Print the two images, before and after, and display side by side.
- If you like, develop the idea into a series using other photos.

Found objects: Objects or artefacts not originally intended as art, found and considered to have aesthetic value. Also referred to as *objets trouvés* (French).

Contemporary art: Work being produced by artists living today or in our times.

STUDENT EXAMPLE: SHINICHIRO YOSHII

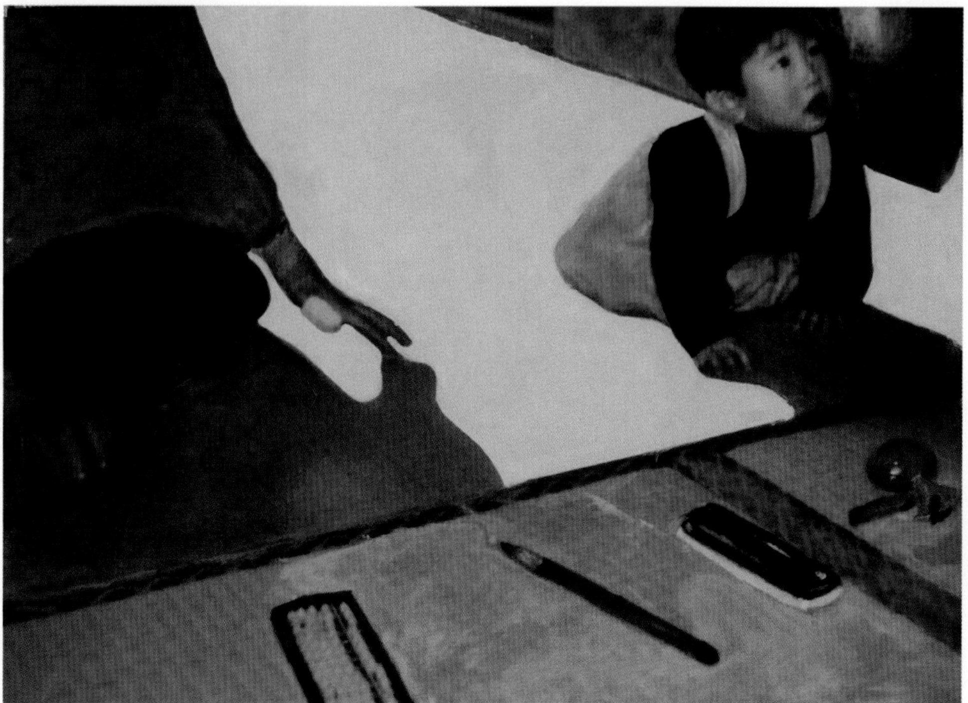

Figure 3.08: *Choice*, by student Shinichiro Yoshii. The student painted over a family photograph of himself as a baby, cropping the composition and drawing attention to the abstract curvilinear forms made by accentuating the light and shadow.

SPOTLIGHT ON THE STUDENT: SHINICHIRO YOSHII

Nationality: Japanese
Born: Fukuoka

Main artistic interests:

- conveying mood and space
- architectural space and icons
- the links between: music, physics, history, mood, emotions
- film work and sociological comments.

Influential artists/thinkers:

- E.H. Gombrich
- William Turner
- Felix Vallotton
- Francis Bacon
- Michelangelo.

3.4 Where am I now? Exploring your surroundings

When investigating the art and culture of a specific place or region it is probably best to avoid **tokenistic** 'cultural projects' that only look superficially at culture, for example famous monuments or other clichéd references. Instead, take a closer look at where you live now, the culture of the country where your school or college is located. Many students come from backgrounds that are culturally different from the country in which they now live and of their host school, and can think about the differences. If you have lived all your life in the same place, you may never have looked into your own cultural background, society or physical surroundings. This section includes a series of activities designed to help you explore your culture and surroundings.

Tokenistic: Doing something only to show that you are following rules or doing what is expected or seen to be fair, and not because you really believe it is the right thing to do.

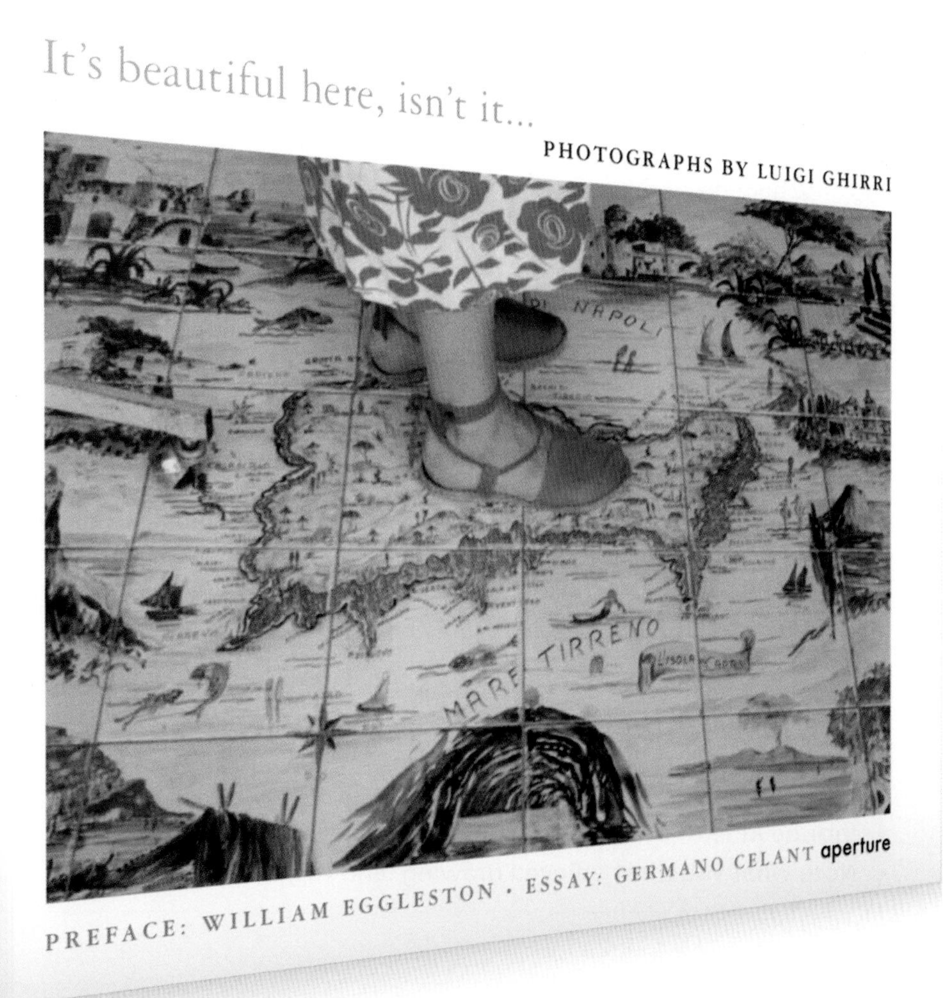

Figure 3.09: Photo taken from *It's Beautiful Here, Isn't It . . .*, a book about the work of 20th-century photographer Luigi Ghirri. Ghirri took whimsical, poetic pictures of his Italian landscape, often employing optical puns and mixing the real and the representational.

Figure 3.10: Paul Gauguin, *D'où venons nous? Que sommes nous? Où allons nous?*, 1897. The inscription in the top left of Gauguin's painting (*Where have we come from? What are we? Where are we going?*) asks a marvellously complex question, one that a lifetime of art-making can only begin to try to address.

Where do we come from? What are we? Where are we going?
(Paul Gauguin)

ACTIVITY 3.6: DRAWING VIEWPOINTS

a) Take some time to visually investigate your immediate surroundings.

- Explore your physical environment: nature, vegetation, the buildings and spaces you live in, the streets and urban areas.
- Make notes and sketches, take photos, make videos: explore it all with an open mind, curiously.
- Note what you find interesting, what is important to you and what you care about in the world around you.

b) Make a series of at least five small sketches of your surroundings in your visual journal.

- Try drawing from different perspectives (for example looking down, looking up).
- Include at least one detail and one panoramic view.
- Note what you most enjoyed drawing, and why.

Figure 3.11: These sketches in ink and wash by student Anastasia Leonovich capture a sense of Barcelona's architecture and its characteristic ironwork. Quick drawings such as these are also a form of visual note-taking that may be developed in studio work later on or included in your pp (covered in Chapter 8).

ACTIVITY 3.7: STREET DRAWING

Draw people in a public place such as a train station or a cafe. Let your drawings overlap each other and fill the page as people enter and leave your view.

You might try using different coloured markers or pens for this, switching colours as you introduce a new figure.

ACTIVITY 3.8: NEW ANGLES: WALKING PHOTOGRAPHY

Take your camera with you for a one-day photography project. Go by yourself so that your whole attention can be focused on observing your surroundings.

- What elements strike you in your cityscape or landscape, or even in an interior space?
- Look for new angles and interesting viewpoints. Try a combination of close-up, medium and long shots.
- Pay careful attention to how you frame each composition.
- Think about colour as an overall tone or a contrasting element.
- Take pictures with strong formal compositions, with the added interest of your observant cultural commentary.
- Try to communicate something about the place, the values and the people.

Take as many photos as you like but then select the ten images that evocatively capture a sense of your place and work together as a mini series.

- What are the unifying threads?
- What formal elements are strongest?
- What do these photos say about your chosen subject?

Give your series a title and write a caption for each image, describing your intentions.

LOOK UP SOME PHOTOGRAPHERS WHOSE WORK EXPLORES A SENSE OF PLACE, SUCH AS:

- William Eggleston
- Luigi Ghirri
- Brian Rose
- Robert Frank
- Ansel Adams
- David Spero
- Andreas Gursky
- Laura Volkerding.

Figure 3.12: *Studio 01*. Student Karen Laanem took her camera with her when she visited the countryside where her family came from in Estonia. These photos were the beginning of a project that developed into a very personal body of work. (You can see more of Karen's work in Chapter 5.)

LOOK AT ARTISTS FROM THE PAST AND PRESENT WHO USE EVERYDAY AND FOUND OBJECTS TO CREATE COLLAGES – AS IN THE EXAMPLE IN FIGURE 3.13 BY KURT SCHWITTERS. FOR EXAMPLE:

- George Braque
- Max Ernst
- Robert Rauschenberg
- Mimmo Rotella
- Eduardo Paolozzi
- Romare Bearden
- Faith Ringgold
- Hannah Höch
- John Stezaker
- Mark Bradford
- Mat Bryans.

Figure 3.13: Kurt Schwitters, *Invisible Ink*, 1947, was made with scraps of paper, tickets and other printed matter. Notice how Schwitters incorporated words and numbers as part of the content.

ACTIVITY 3.9: TRACES OF PLACES: COLLAGE

Over the course of several days or more, collect small objects, natural and manmade: scraps of paper, a bus ticket, a leaf, things that tell stories of the place where you are. If it is a new place, this will have a quality of discovery, maybe writing in another language, a foreign coin. If the place is familiar, the objects you collect may tell a personal story: your own path through the landscape, and the interactions and stories that belong to this particular space.

- Arrange your objects onto a support (heavy paper, cardboard, wood – anything that provides a structure and holds it together).
- Create a pleasing composition.
- Think about the story that objects tell when placed together in a certain way.

Bird's-eye view: An overview, or a general view from above, as seen by a bird.

Figure 3.14: This 19th-century woollen shawl from Kashmir, India, has been embroidered with a pictorial map of Srinigar, showing canals, bridges, boats and people in a bird's-eye view.

ACTIVITY 3.10: ALTERED MAPS

Before you begin to make your own altered map, look at maps from different contexts. Old or ancient maps and charts are great for getting graphic ideas, such as the embroidered map depicted in Figure 3.14.

LOOK UP AT LEAST ONE OF THESE CONTEMPORARY ARTISTS WHO USE MAPPING AS AN EXPRESSIVE FORM:

- Alighiero Boetti
- Kathy Prendergast
- Julie Mehretu
- Richard Long
- Guillermo Kuitca
- Simon Patterson.

To make your altered map:

- Find an existing map of where you are.
- Make some photocopies of it and experiment on these before using the real map.
- Alter the map by drawing, cutting, folding, writing over, or otherwise transforming it.
- Superimpose your own landmarks, special places, memories and encounters
- Create a key (or code) for reading the map.

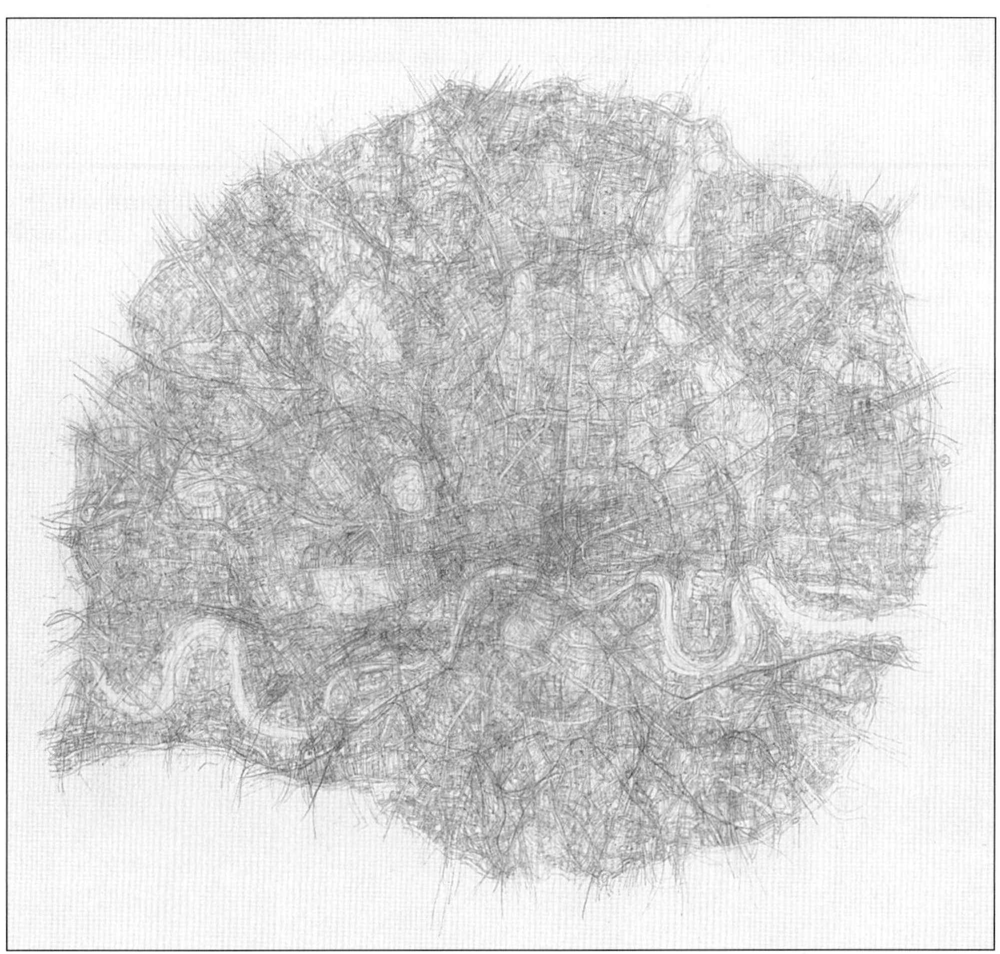

Figure 3.15: Kathy Prendergast, *City Drawings* series, 1997, pencil on paper.

This delicate pencil drawing of a map of London is by contemporary Irish artist Kathy Prendergast – one of her many drawings of the world's capital cities. She begins at the center of a small sketchbook page and works slowly outwards, the city spreading like a complex tangle of threads floating in space.

3.5 Making connections

In section 3.4 you explored a range of media and different visual and conceptual approaches to your surroundings. Let's pause to reflect on these experiences and make some connections between ideas, materials, artists and environment.

ACTIVITY 3.11: ADDING REFLECTIVE CONTENT

Adding text to your images on place will give the images contextual gravity and help to explain your thinking behind the making. You can incorporate your written reflections around your existing drawings or you can create new visual journal pages.

Use the following questions to help guide your written reflection in your visual journal.

- How do your ideas communicate through different media and materials?
- Which medium do you feel suits your own expressive intentions best?
- How have you made connections between other artists' ways of working and your own?
- What have your studies revealed to you about your environment?
- What relationships do you see between your different pieces?
- What interests you and what would you like to explore further?

Tip: Make small sketches or diagrams of your linked artworks in your journal with your written reflections explaining the connections between them. You can do the same with artworks that have influenced your thinking. Be sure to acknowledge artists and cite your sources!

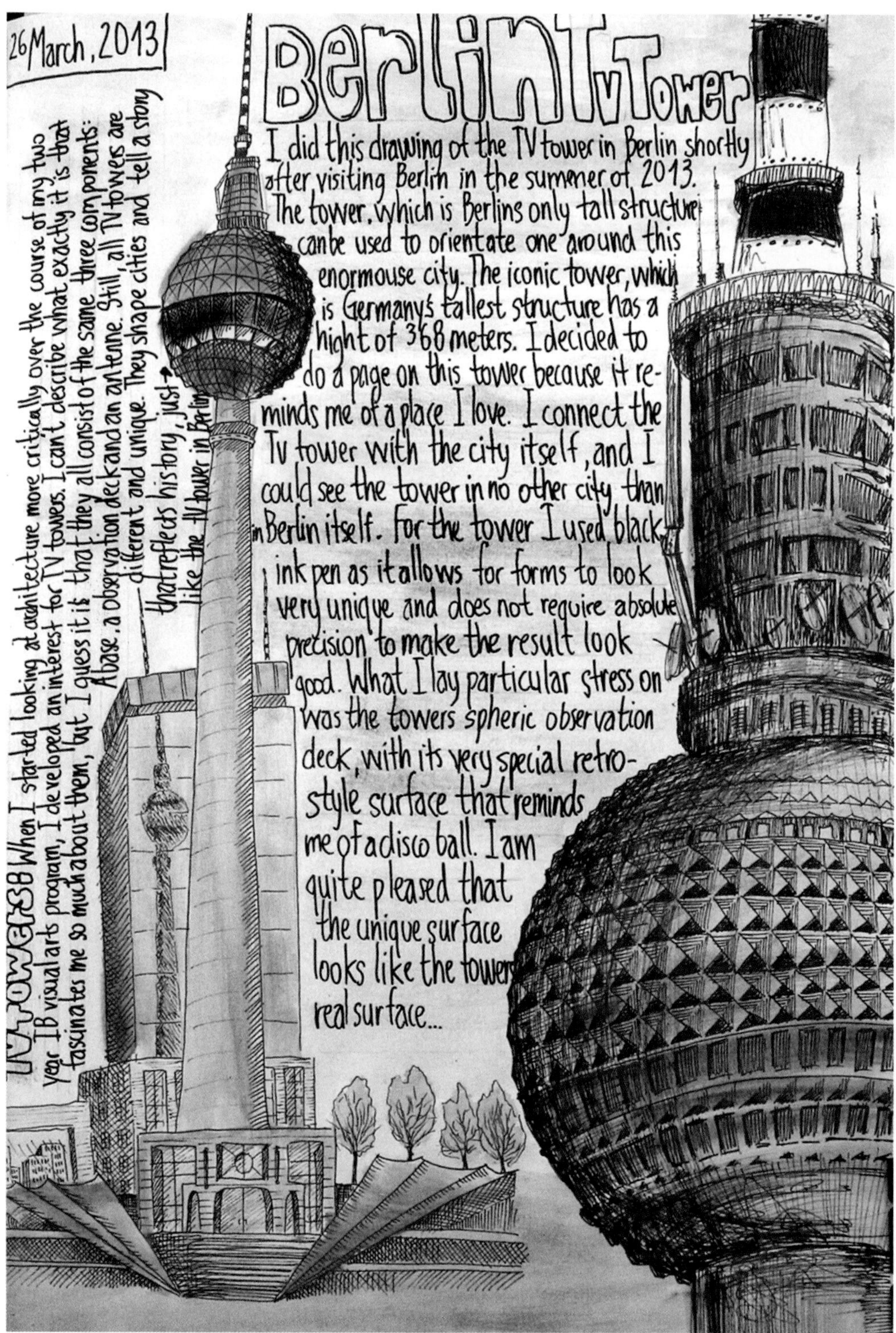

26 March, 2013
Berlin TV Tower
TV TOWERS58 When I started looking at architecture more critically over the course of my two year IB visual arts program, I developed an interest for TV towers. I can't describe what exactly it is that fascinates me so much about them, but I guess it is that they all consist of the same three components: A base, a observation deck and an antenne. Still, all TV towers are different and unique. They shape cities and tell a story that reflects history, just like the TV tower in Berlin
I did this drawing of the TV tower in Berlin shortly after visiting Berlin in the summer of 2013. The tower, which is Berlins only tall structure can be used to orientate one around this enormouse city. The iconic tower, which is Germany's tallest structure has a hight of 368 meters. I decided to do a page on this tower because it reminds me of a place I love. I connect the TV tower with the city itself, and I could see the tower in no other city than in Berlin itself. For the tower I used black ink pen as it allows for forms to look very unique and does not require absolute precision to make the result look good. What I lay particular stress on was the towers spheric observation deck, with its very special retro-style surface that reminds me of a disco ball. I am quite pleased that the unique surface looks like the towers real surface...

Figure 3.16: Visual journal page by student James McGoldrick. By adding text to his fine pen renderings of the Berlin TV tower, James gives the drawings a contextual reference and explains his interest in the TV towers as both structures and icons.

A personal response

So far in this book you have explored several art-making forms including drawing, photography, collage and map-making, and looked at artwork in these forms made by several artists. The activities you have done in section 3.4 will be excellent preparation for your next piece of work.

Based on these experiences and the information you have gathered, can you come up with an individual response to your surroundings in the medium of your choice?

STUDENT EXAMPLE: MAHSHAD REZAEI

Figure 3.17: *Passive Destruction* by student Mahshad Rezaei. Place can also be an intimate setting, like this painting in oil and acrylic on board. Mahshad has combined three different sketches of interior views of his house into one dreamlike sequence, evoking a personal, private space.

SPOTLIGHT ON THE STUDENT: MAHSHAD REZAEI

Nationality: Iranian
Born: Tehran

Main artistic interests:

- the role of women in Iranian culture
- finding a balance between the western and Middle East ways of thinking
- love for design and pattern making
- finding uniqueness in different cultures.

Influential artists/writers :

- Angela Carter
- Francis Bacon
- Shirin Neshat
- Mohammad Ehsai
- Hoda Afshar.

3.6 Site-specific art

A **site-specific** artwork is done in response to a specific place and is in direct relationship with its surroundings. Site-specific art includes a range of practices from large-scale land art to urban street art. Sometimes the artwork can be moved and still be relevant in another setting but usually it is tied to the original place. Viewers are very much involved in the work as they are present on the site too and engaging with the same surroundings as the artist. Site specific can also refer to the very specific placement of artwork within gallery spaces, responding to the elements or furniture within the gallery space.

Site-specific art: A work of art designed for a specific location that has a meaningful relationship with that place.

Site specificity is not a modern invention, although we tend to think of it as a contemporary art movement. Much of the art of the past was site specific, created specifically for a certain building or place, often commissioned by a religious entity. Think of the frescos by Michelangelo in the Sistine Chapel, the mosaics in the Great Mosque in Damascus, or the great pyramids of Giza.

Culture and place

Religious art has often been in response to a particular site, but lay artists have also worked site specifically in the past. And broadly speaking, all architecture and garden design (an early form of land art) is of course site specific. So nothing new here!

Figure 3.18: Stonehenge (Great Britain, 3000 BCE) is a site-specific Neolithic monument, designed in perfect alignment with the solar and lunar calendar. It was made in a very specific place and its significance depends on its relationship to that place.

Christo and Jeanne-Claude, a pair of artists who were partners in life and in art, created site-specific art all over the world from the 1970s onwards. Together they planned and oversaw massive-scale projects such as *Wrapped Coast* in Sydney, *Valley Curtain* in Colorado and *Surrounded Islands* in Florida. Their work also addressed urban landmarks such as the Pont Neuf in Paris, the Reichstag in Berlin, and the gates of Central Park, New York City. By wrapping and concealing aspects of familiar landscapes, the artists created new ways for us to experience them.

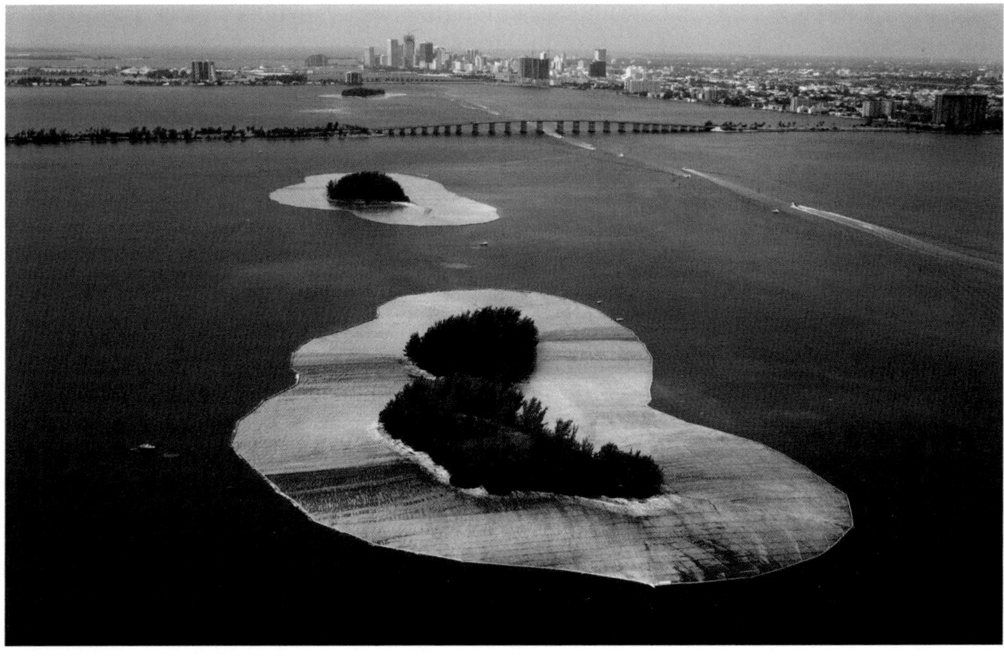

Figure 3.19: For *Surrounded Islands* in Biscayne Bay, Florida, 1983, Christo and Jeanne-Claude surrounded 11 islands with pink nylon fabric that followed the contours of the islands, creating a luminous and playful contrast.

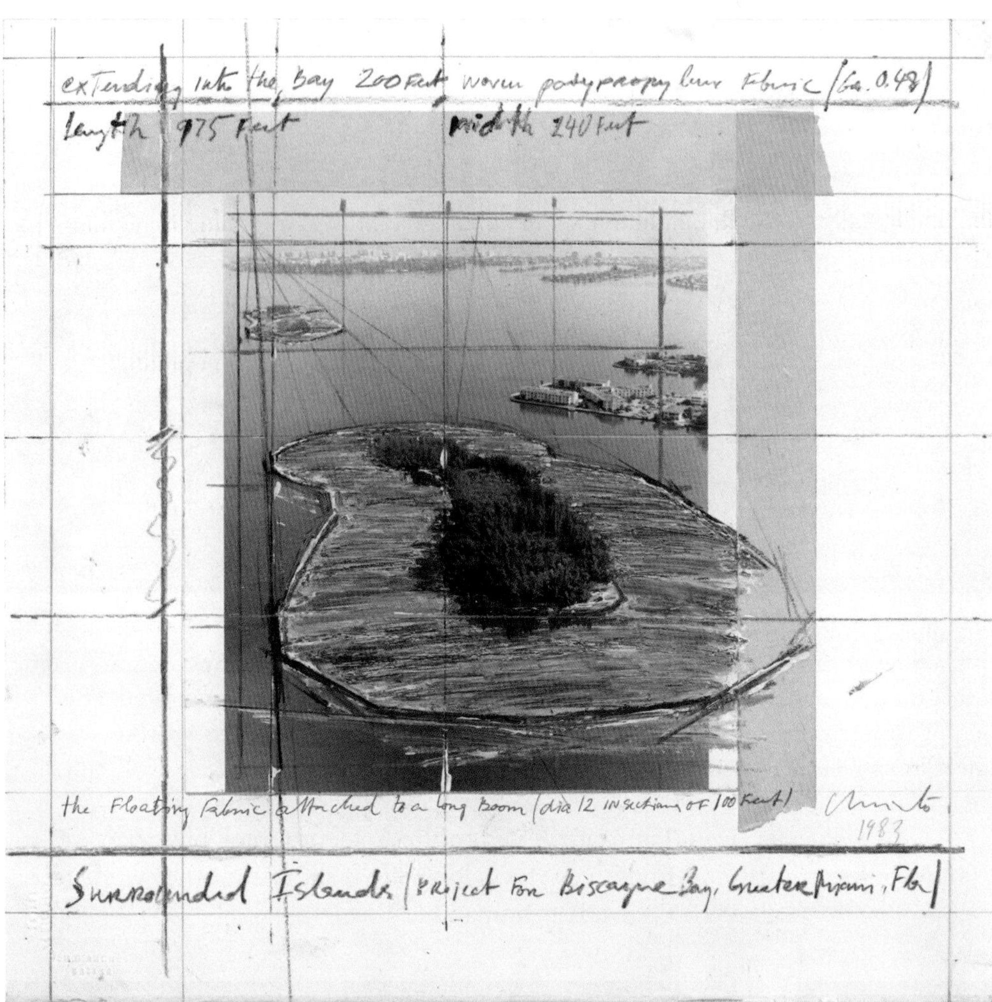

Figure 3.20: The drawings and collages made by Christo and Jeanne-Claude are what remain after the large-scale installations are taken down. The artists used the proceeds from the sale of these works on paper to finance their projects.

ACTIVITY 3.13: ACT LOCAL

Try the opposite approach to Activity 3.12 and make something low impact and non-invasive in your own environment. This could be in a natural or urban environment.

Note: If you want to make street art or paint a graffiti wall, make sure that you have permission to do so in that particular place and that you respect the property of others. There are many situations in which artists are welcome to make works in public places: with a bit of research you can find out where that might be in your community.

Installation art

The term **installation art** describes an artistic genre that involves a transformation of a space. Generally, the term is applied to interior spaces, whereas outdoor interventions are often called **land art**, but the boundaries between these terms overlap.

ACTIVITY 3.12: DREAM BIG

In your journal, design a large-scale land art project for a specific place in the world. You are only making the **plan** so you might as well dream big. Unless you get crowd-funded, you probably wont be making the actual piece – at least not yet! Write a short rationale to support your idea.

Figure 3.21: In this photo a student at La Vigna Art Studios, Pisa is making a site-specific artwork. She is wrapping cotton yarn around the knots in the trees to accentuate the natural shapes that bear an uncanny resemblance to eyes.

Installation art can be either temporary or permanent. Many installations are site-specific in that they are designed to exist only in the space for which they were created. This kind of art opens up a broader sensory experience, rather than focusing on a single object like a painting on a wall or a sculpture on a pedestal.

Ars longa, vita brevis (Latin, attributed to the Ancient Greek physician Hippocrates, translates in English as 'Art is long, life is short'. In other words, art outlasts human life.)

Ephemeral: Existing only for a short time, impermanent, transient.

Figure 3.22: Berndnaut Smilde, *Nimbus d'Aspremont*, 2012 (ephemeral materials). Dutch artist Berndnaut Smilde creates installations of clouds suspended in space for only a few moments and captured through video documentation and photography. These ephemeral installations are also site specific, the setting contributing significantly to the overall experience.

Transient or ephemeral artworks are those that exist only for a determined period of time – they are not intended to last.

- Does this make it any less valuable as an art piece?
- Does art need to be permanent to endure in our minds?
- Does this challenge the notion that art outlasts human life?
- What does the interest in ephemeral, less solid materials say about the world we live in?

ACTIVITY 3.14: DISCOVER AN INSTALLATION ARTIST

Choose an artist from the list, then use the following questions to help you write about the artist's work.

- What is the relationship of the work to the space it is shown in?
- What kinds of materials does the artist use and how do they play a role in the outcome?
- Is this work permanent, temporary or ephemeral? Does time play a role?
- How does the viewer interact with the work? Is it participative?
- What do you think is the artist's intention in making this work?
- How do you relate to this work? What appeals to you about it or not?

INSTALLATION ARTISTS:

- Jeanne-Claude and Christo
- Louise Bourgeois
- Gabriel Orozco
- Allora & Calzadilla
- Emily Jacir
- Olafur Eliasson
- Doris Salcedo
- Rachel Whiteread
- Ann Hamilton
- Cornelia Parker
- Ernesto Neto
- Fischli/Weiss.

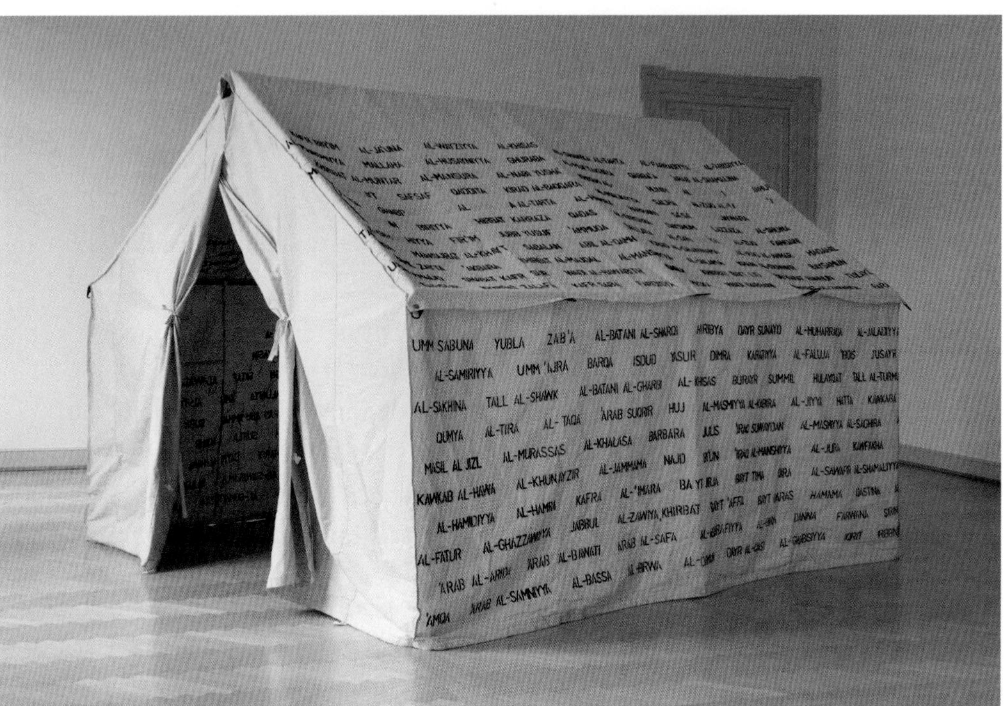

Figure 3.23: Emily Jacir, *Memorial to 418 Palestinian Villages Which Were Destroyed, Depopulated and Occupied by Israel in 1948*, 2001. Palestinian-American artist Emily Jacir, best known for her politically charged conceptual photography, video and installation projects, was an IB art student herself. This installation features a refugee tent, embroidery thread, and a log book of all the people who came to her studio and participated in stitching the names of the villages on the tent.

For two months, I opened my studio to anyone who wanted to sew with me on this Memorial. Over 140 people came, the majority of them I had never met before. They came as lawyers, bankers, filmmakers, dentists, consultants, musicians, playwrights, artists, human rights activists, teachers, etcetera. They came as Palestinians (some of whom come from these villages), as Israelis (who grew up on the remains of these villages) and people from a multitude of countries. (Emily Jacir)

Places, materials, ideas

An installation can begin with a **place** or **space**. You can create a work for a specific space: small, large, open or closed.

An installation can be born from **materials**. You can create an installation piece using materials as a starting point. Collect materials or use found or discarded materials.

An installation can emerge from an **idea**. A concept or idea, such as **exclusion** or **inclusion**, can be the starting point for an installation.

If you have a thematic focus already in your work then this will provide a starting point for thinking about an installation piece. If you don't have a theme or an idea in mind, begin with choosing **where** you want to make your installation, and let the concept be led by the place.

When choosing a place to create an installation, think about the significance of the space. Is it intimate and enclosed (like a wardrobe), or is it an open public space (like the school cafeteria)? Who will see this and under what circumstances? Consider the viewer's experience.

Make notes and sketches to plan your work. Watch how ideas develop and change as you begin to encounter the physical reality of making the work. You may end up with something completely different from the idea you started with . . . that's art!

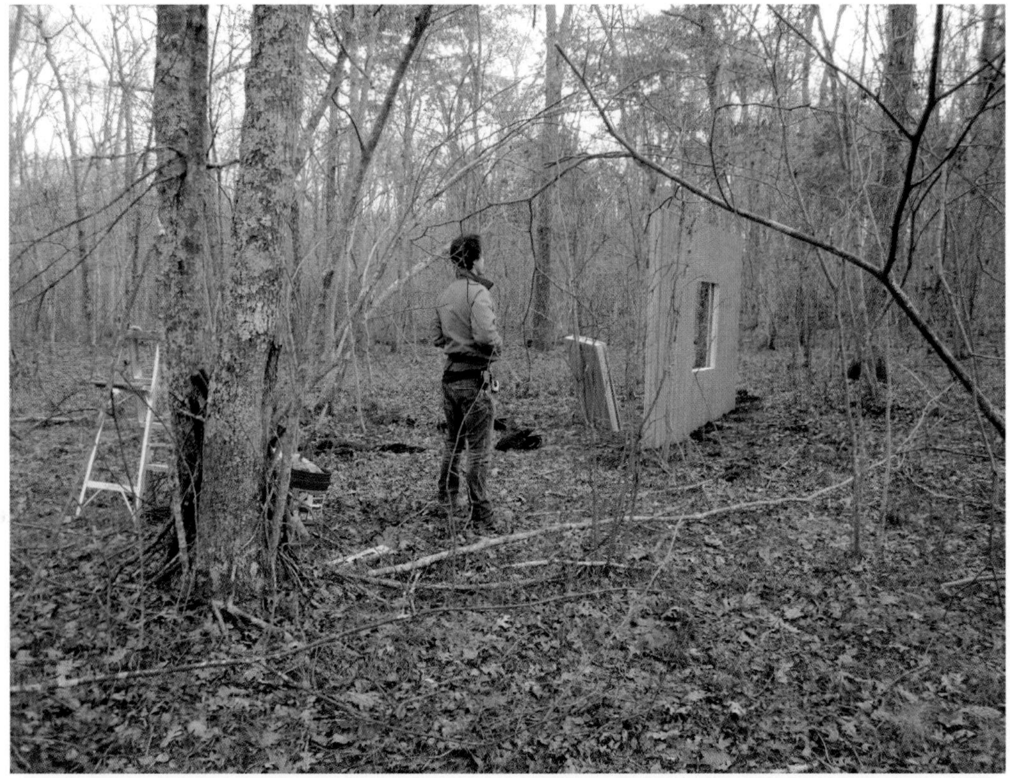

Figure 3.24: Don Edler, work in progress. The artist surveys his site-specific installation: a plasterboard wall with a cut-out window in the woods at I-Park in rural Connecticut, an entirely useless but nevertheless evocative object. The construction will remain indefinitely, provoking curiosity from the passing hikers.

ACTIVITY 3.15: SITE-SPECIFIC INSTALLATION

Make a site-specific installation piece of your own. Choose one of these starting points.

- Create an unexpected barrier or a wall within a space or outdoors.
- Use cast-off and found objects, create and furnish a 'room' or, on a smaller scale, a shelf or miniature room in a box.
- Make an alteration to a space that creates subtle visual confusion (for example, turn the pictures on a wall upside down).
- Move something out of its context and environment (for example, a boat on a rooftop).

Tip: Document your work thoroughly with photos and video; the installation may be temporary but the documentation is the testimony that remains. You will need a good record of it if you decide to include this work in your final assessment.

Summary

In this chapter you have witnessed how looking at the culture and context from which art arises can help broaden our understanding of art.

Through a series of art-making activities that explore different media and conceptual approaches, you have experienced new ways of thinking about place and culture. You have considered the impact of place and time on a given artwork and reflected on how your own work can be influenced by your surroundings and personal cultural background. You have learned about site-specific art and how place and space can impact the viewer's experience.

Chapter 4 Materials and meaning

Introduction

This chapter investigates the cultural significance of materials, looking at both traditional fine arts media and the uses of new and emerging media in contemporary practice. You will reflect on art and meaning and how the specific materials that an artist (including yourself) chooses contribute to constructing meaning.

As IB visual art students you are encouraged to explore different art forms, materials, techniques and conceptual approaches and to choose which of these to elaborate in your studio work and show in your process portfolio (PP; covered in Chapter 8). In this chapter you will explore diverse art forms, looking at examples of student work from the range of art-making forms set out in the *IB DP Visual Arts Guide*.

Note: The examples presented in this chapter are only a sampling of kinds of student artwork that are possible: not all art forms are represented. The work shown includes examples of resolved artworks and some visual journal pages/PP screens. The resolved studio work would be included in the student's final exhibition (see Chapter 9) rather than submitted in their PP.

LEARNING OBJECTIVES

- Gain familiarity with a range of techniques and art-making forms.
- Explore two-dimensional art forms.
- Explore three-dimensional art forms.
- Explore lens-based, electronic and screen-based art forms.
- Explore conceptual and material significance.

4.1 Techniques and art-making forms

Art is magic delivered from the lie of being truth.
(Theodor W. Adorno)

There are as many approaches to making art as there are artists. Your own practice will grow and change throughout the course as you engage in a variety of art-making forms and techniques. The artists that you study, the materials you choose to work with and the concepts (ideas) that you decide to explore will all help to shape and guide your development as an artist.

Choosing a medium that is appropriate to your concept is the key to the success of your artwork, not only for conceptual pieces. The materials you use, the surfaces you work with, the marks you make, the colours you choose, the scale of the work – all of these contribute to the overall effect and how the work communicates. You will be able to make these choices more easily once you have experimented with a variety of materials and techniques.

All students are required to work across different art-making forms in their PP in order to gain some familiarity with techniques and materials. The IB art-making forms table is divided into three columns:

Two-dimensional forms	Three-dimensional forms	Lens-based, electronic and screen-based forms

(The different requirements for SL and HL are discussed in discussed in Chapter 8.)

What art-making form is it?

There are times when a piece of artwork could fit into more than one column of the IB art-making forms table. A collage may become a three-dimensional assemblage, depending on the materials used. A graffiti mural may be both two-dimensional (a spray painting) and three-dimensional (carried out on a site-specific wall). A video (lens-based) may be part of a sculptural (3D) installation. In these cases you may discuss with your teacher where to place the work in relation to the art-making forms requirements (described in Chapter 8).

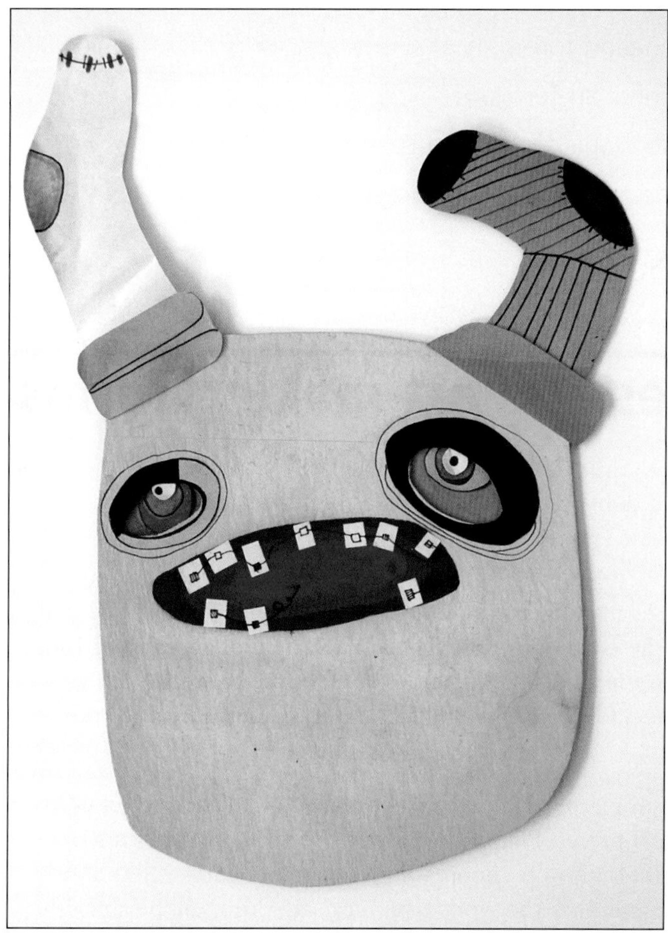

Figure 4.01: *Sock Monster* by student Sage Dever is a mixed-media collage/ assemblage. Sage uses an expressive combination of materials (felt, paper, markers, thread, buttons), colours and shapes for this whimsical character.

4.2 Two-dimensional art forms

Two-dimensional work encompasses a huge range of techniques and processes for creating imagery. It includes all kinds of drawing, painting, printmaking, graphics, frottage, collage, and anything that has a two-dimensional form.

Drawing

Drawing is a visual artist's thinking tool: it helps us to understand the physical world in terms of form, space and line and is a 'way in' to visual thinking. Drawing used to be considered mainly as a preparation for making art in other forms such as painting or sculpture, but today it stands as its own unique art form. Contemporary drawing encompasses a wide range of approaches, from hyper-realistic to purely abstract, from expansive wall drawings to postage-stamp-sized miniatures, and an equally wide range of **mark-making**.

Here, contemporary British artist Grayson Perry talks about how he makes use of many sources and experiences to create his splendidly wacky drawings, for example, Figure 4.2.

> Until we can insert a USB into our ear and download our thoughts, drawing remains the best way of getting visual information on to the page. I draw as a collagist, juxtaposing images and styles of mark-making from many sources. The world I draw is the interior landscape of my own personal obsessions and of cultures I have absorbed and adapted, from Latvian folk art to Japanese screens. I lasso thoughts with a pen.

Figure 4.02: Detail of *Map of an Englishman* (detail of a much larger piece), 2004. Grayson Perry uses the format of an antique map and the cosy drawing style of an old-fashioned illustrated children's book to create his imaginary 'map', playing with language, humour and contemporary British culture.

Tip: Make notes in your visual arts journal of the medium and the techniques you are using as you go along. Any work you put in your PP should be accompanied by a written explanation of why you have included it. Any work that you choose for your exhibition should be accompanied by an exhibition text that states the medium used. (Note that the requirements shown in the art-making forms table do not necessarily apply to work you select for your exhibition.)

Mark-making: Marks are used to create an image but mark-making can also be explored for its expressive value. The quality of the mark depends on many factors: the tool used, the medium and the surface, as well as the hand making the mark.

Materials and meaning

Still life: A still life is an arrangement of inanimate objects.

If you want to improve your drawing skills, start drawing from life. You will gain understanding of volume and space by observing the three-dimensional world directly rather than looking at it flattened on a screen or copying images of images. Begin practising observational drawing with a **still life** or a self-portrait, or look to nature for complex, beautiful and challenging forms 'in the round' (in three dimensions). Activities 4.1–4.3 focus on observational drawing.

ACTIVITY 4.1: OBSERVATIONAL STILL-LIFE DRAWING

Make an observational drawing (drawn directly from life, not from a photograph or from memory).

- Choose several objects that work well together or tell a story.
- Set up a composition of the objects on a table surface, adding visual interest (for example, include a patterned cloth on the table or as the background).
- Create a direct light source.
- First, map out your composition lightly with a pencil.
- Adjust the proportional relationships between objects, looking at the negative space around the objects.
- Complete your drawing using charcoal or an ink wash.

Tonal values: This refers to the degree of light or dark on a grey scale (from white to black).

Figure 4.03: Drawing (charcoal on paper) by student Enrico Giori. He has chosen a cleaning cupboard as the subject of this still life, in line with his personal exploration of domesticity. The clutter of the closet is rendered with bold gestural mark marks and strong diagonal lines. He uses a range of tonal values achieved by using both vine charcoal (lighter) and compressed charcoal (darker).

ACTIVITY 4.2: SELF-PORTRAIT VIEWPOINT

Draw yourself in a mirror. This is not an idealised 'selfie' – your objective is not to flatter but to observe carefully.

For a different viewpoint, try one of these variations:

- Place the mirror above or below you for a bird's-eye or fish-eye view.
- Use a convex mirror to create a distorted effect.

STUDENT EXAMPLE: POLINA ZAKHAROVA

Figure 4.04: Pencil and ink drawing by student Polina Zakharova. This drawing uses observational, expressive and imaginative drawing styles. Polina has devised a composition that creates tension through a compressed and claustrophobic space, the three figures framed by the disjointed arms.

Here, student Polina Zakharova tells us about her passion for drawing people that are important to her:

> Drawing became a new way for me to express my feelings. I started off from drawing portraits, and people still are my favourite subject matter. However, it is necessary to highlight that it is important for me to have feelings for the person I am drawing or painting. It can be feeling of respect of friendship, but is mostly affection, care and tenderness that provoke to make a portrait. To me it is a special way of making a photograph – however, a photograph is not as personal as the process of drawing or painting, I prefer the last two. I want to keep the person in my sketchbook, or in my portfolio, and keep it there, just as others keep photographs of their loved ones in their purse.

ACTIVITY 4.3: GHOST DRAWING

This exercise gives new life to an old pencil drawing and encourages you to revisit a piece of your work that you aren't happy with.

- Choose a piece of work to revisit.
- Smudge it all over really well.
- Gently erase some lines through it until you can barely recognise the image.
- Redraw the same image over the top of the old, letting the old image be the 'ghost' of the new.

STUDENT EXAMPLE: JAMES McGOLDRICK

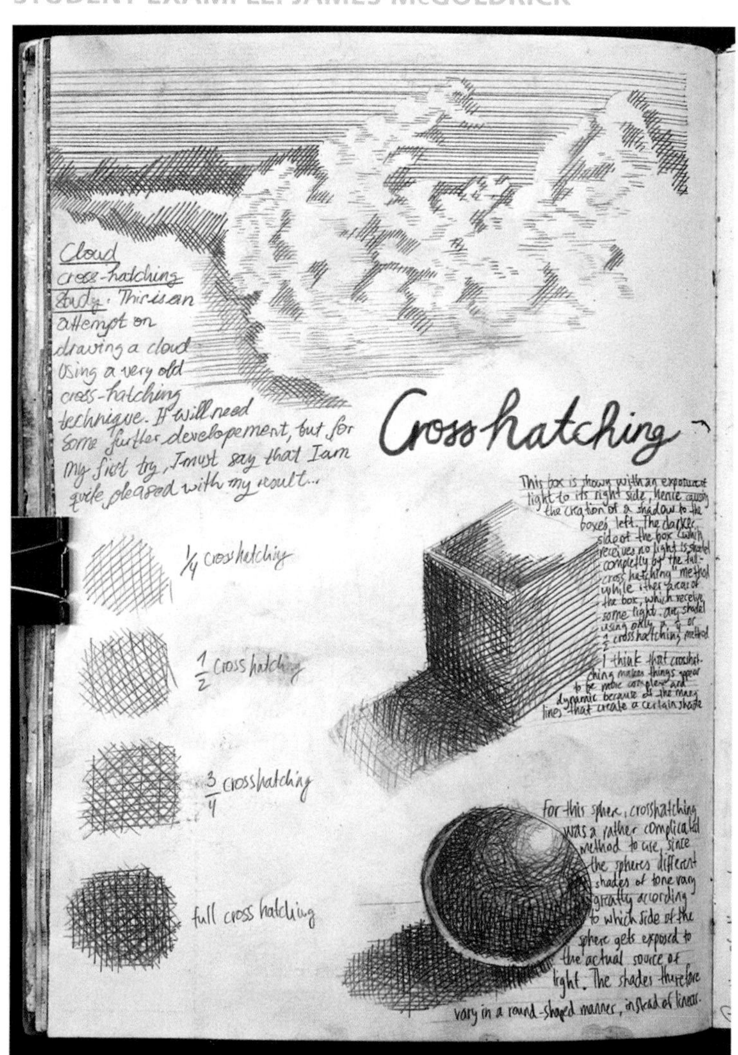

Figure 4.05: In this visual journal page, student James McGoldrick explores cross-hatching as a kind of mark-making to build up areas of shadow. He also applies cross-hatching to different shapes to create volume.

ACTIVITY 4.4: MARK-MAKING: FOUND LINES

- Observe different kinds of lines in your environment: the cracks in the pavement, a piece of found wire, a tangle of cables, a knot of delicate hair.
- Make a series of line drawings of these in your journal, using various drawing media: pencil, pen, marker, biro and graphite, adding descriptive notes.

Figure 4.06: *Drawing #12* by student James McGoldrick. This ink-pen drawing is built up of multiple marks, loosely cross-hatched and layered. The student is developing his own personal style with expressive mark-making and curvilinear forms.

Here, student James McGoldrick tells us how his work has been influenced by his investigations into German art:

> In my art, I try to show the German culture and mentality as I experienced them prior to moving to a country that is, in many ways, different from my own. Art has been the tool that I turned to in order to express the ardent bond I feel with my native culture. By experimenting with different media, such as linocut, 3D model-building and photography, I tried to depict what I thought German culture truly resembled to me. Influential German artists, such as painter Otto Dix, and printmaker Albrecht Dürer, created a foundation of inspiration for my own artwork.

Drawing surface: This refers to the paper or any other support – for example, wood, cardboard, a tablet, a wall – on which a drawing is made.

Tip: Document all of these activities in your visual arts journal with notes about the materials and techniques you are using, your observations and photos of the process. This will be useful when assembling your PP.

ACTIVITY 4.7: MARK-MAKING WITH NATURE

Experiment with using natural materials or processes to make marks. Keep a scientific record of the process.

- Try making marks with plants, berries, stones, ash or other natural substances.
- Leave a piece of paper out in the rain or the sun for a day or a few days; see what happens. Use this surface as a starting point for a drawing.

ACTIVITY 4.5: DRAWING THE NEWS

This activity is a response to current events in the world and requires you to select your content carefully.

- Make a drawing that is an exact copy of a section of a newspaper page, including both image and text.
- Explain why this topic is interesting to you.
- What are you saying about it by copying it?
- Enlarge or crop the image as suits your intentions.

You can draw on practically any kind of **surface** and you can use any number of tools to make marks. Depending on type of paper, rough, smooth, coloured, printed, you can create different textures, colours and contexts for your drawing.

ACTIVITY 4.6: DRAWING ON FIVE SURFACES

Create a series of drawings of the same subject on five differently textured or coloured surfaces and discuss in your journal how each surface impacts the drawing.

Suggestions:

- graph paper
- tracing paper
- toned paper
- book pages
- found paper
- corrugated cardboard
- sandpaper
- fabric.

Drawing on walls or floors or any (nearly) undefined surface allows the drawing to flow over edges into other spaces, suggesting continuity and expansion. A drawing or painting on a wall or another built surface could be considered as a 3D art form.

Painting, collage and 2D mixed media

Painting, another major player in two-dimensional forms, includes a vast range of media and techniques such as oil, acrylic, egg-tempera, watercolour, gouache, ink, and mixed media. There are as many ways to apply paint as there are surfaces and subject matter.

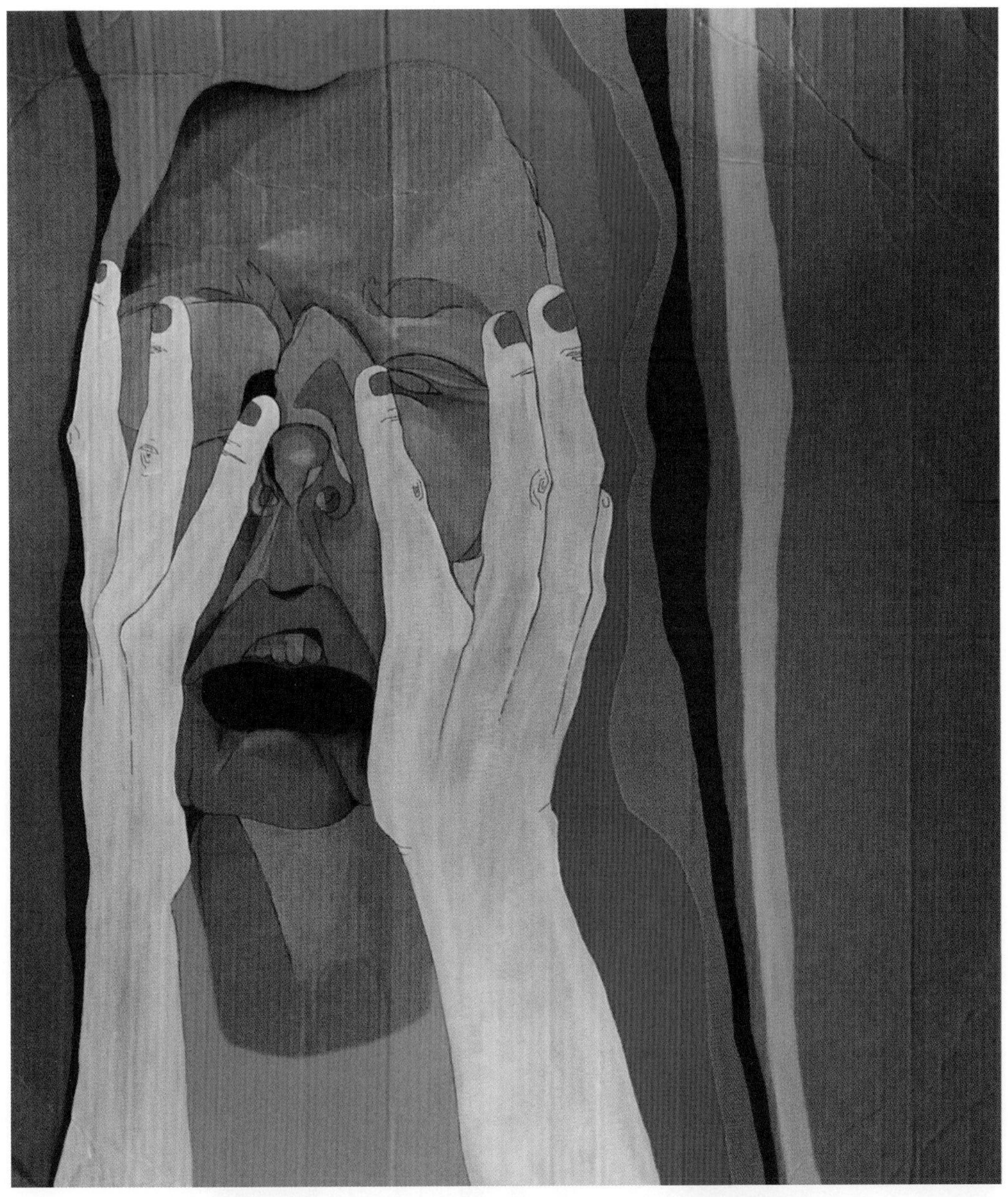

Figure 4.07: ***Noa*** **by student Sage Dever is an acrylic painting on cardboard. Strong drawing skills and good understanding of colour underpin this composition.**

The support that is used to paint on can also communicate meaning. In *Noa* (Figure 4.07), student Sage Dever uses cardboard as the support for her acrylic painting. Cardboard has a throwaway aesthetic – in other words it doesn't feel very precious, and it is cheap and easy to find. She paints on an unprepared surface, leaving the raw cardboard as the background colour and texture. The face is also exposed cardboard, making a marked contrast to the ghoulish white of the hands. Influences of Egon Schiele, an artist Sage studied, are clearly discernible in the angular, exaggerated drawing of hands and facial features. The stylised hair is painted in bright, saturated colours, which contrast with the dull brown of the cardboard.

Supports

A support is the material or surface on which a painting is created, usually paper, canvas or a wooden panel.

Collage: Collage comes from the French word *coller*, to glue. A collage may include all sorts of paper and other materials, newspaper clippings, coloured or hand-made papers, portions of other artwork or texts, photographs and other found objects, all glued to a support.

Supports include:

- **Paper:** good for light work, **collage**, sketching and drawing, using inks and watercolours, gouache, acrylic and so forth. Paper comes in a huge range of textures, weights, tones and colours.
- **Cardboard:** slightly stronger than paper, it's cheap, but creates a certain effect, a 'throwaway' aesthetic.
- **Wood panels:** a board is more rigid than canvas and useful in circumstances where a strong support is needed. Panels can be used with traditional gessos, or when a fine, detailed finish is required.
- **Canvas and linen:** these need to be stretched on a frame (stretcher) and prepared with gesso or sized. Canvas is normally used for oil or acrylic paintings. Try stretching your own rather than buying a pre-fabricated canvas; you will notice the difference.
- **Stretcher:** the wooden supports for the canvas.

There are many other two-dimensional art-making forms to explore besides drawing and painting: for example, collage, printmaking, camera-less photography, paper-cutting, graphic design and illustration – almost anything on a flat surface. Experiment widely and fearlessly!

Figure 4.08 Mixed media collage by student So Young Lim. She uses a combination of drawing, photographs, watercolour and acrylic paint and marker pens to create this dynamic, contemporary take on the classic fairy tale *Hansel and Gretel*.

Printmaking

Printmaking is an art form in which multiple prints are produced from a single image. The original image is transferred by inking and printing from a printing plate, block, stamp or stencil. Because you are able to create multiples of any print, you have the possibility of working work back into them, drawing over, collaging onto, generally experimenting without the fear of spoiling the single piece.

STUDENT EXAMPLE: KSENIA KLIMOVA

Figure 4.09: Close-up from a monotype series, *Movement of Pain*, by student Ksenia Klimova. This expressive image has a sense of immediacy but also of intimacy. Ksenia made drawings from photographs of children at the Imperial War museum's *Holocaust* exhibition in London, which she felt resembled a dance/movement of pain. She then used the monotype printing technique, which permits a loose, gestural drawing style and which she felt expressed the morbid character of her subject.

Monotype: A monotype is painted directly on a piece of glass or plastic and printed onto paper. It is usually a one-of-a-kind print, although you can make variations.

Printmaking terms

Relief print: A print which is made from the raised portions of a carved block, like a rubber stamp.

Linoleum print: A relief print carved into linoleum.

Intaglio print: A print made from ink forced into the recessed lines of a block or plate, like etching or engraving. This technique requires a press.

Embossing: A raised pattern or design created by pressure without any ink.

Frottage: The technique or process of taking a rubbing from an uneven surface to form the basis of a work of art.

SPOTLIGHT ON THE STUDENT: KSENIA KLIMOVA

Nationality: Russian
Born: Moscow

Main artistic interests:

- Russian cultural heritage
- simple and ordinary people
- emotions, neuroscience
- politics.

Influential artists:

- Anselm Kiefer
- Jindřich Štreit
- Ryan Tippery
- Harding Meyer
- Jenny Saville
- Henry Moore.
- Tommy Lee Hunson.

Frottage

ACTIVITY 4.8: FROTTAGE TEXTURES

Look for low-relief textures and patterns in your environment: for example in iron-work or textured wallpaper:

- Make a **frottage**, placing paper over the texture and rubbing with a graphite stick.
- Note where each texture/pattern was found.
- Make an artwork that incorporates these textures.

Tip: For assessment purposes, graphic design work may be considered either as a 2D or as a digital art-making form.

Graphics and illustration

Graphic design is a form of visual communication that includes combinations of text, photos, illustrations, logos and symbols, and is often seen in advertising, book and web design. If you are working with this art-making form, you might use a combination of digital and fine-arts media.

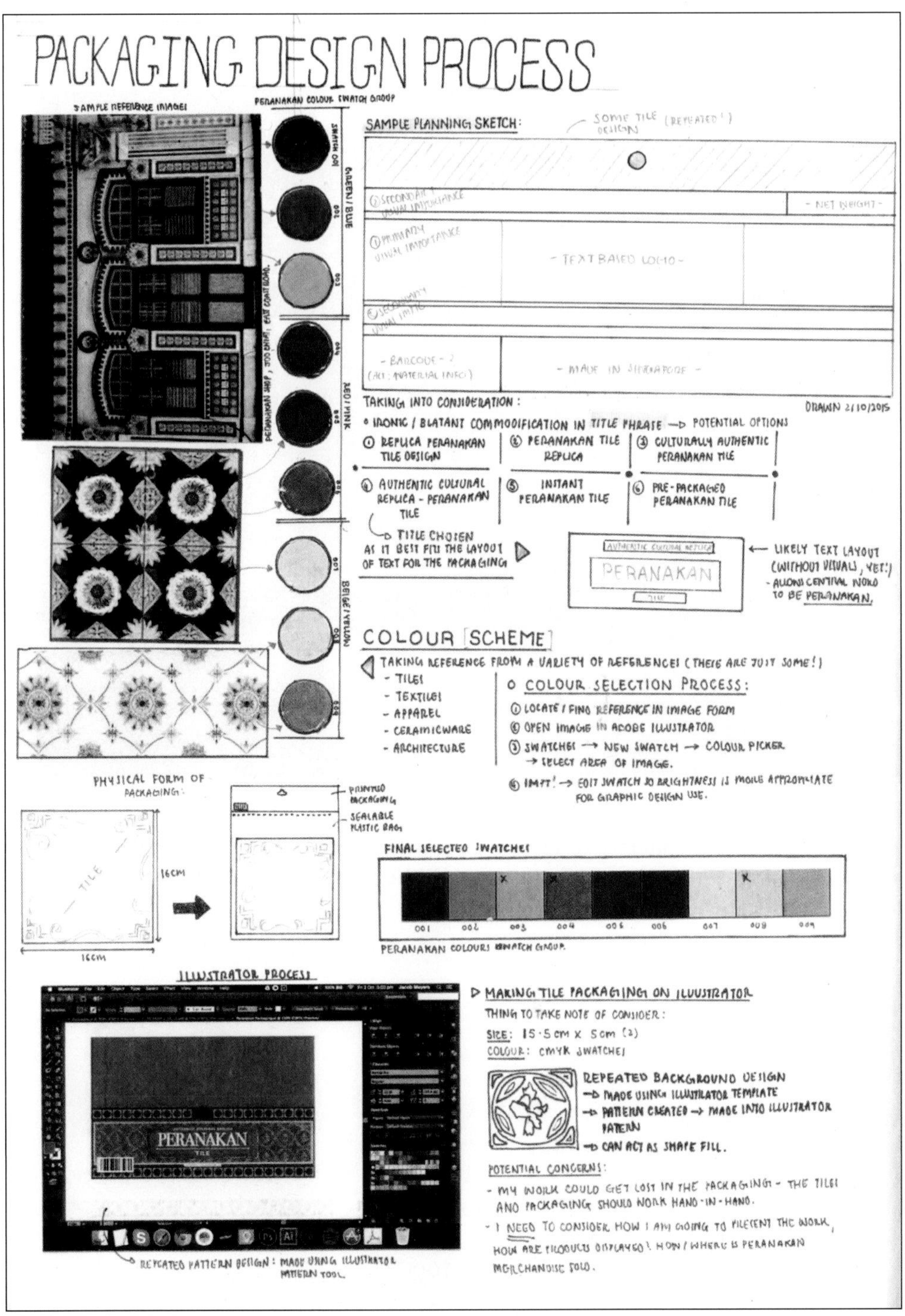

Figure 4.10: A visual journal page by student Jacob Elias Meyers Jing Long planning a packaging design using Adobe Illustrator. The product is Jacob's own clay tile designs, so he is making a 3D form, designing the packaging (2D) as shown here, and creating the package (digital media).

Illustration is also a form of graphics that illustrates a subject or an idea, often with a narrative content, and includes book illustration, fashion illustration, cartoons and graphic novels.

STUDENT EXAMPLE: JULIA GRANILLO TOSTADO

Figure 4.11: *In bocca al lupo* by student Julia Granillo Tostado. Julia created illustrations drawing on imagery from fairy tales in European culture. The title (Italian) translates literally as 'Into the mouth of the wolf' and is used to offer support, as in 'Don't be scared'.

SPOTLIGHT ON THE STUDENT: JULIA GRANILLO TOSTADO

Nationality: Mexican
Born: Mexico City

Main artistic interests:

- spaces which transmit emotion
- stories without words
- combination of naive and sinister worlds
- Mexican folklore
- applying fairy tales to tell a personal story
- sexual awakening and loss of innocence.

Influential artists/writers:

- Edward Gorey
- Henri Matisse
- J.M.W. Turner
- Lewis Carroll
- The Grimm Brothers
- Hans Christian Andersen.

4.3 Three-dimensional art forms

The second column of the IB art-making forms table refers to three-dimensional work, which includes a huge range of media and techniques. **Sculpture** of all kinds is included: ceramics, wood, metal, glass, resin, **assemblage**, found objects, collections, casts, moulds and mobiles. Designed objects such as vessels, furniture, fashion and accessories may be considered three-dimensional work. Textiles, tapestries and fibre art, environmental art and site-specific installations – there is all of this and more to explore.

Sculpture: Three-dimensional art form where objects that represent a person, idea or thing are formed out of material(s) such as clay, stone, wood, metal, metal, styrofoam.

Assemblage: Three-dimensional collage work produced by the incorporation of everyday objects into the composition.

Sculpture and assemblage

Sculpture may be carved, cast, moulded, modelled, welded or assembled using a wide range of materials, traditional and non-traditional.

Tip: If you are using found objects to create a new artwork, the resulting combination of objects can be considered an original art piece. (See also Chapter 9.) When working with found or sourced objects always label them as such in your exhibition text.

Figure 4.12: Student work (low-relief assemblage) made in a masterclass with sculptor Andrea Locci at La Vigna Art Studios. These whimsical characters are made of recycled materials assembled with drills and screws (not glue) and mounted on a painted wood base.

ACTIVITY 4.9: MIXED-MEDIA ASSEMBLAGE

Create a character assembled from different materials.

- Collect different kinds of printed material, buttons, sequins, hardware and so on.
- Cut and prepare a base shape from wood, metal or cardboard.
- Add features and details by collaging or assembling from your collected material.
- Mount your character on a base or attach a hook on the back to hang on a wall.
- Explain the reasons of your choices of specific media and how these materials communicate your artistic intentions.

STUDENT EXAMPLE: MARCUS SPECHT

Figure 4.13 ***Symphonic Dissonance, or The Orchestra of the World,*** **a sculptural installation by student Marcus Specht, consists of musical instruments hand-crafted by him. The instruments are based on different regions of the world, and are both real and imagined.**

Here, student Marcus Specht writes about the thinking behind his piece:

> I am trying to represent the possibility of an 'orchestra of the world' made up of seemingly conflicting ideas that, although they may produce dissonance, do not necessarily result in cacophony. I am using the metaphor of the symphony, composed of all kinds of instruments, real and imagined, European, African, Australian to show diversity and to explore my thoughts on living in a globalised world made of many cultures and sounds.

Tip: When photographing your work for your exhibition (Chapter 9), remember that this is the evidence the examiner will see. Figure 4.14 is a good example of properly photographed 3D artwork: the photograph is evenly lit and sharply focused against a solid black background.

STUDENT EXAMPLE: ELEANOR WELLS

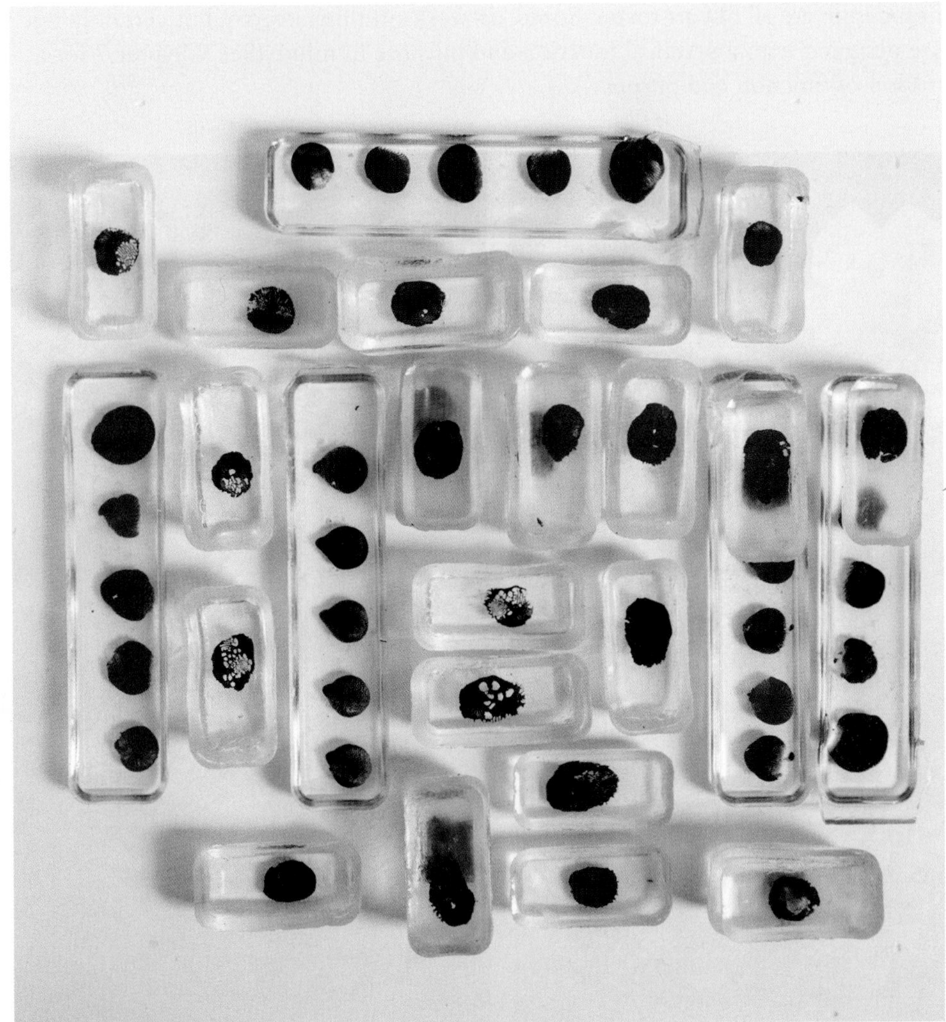

Figure 4.14: *Leave No Trace* (resin and acrylic paint) by student Eleanor Wells.

Here, Eleanor writes about the meaning of her art work:

> This piece is made of various resin blocks with my fingerprints cast inside in black and red acrylic paint. Fingerprints are a sign of our individuality – no one has the same fingerprint. I used fingerprints because we leave them everywhere, yet cannot see them. They are used to identify us, but tell us nothing of who we really are.

Designed objects, textiles and fashion

Furniture, vessels, designed objects, textiles, weaving, printed fabrics, architecture and fashion design are all 3D art forms. Some art works in this category, but certainly not all, are designed with a practical function and purpose in mind. (See Chapter 7 for a discussion of function and purpose.)

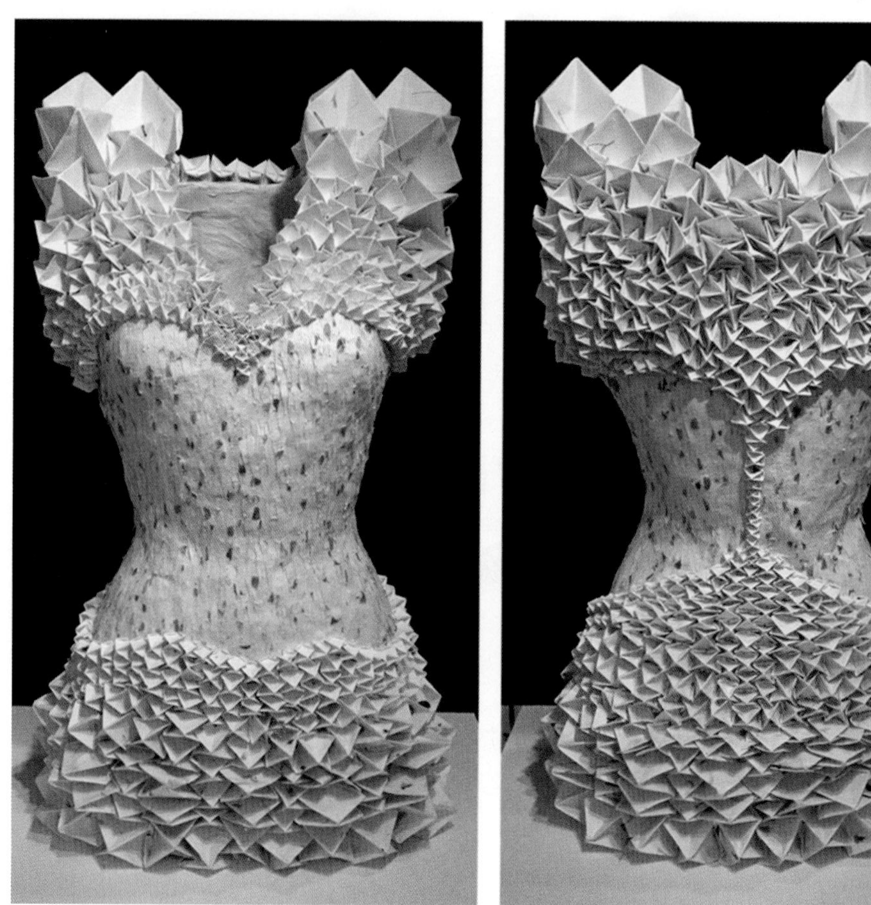

Figure 4.15: This sculptural (non-wearable) dress by student Shihaam Adams is made of paper and mixed media constructed on a rigid support. Shihaam was inspired by Alexander McQueen's fashion designs and by origami folding.

Site-specific and ephemeral materials

Site-specific art, land art, installations and murals are considered part of 3D art forms. (See also Chapter 3, which introduces site-specific and installation art in the context of environment and place.)

The concept of what can be used to make art today includes materials unthinkable a hundred years ago: crystals, pollen, blood, rain, the internet, clouds . . . There is a move in contemporary art practice towards more ephemeral materials, things that have no longevity or durability. Installations are dismantled after a brief period of time, live performance pieces finish, organic material disintegrates. These impermanent works are documented with video or still photography and the documentation is usually what remains of the artwork.

STUDENT EXAMPLE: WONHEE LEE

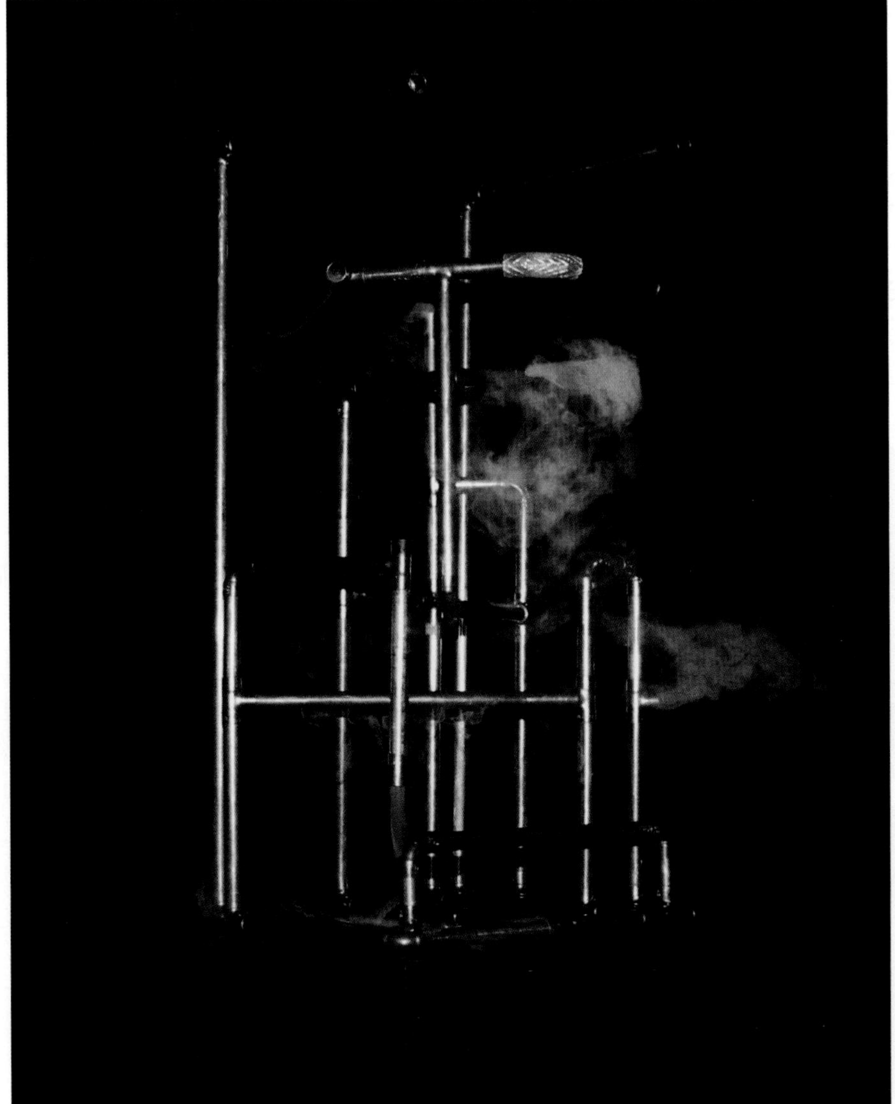

Figure 4.16: *Steamvine* by student Wonhee Lee is constructed from 12 mm copper pipes, epoxy adhesive, wood, nails, acrylic paint, fishing wire, and a humidifier in a black box. This sculptural installation has ephemeral, sensory qualities (steam, heat) that are best experienced live.

Here, Wonhee writes about the inspiration for *Steamvine*:

> This experimental sculpture explores the element of steam and the power of heat. I was initially inspired by the Israeli artist Sigalit Landau and her project *One Man's Floor is Another Man's Feelings* (2011), which used water instead of steam. Vapour, like blur, for me evokes imagination and memories.

(You can learn more about the thinking process and construction of Wonhee's work in Chapter 8.)

ACTIVITY 4.16: UNCONVENTIONAL MATERIALS

Think of an unusual material that you feel has a powerful charge in itself. Brainstorm an art piece using this material. Make it!

- Record your process with notes and images in your visual journal.
- Document the finished piece with video or photos.
- Written reflection: Do materials have power of their own or does the artist imbue the material with its power?

4.4 Lens-based, electronic and screen-based art forms

Tip: When documenting time-based work for your final exhibition, be sure to state clearly in the exhibition text in what medium you presented it: was it a live performance piece or a video projection of the performance?

Column three of the IB art-making forms table includes time-based and sequential art such as animation and performance art, lens-based photography and moving image, lens-less media such as photogram/rayograph, pinhole photography, cyanotype, digital collage and montage, video, projections, screen-based graphics and software generated design.

Time-based and sequential art forms

Time-based and sequential art forms include animation, storyboard, performance art and any work that takes place over a period of time.

Figure 4.17: This time-based performance piece by student Alberte Holmø Bojesens is documented in a seven-minute film. Alberte describes the performance in her exhibition text: 'The piece depicts how adolescents dance around in their own little world, egoism made visual through dance and music. The eerie feeling is created by sheets and blue light, inspired by the choreography in the film *First Born* [dir. Isaac Webb] and by Christo's *Running Fence*. The original dance and sound are inspired by the musician Nick Cave's performances.'

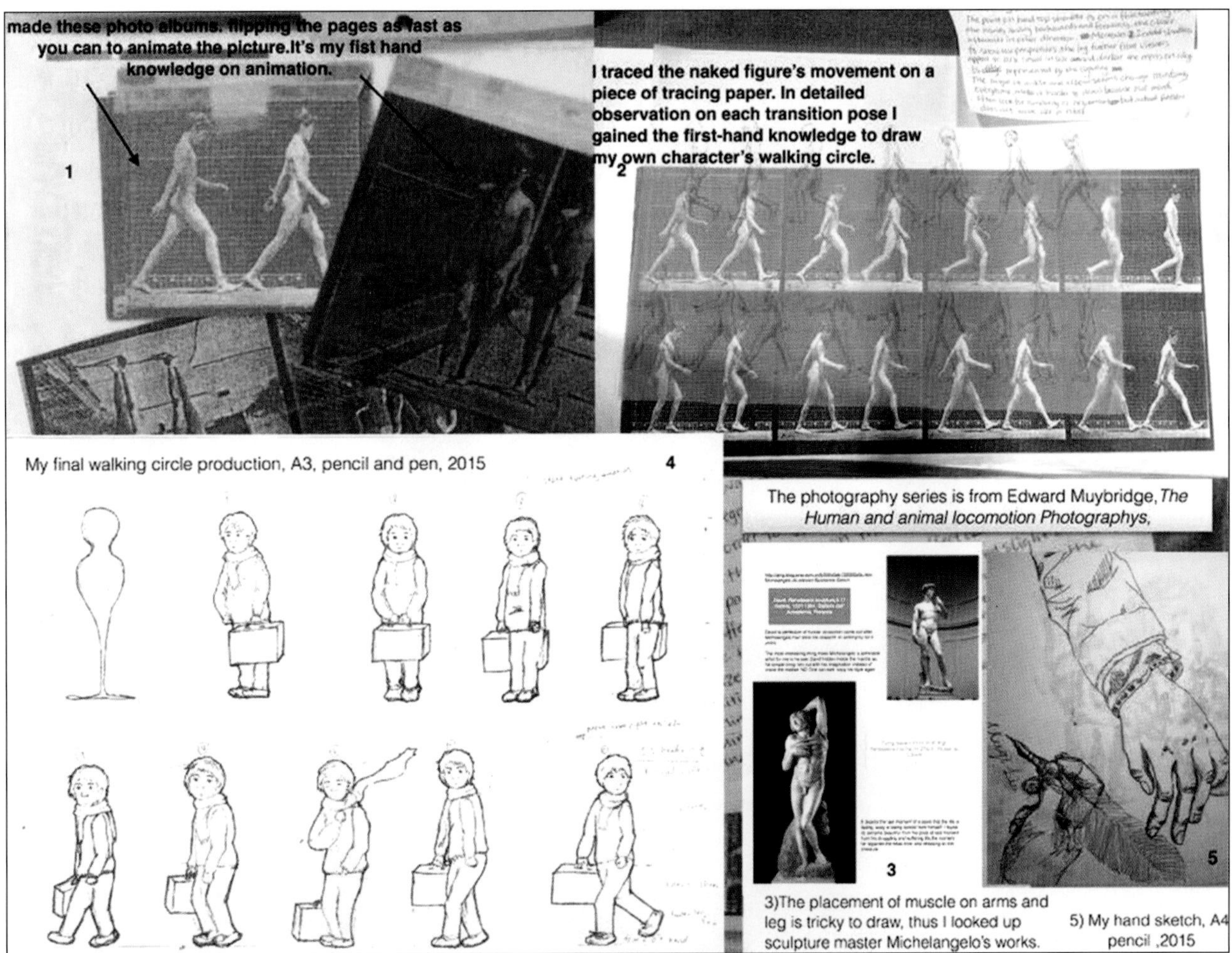

made these photo albums. flipping the pages as fast as you can to animate the picture.It's my fist hand knowledge on animation.
1
I traced the naked figure's movement on a piece of tracing paper. In detailed observation on each transition pose I gained the first-hand knowledge to draw my own character's walking circle.
2
My final walking circle production, A3, pencil and pen, 2015
4
The photography series is from Edward Muybridge, The Human and animal locomotion Photographys,
3
3)The placement of muscle on arms and leg is tricky to draw, thus I looked up sculpture master Michelangelo's works.
5
5) My hand sketch, A4 pencil ,2015

Figure 4.18: Process portfolio screen by student Meiqi Liu. On this screen she is figuring out how to make the figure move across the page by studying Eadweard Muybridge's photos and Michelangelo's sculptures of the human body. She is working out transitions for her own hand-drawn animation *Unexpected Encounter* about a boy on a journey of discovery.

ACTIVITY 4.17: DRAWING ANIMATION

A simple animation can be created with a series of drawings and still photos.

- Draw a storyboard to plan the flow of your sequence.
- Draw each frame and photograph it (try black marker line drawings for a simple effect, or use charcoal and erasure (as in the work of **William Kentridge**) reworking the same drawing for each frame).
- Use computer software programs (such as iMovie, Keynote) to turn your drawings into an animation.

William Kentridge: William Kentridge is a South African artist well known for his animated films, as well as his drawings and prints. Kentridge makes his animations by filming a charcoal drawing, making slight changes (adding or erasing), filming again and continuing like this for each frame until the end of the scene.

Lens-based and digital/screen-based art forms

Lens-based media includes photography, montage projections and any work captured through a lens. Digital and screen-based forms include software-generated images, vector graphics and vector design.

STUDENT EXAMPLE: ELISABETH LAUER

Here, student Elisabeth Lauer writes about her challenges in making *Me and Animal*:

> In order to fuse two images to look like one picture I had to use two images of similar quality, adjusting size and colour. I did my animal/human face series more for fun than as a statement, but I researched Le Brun's *System on Physiognomy* and discovered that historically humans have long assigned meaning to facial features reminiscent of animals.

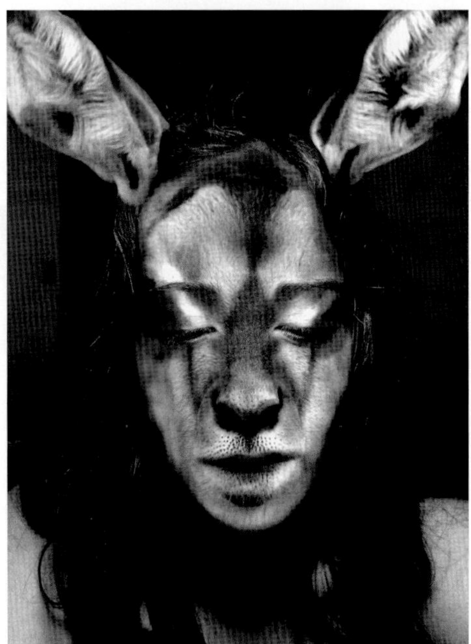

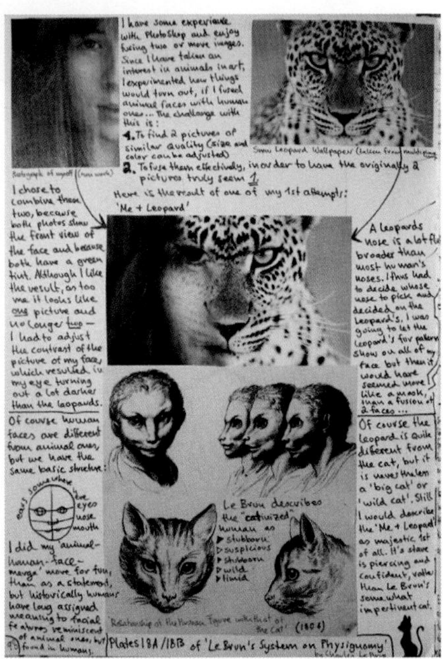

Figures 4.19 and 4.20: *Me and Animal* (left) by student Elisabeth Lauer is a digital image created in Photoshop, part of a series in which she merges her own self-portraits with different animal faces. Her journal page (right) shows part of the process and development of this series. This page discusses a different image in the series, a leopard, which uses the same concept and technique as in Figure 4.19.

Elisabeth's journal page (Figure 4.20) shows the development of her ideas and the steps involved in creating the images in her series of prints.

Tip: When using digital media it is equally as important to document the process as with other techniques, so take lots of screenshots! You can include the documentation in your visual journal or directly in your PP.

Figure 4.21: Collage montage from the series *Urban Collages* by student Jacob Elias Meyers Jing Long. Jacob created them by manipulating and reassembling his photographs of buildings in his environment. He says he is interested in forming an 'artificial urban identity using images of physically existing structures'. The work explores composition, space and perspective by cropping and combining different viewpoints.

STUDENT EXAMPLE: GARANCE COURBON

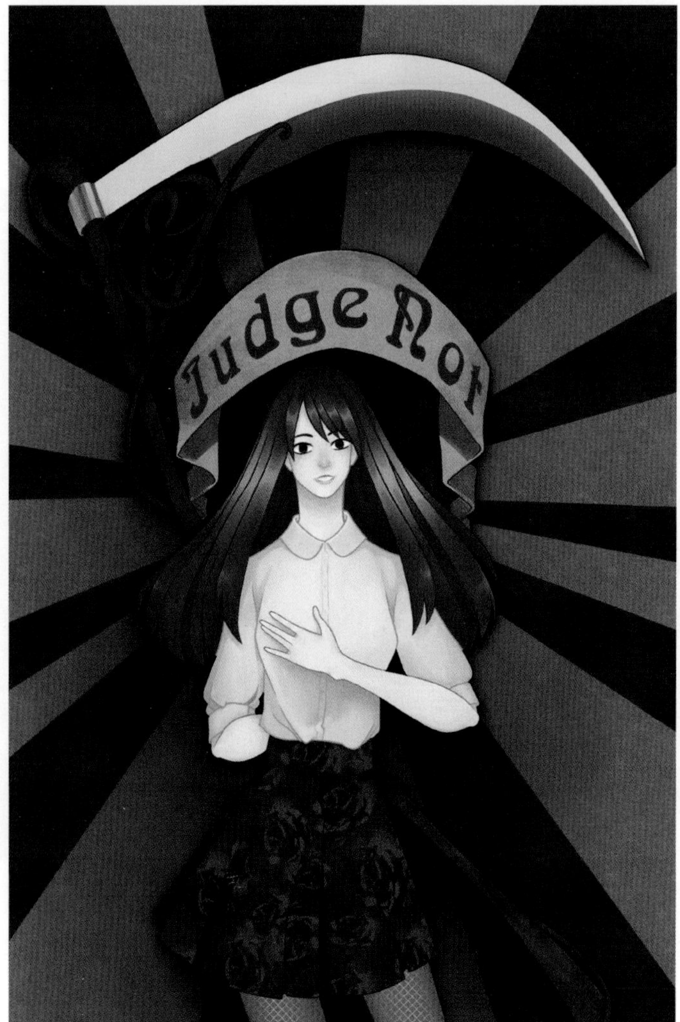

Figure 4.22: *Judge Not* by student Garance Courbon is a digital software-generated image of her original design and concept. She exhibited the work as a digital print, poster size 29.7 × 21 cm.

Here, student Garance Courbon reflects on the meaning of her imagery and the influences on her work in this comment from her curatorial rationale:

> This is an illustration of a quote by Nietzsche: 'One must not let oneself be misled: they say "Judge not!" but they send to Hell everything that stands in their way.' I picked this quote because I am interested in the theme of existentialism and because I felt it represented our race very well. The scythe represents the 'send to hell' part as it reminds us of reapers. She has her hand on her heart to show the will not to judge and to be good. The scythe is hidden behind her to illustrate the deceiving nature of humans. My artistic influences are a mixture of Art Nouveau, from my French background, and a personal interest in *manga*. The Art Nouveau style influenced the scythe, the banner and the gender of the character.

New media

As IB Visual Art embraces the 21st century, it encourages students to become aware of the uses of emerging media as well as traditional artistic media. This does not mean that you should not continue to use traditional techniques and fine-art media. An understanding of form, line, composition, light and shadow, depth and volume is essential for training your eye and your mind to see, whether you are working with traditional or new media. New media (sometimes called **emerging media**) often includes technology as part of the process, but it isn't necessarily digitally made. New media refers to media that explores new territories, the crossroads of art, innovation, technology, science, communication, collaborative practices, social activism, appropriation, open sourcing . . .

ACTIVITY 4.18: NEW TERRITORIES

Make a mixed-media artwork that combines traditional and new media, such as drawing and video, or photography and social activism. What uses of new or emerging media can you come up with in each of these areas:

- appropriation: intentionally using material from other sources?
- social networking?
- collaborative work?

Figure 4.23: This interactive digital artwork *Crying Sirens* by student Sara Sashar is an series of animated sketches displayed on iPads. She combines drawing and technology, photographing her pen sketches and using an app on her phone to animate them. The animations repeat whatever the viewer says to them, like nine talking parrots. Sara writes in the exhibition text 'my intention is to communicate the identities of each individual imitating one another and society's speech and thoughts'.

4.5 The medium has a message

Choosing an appropriate medium that is best suited to your intentions is like finding the right words to express your ideas. The materials and techniques an artist uses, the way the medium is handled, the surfaces, the kind of mark-making, all of these contribute to the mood and meaning of the work. Each medium has its unique visual qualities, but it also has conceptual connotations related to the physical nature of the material and to its cultural, historical and social significance.

STUDENT EXAMPLE: YASMIN BARATOVA

Student Yasmin Baratova looked beyond the traditional art supplies typically found in the studio and came up with her own unique use of materials to communicate meaning.

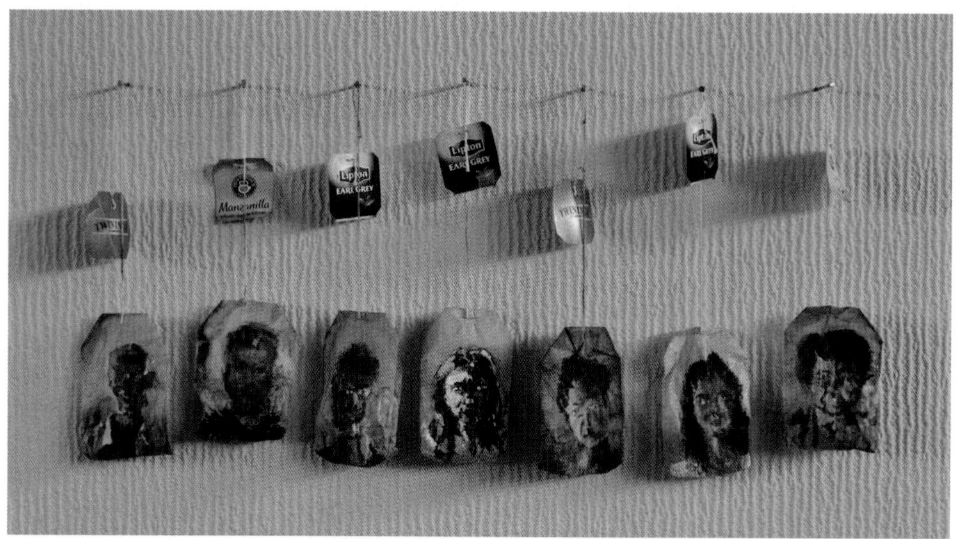

Figure 4.24: ***Sem Ya*** **(acrylics on teabags) by student Yasmin Baratova. For this piece, Yasmin painted a series of portraits of her family members on seven teabags.**

Here, Yasmin provides a thoughtful and articulate rationale for her artistic decisions, commenting on the choice of materials (teabags), which reflects her Uzbek culture and family traditions, the number seven, which has multiple meanings including a play on words, and the consideration of a presentation format. This is indeed a successful marriage of materials and meaning!

> Tea-drinking is a large aspect of my (Uzbek) culture. My family in particular drinks a lot of tea, especially in the winter. Upon observing how quickly boxes of tea become empty, I realised that we must throw away a huge quantity of teabags yearly. I decided that throwing them away is a waste, and started saving them up. After experimenting with mediums (*Sharpies*, oil, watercolour) and subjects (random people, friends, myself) and ways of presenting (wind-chime-style, on wire skewers, etc.) I came to the idea of painting seven of my family members (including myself). The significance of the number 7 resonates on many levels: 7 is a conventionally 'lucky' number, I consider these seven people the closest family I have, and family is *semya* in my mother tongue (Russian, the Russian word for seven being *sem*, thus creating a sort of pun). I decided that since the idea is already sophisticated enough, the presentation should be simple, such as nailing them to a wall in a straight line.

Cultural and historical significance

A well-chosen medium can give an artwork further layers of associated meaning. An artist may intentionally reference an aspect of culture or history through the choice of a particular medium or style.

For example, the contemporary miniature painting shown in Figure 4.25 is a cultural reference to the Mughal tradition of miniature paintings from the 16th and 17th centuries, which historically depicted religious, military and courtly scenes. This cultural reference has its particular set of historical, traditional and expressive associations that carry over into the meaning of the new artwork. The artist Imam Qureshi brings the historically rooted art of miniature painting into the present day and uses it to address current issues. The characters in his paintings are contemporary Muslims peacefully engaged in everyday 21st-century activities: carrying shopping bags or laptops, wearing 'cargo' trousers, lifting weights, blowing bubbles – relaxed and idyllic, and gently challenging western notions of Islamic culture.

Imran Qureshi painted this series of portraits (*Moderate Enlightenment*) when he realised that, after 9/11, the world insisted on segregating religious people. One form of segregation to which Qureshi points in his work revolves around choices in clothing or activities. He notes that 'a religious person wearing camouflage socks is perceived as threatening, but in other cases, it is mere fashion'. His work challenges narrow-minded assumptions that exist on a societal level and complicates traditions of art-making, specifically the perceived disparity between miniature painting and contemporary art.

Figure 4.25: In this image from the series of miniature watercolour and gold leaf paintings *Moderate Enlightenment*, 2009, Pakistani artist Imran Qureshi introduces contemporary content into a traditional format. Qureshi uses the technique and style of traditional Mughal miniatures: small scale paintings of figures depicted in flat space, delicately painted decorative motifs, jewel bright colours and gilded edges.

ACTIVITY 4.18: CULTURAL CONNOTATIONS

This activity explores the relationship between techniques and culture, and how a traditional technique carries a powerful cultural message

- What cultural and historical connotations does the work from the series *Moderate Enlightenment* carry?
- How does using a historical technique impact this contemporary artwork?
- How does Qureshi's work challenge assumptions and stereotypes?
- Can you identify a technique you have used that has a particular cultural association?

Social, political and personal significance

A material or medium may also have its own set of social or political signifiers: for example, embroidery carries associations with the feminine, and gold symbolises wealth and power or the divine, depending on the cultural context. Artists may also use materials that have strong associations to personal experiences. For artist Joseph Beuys, felt and fat were materials linked to his memories of experiences during the Second World War. The artist Louise Bourgeois often worked with textiles in her art: tapestry restoration was her family's business when she was a child.

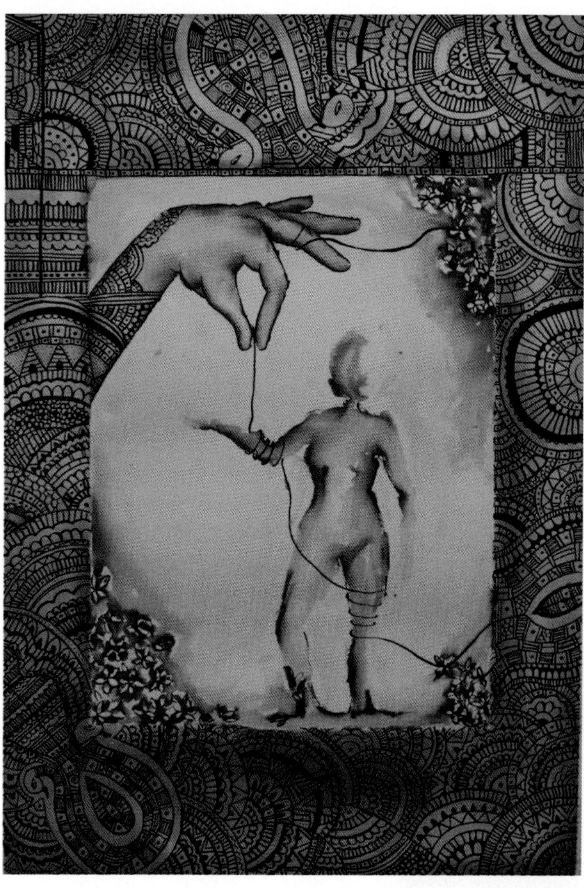

Figure 4.26: Work in watercolour and pen on paper by student Ida Karászy. Ida was looking at traditional Pakistani miniatures and at the work of Shahzia Sikander, a contemporary Muslim artist who integrates traditional forms of Mughal (Islamic) and Rajput (Hindu) styles and culture in her multimedia work. Ida was particularly interested in the cross-cultural elements in Sikander's works exploring western and traditional depictions of the female figures.

How do the materials that an artist chooses contribute to constructing meaning?

TOK and art: Art and meaning

- Does art have to have meaning?
- Conversely, if something is meaningless, can it be art?
- Who decides what is art? Are there limits to what we can call art?
- Is there a distinction between high art and low art? Between art and craft? If so, what might this be?
- Is there a common ground for what constitutes art?
- When does performance become art?
- Is there a line between the different art forms?
- Is life art?

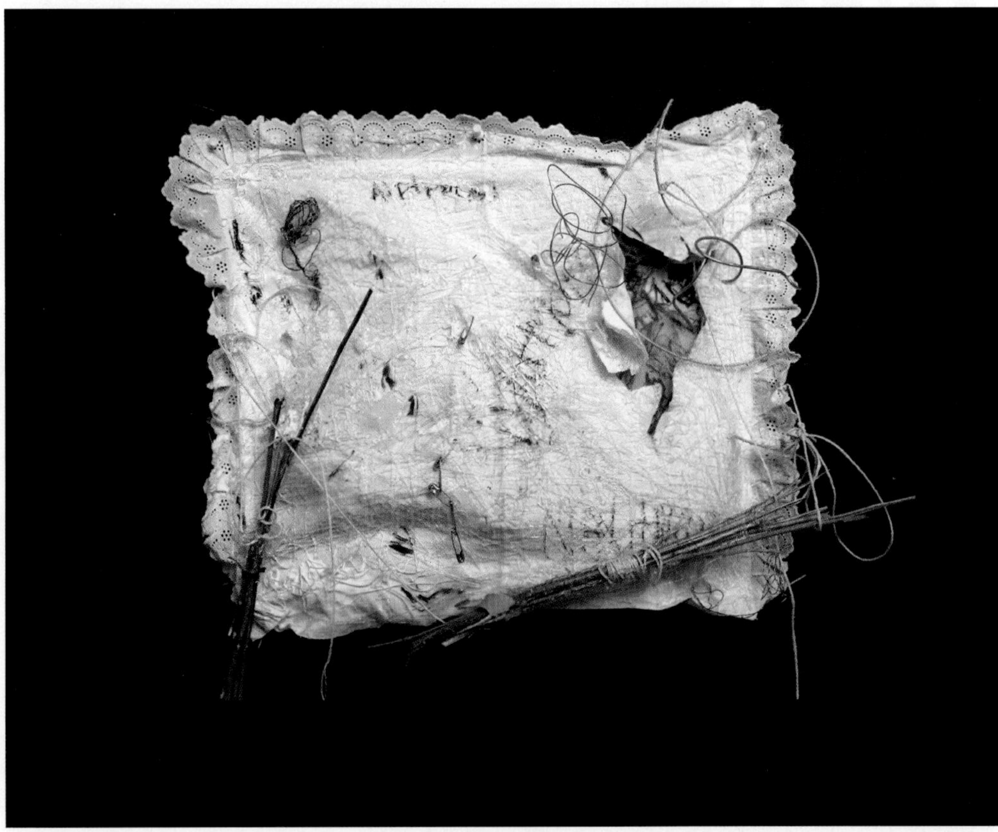

Figure 4.27: *Nightmare* by student Roberta Shreyer. This work is made of found objects, textiles and mixed media. Roberta writes, 'Pillows are archetypal symbols and supposed to be part of one's comfort zone. This pillow represents my nightmares, not my comfort zone. I added cold, uninviting materials and tokens that stand for "worry dolls", which are supposed to take nightmares away.'

Summary

In this chapter you have seen many examples of student work in a diverse range of media from all three columns of the IB art-making forms table and discussed how the materials that artists choose contribute to constructing meaning. You have looked how cultural, historical and social references can be communicated through materials and techniques. You have explored new territories in contemporary art practice, including the relationships that materials being used by artists today have with society. You have also considered whether materials have a power of their own.

Chapter 5 Developing focus

Introduction

Each student charts their own particular journey in IB DP Visual Arts. Of course, you are required to complete certain tasks, but your route is an individual one and requires you to have an independent, self-directed approach.

When you present your work for your final exhibition (covered in Chapter 9) you need to show a selection of pieces that work together. A coherent body of work is much more likely to result when you pursue your ideas with focus and develop them over a period of time.

This chapter offers strategies for helping you to identify your own areas of interest and to develop a body of work, supported and informed by your investigations in your process portfolio (PP) and comparative study (CS). You will explore cross-curricular connections, art styles and genres from art history, and consider what is meant by ethical values in art and what this means for you.

You will look at examples of how other IB students have developed focus and continuity in their investigations and how coherent and meaningful bodies of work evolved from this.

Figure 5.01: Visual journal page by student So Young Lim, in which she 'draws the lyrics' to the music she is listening to, each song conjuring up new imagery. Imaginative response to music is an area of interest with potential for many historical and cultural connections.

LEARNING OBJECTIVES

- Identify areas of interest and focus.
- Investigate cross-curricular connections.
- Consider ethical expression and sensitive topics.
- Explore art genres and styles related to your interests.
- Begin to create a body of work with clear artistic intentions, supported by your work throughout the course.

5.1 Identifying areas of focus

Finding meaningful subject matter can be a challenge. In the past, artists had less choice – subjects in demand were historical or religious scenes, portraits, landscapes, maybe a still life – but today, the choices for an artist are wide open.

Your hobbies and interests, music, literature, films, pop culture, your environment, all are possible areas for you to explore in your art. The personal relevance and importance of the topics you choose will have a direct on the quality of the work you make. Technical skills are not the only key to a successful art portfolio: clear, focused, adventurous ideas carried forward in a spirit of curious investigation are equally important.

(Art-making skills and developing a good understanding of your chosen techniques and media, are discussed in Chapter 4.)

> Attention is vitality. It connects you with others. It makes you eager.
> (Susan Sontag)

What interests you?

An area of interest can be a **subject**, such as the human figure or landscape, or a **concept**, such as identity or transformation. You might be interested in exploring **elements of art,** like light and shadow, or **material concerns**, like transparency or texture. Any area of interest can be pursued in depth and breadth across a range of media, subjected to various influences and experimentation.

You will probably be able to identify certain areas of interest that derive from your experiences and your curiosity towards the world. You can build upon these natural inclinations through your investigations, the artists you study, your experiments with materials and techniques, and your continued reflection and attention.

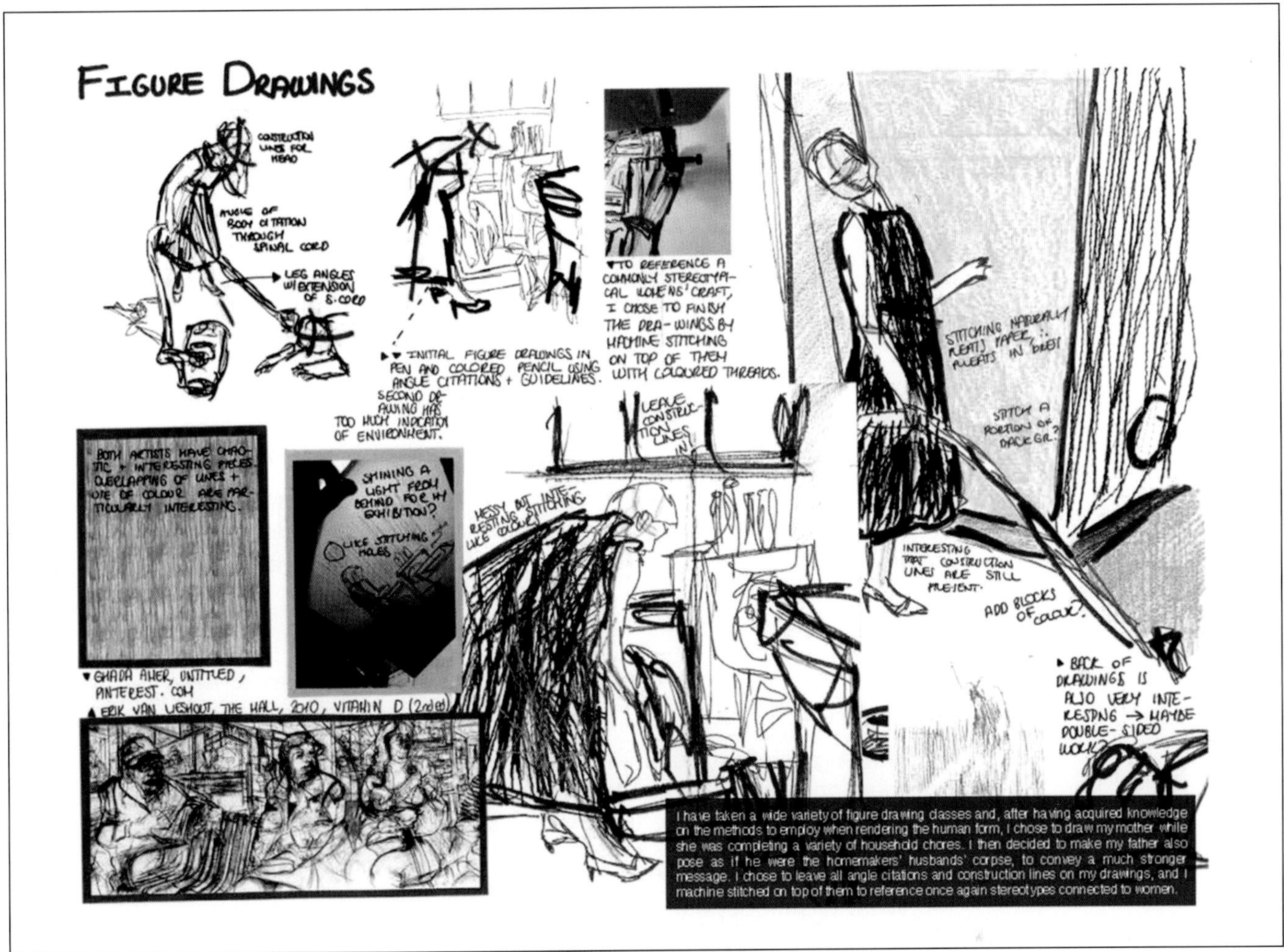

Figure 5.02: Process portfolio screen by student Enrico Giori exploring his interest in drawing the figure and experimenting with sketching and machine stitching as mark-making. In this page he began to develop the ideas elaborated in his studio work, as you will see in section 5.5, 'Building a body of work'.

Should you have a theme?

It is certainly not a requirement to have a theme, and themes should never be imposed. Continuity can be developed from one piece to the next, a progression of coherent linking ideas that aren't necessarily thematic. If you do choose to work with a theme, it is important not to be limited by it: do not try to force everything to 'fit in' to your theme but rather let it evolve naturally. The examples in this chapter (and the case study in Chapter 10) provide evidence of focused work that grew out of personal interests, showing a fluid progression of ideas and development of work.

Tip: If you are not already familiar with the IB design cycle (a tool used in the Middle Years Programme) you may want to take a look at it. The design cycle consists of five fluid steps (investigate, plan, design, create, evaluate) to help you find solutions in response to challenges faced.

Creative choices

For an artist there are always choices: about subject matter, medium, colour, surface, scale, materials, mark-making, meaning, presentation, and about how you want your work to be perceived. Each step of art-making presents opportunities for creative decisions along the way. This doesn't mean that you know what is going to happen in your artwork or what the end result will be. The point is that you take the time to explore a concept through various stages of development. This process includes research, experimentation, trial and error, reviewing and refining, and evaluation (not necessarily in that order). You are in charge of making these decisions: no one else can do it for you.

What are your strengths?

As you begin to identify areas of interest, discover artists you like and experiment with techniques and genres, pause and reflect on your own development in your journal. It can be hard to see your own artwork with an objective eye. There may be an area of particular strength or quality in your work that you don't see but a teacher or peer can help you to recognise.

ACTIVITY 5.1: INDIVIDUAL REFLECTION: SELF-KNOWLEDGE

Identifying your natural areas of strength will allow you to make the most of them and guide you towards making work that you really enjoy. Use the following questions to reflect on your strong points:

- What are my strengths as a visual artist?
- What techniques and media do I find naturally appealing?
- Do I like to work with design?
- Does my work have a narrative content?
- Am I interested in conceptual art?
- Am I drawn to figurative representation?
- Do I enjoy craftsmanship?
- Do I work slowly and methodically, or quickly and impulsively?
- What matters to me when I make art?
- What artists do I love?

5.2 Cross-curricular connections

Art is like frozen music. (10-year-old art student)

Collaboration between the arts and other subject areas has the potential to create new knowledge, and cross-fertilise ideas and processes in both fields. Art-making can be inspired by encounters or connections made through literature, music, maths, geography, psychology, geology, chemistry, even economics and statistics! Each discipline approaches creativity, exploration and research in various ways and from different perspectives; when working together they open up new ways of seeing, experiencing and interpreting the world around us.

By exploring other Diploma Programme subjects from an artistic standpoint you can gain an understanding of the interdependent nature of knowledge. The IB core (the extended essay, CAS and TOK – discussed in the Introduction to this book) also presents opportunities for making connections that will inform your current artwork. In TOK you explore forms of knowledge through the natural sciences, the social sciences, ethics, history, mathematics, religious and indigenous knowledge systems, as well as the arts. It also requires you to reflect on different ways of knowing, including reason, emotion, sense perception, intuition, imagination, faith and memory, and consider how knowledge is arrived at in the various disciplines.

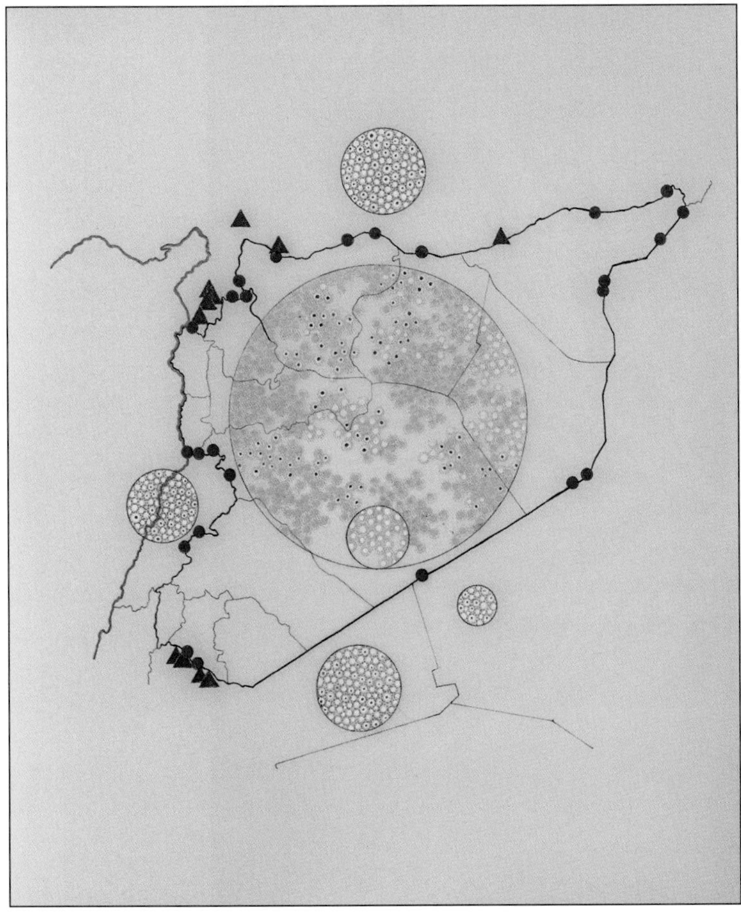

Figure 5.03: *UNCHR/Reuters Syrian Refugee Crisis – Refugees as of 02 Sept 2012*, 2014 (oil and ink on vellum and paper). This is one of a series of cartographic drawings about Syrian refugee migration by the Vietnamese artist Tiffany Chung. The image is based on information from geography and statistics. The artist addresses a humanitarian crisis using graphic information (the drawing charts the dispersion of the refugee population).

Exploring art and science

There is a growing interest in collaborations between art and science, which makes this an exciting area for scientifically inclined students to explore (or anyone interested in materials, processes, technology, cycles, knowledge, growth . . . life in general). Artists working today in the overlap between art and science are many, but if you look back through the history of art you will find artists have always experimented with materials and substances, investigated botany, anatomy, physics, chemistry and the natural sciences.

Art is meant to disturb, science reassures. (Georges Braque)

Chemistry and visual arts collaboration: cyanotype prints

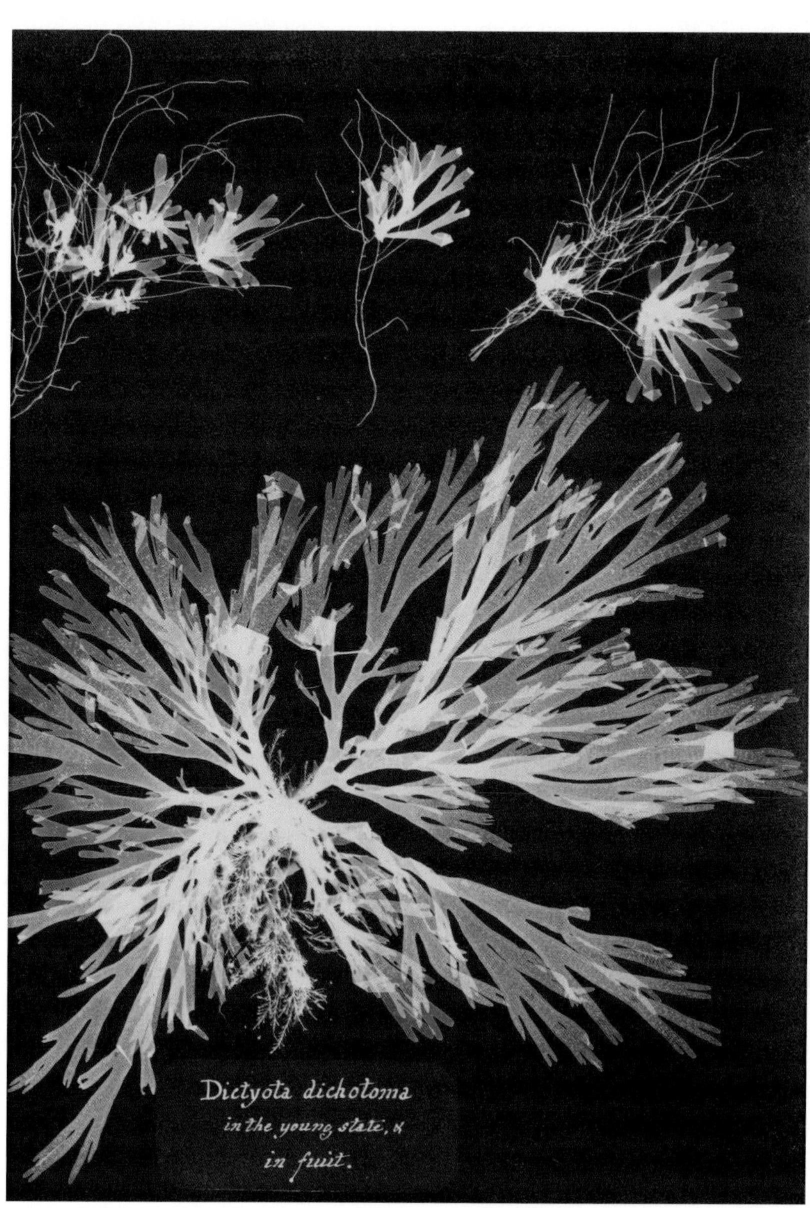

Figure 5.04: Anna Atkins, one of the first women photographers, used cyanotypes to print *Photographs of British Algae: Cyanotype Impressions* in 1843, the very first book of printed photographs and text. The cyanotype process is about 150 years old.

This chemistry and art collaboration shows the alchemical nature of artistic experimentation. Cyanotypes are sometimes referred to as 'sun prints' since the final image appears only with the aid of ultraviolet light, or sunlight.

Making a cyanotype print involves placing a negative image, either a photographic negative or an object, on paper or fabric that has been brushed with an iron-based solution (Prussian blue). The support with the negative image is placed under ultraviolet light or in direct sunlight to develop. The colours can range from pale to deep blue tones and everything in between.

STUDENT EXAMPLE: WONHEE LEE

SL student Wonhee Lee became interested in the properties of heat after encountering the work of Danish-Icelandic artist Ólafur Eliasson, who is famous for large-scale installation works, such as the weather project (2003), that use natural elements such as light, fog, water or air.

Wonhee was interested in using the elements of heat and light as part of his artwork. For *The Phoenix* he first conducted experiments with heat and light radiation using a candle. Inspired by Eliasson, he also experimented with light and video projections.

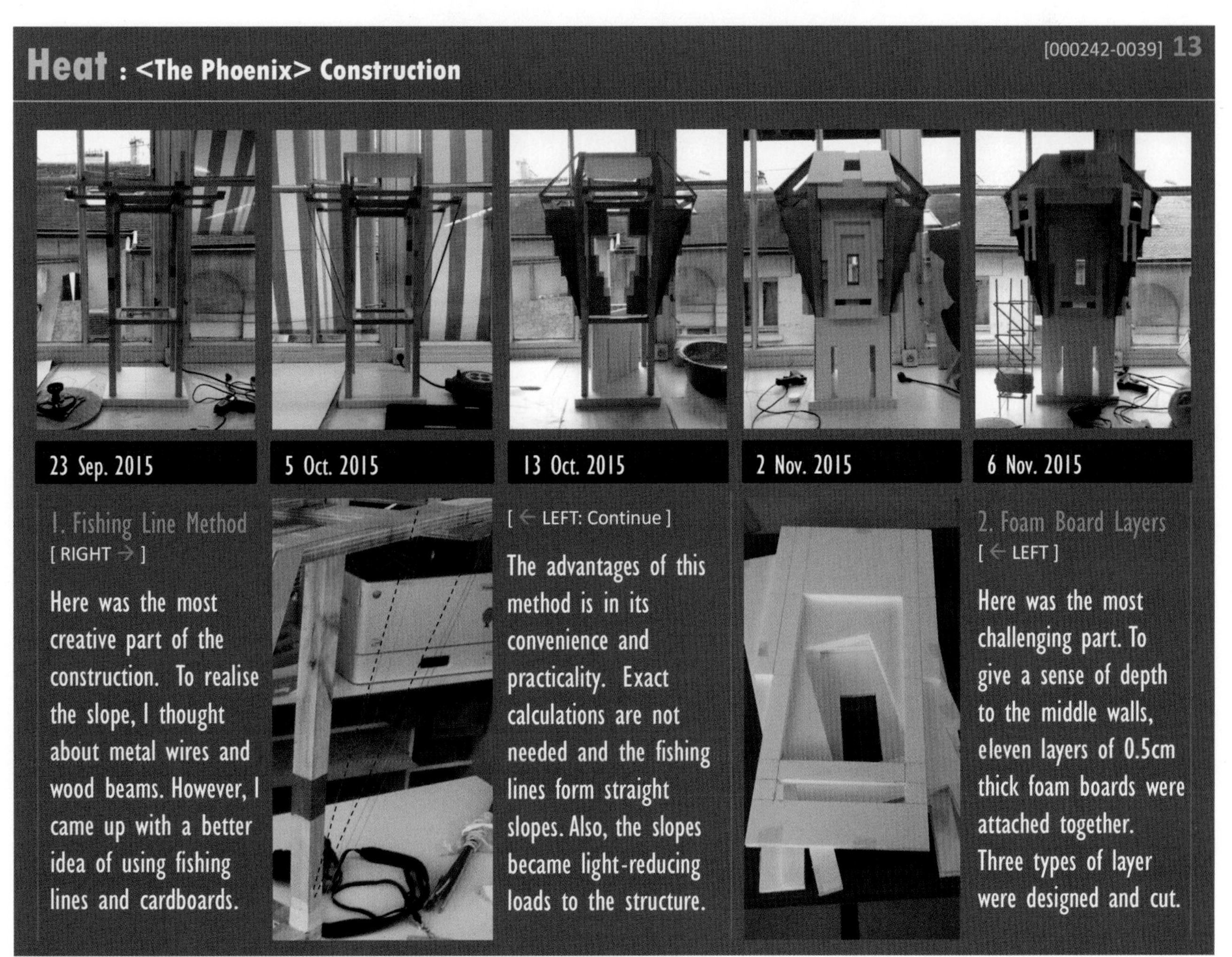
Heat : <The Phoenix> Construction
[000242-0039] 13
23 Sep. 2015
5 Oct. 2015
13 Oct. 2015
2 Nov. 2015
6 Nov. 2015
1. Fishing Line Method
[RIGHT →]
Here was the most creative part of the construction. To realise the slope, I thought about metal wires and wood beams. However, I came up with a better idea of using fishing lines and cardboards.
[← LEFT: Continue]
The advantages of this method is in its convenience and practicality. Exact calculations are not needed and the fishing lines form straight slopes. Also, the slopes became light-reducing loads to the structure.
2. Foam Board Layers
[← LEFT]
Here was the most challenging part. To give a sense of depth to the middle walls, eleven layers of 0.5cm thick foam boards were attached together. Three types of layer were designed and cut.

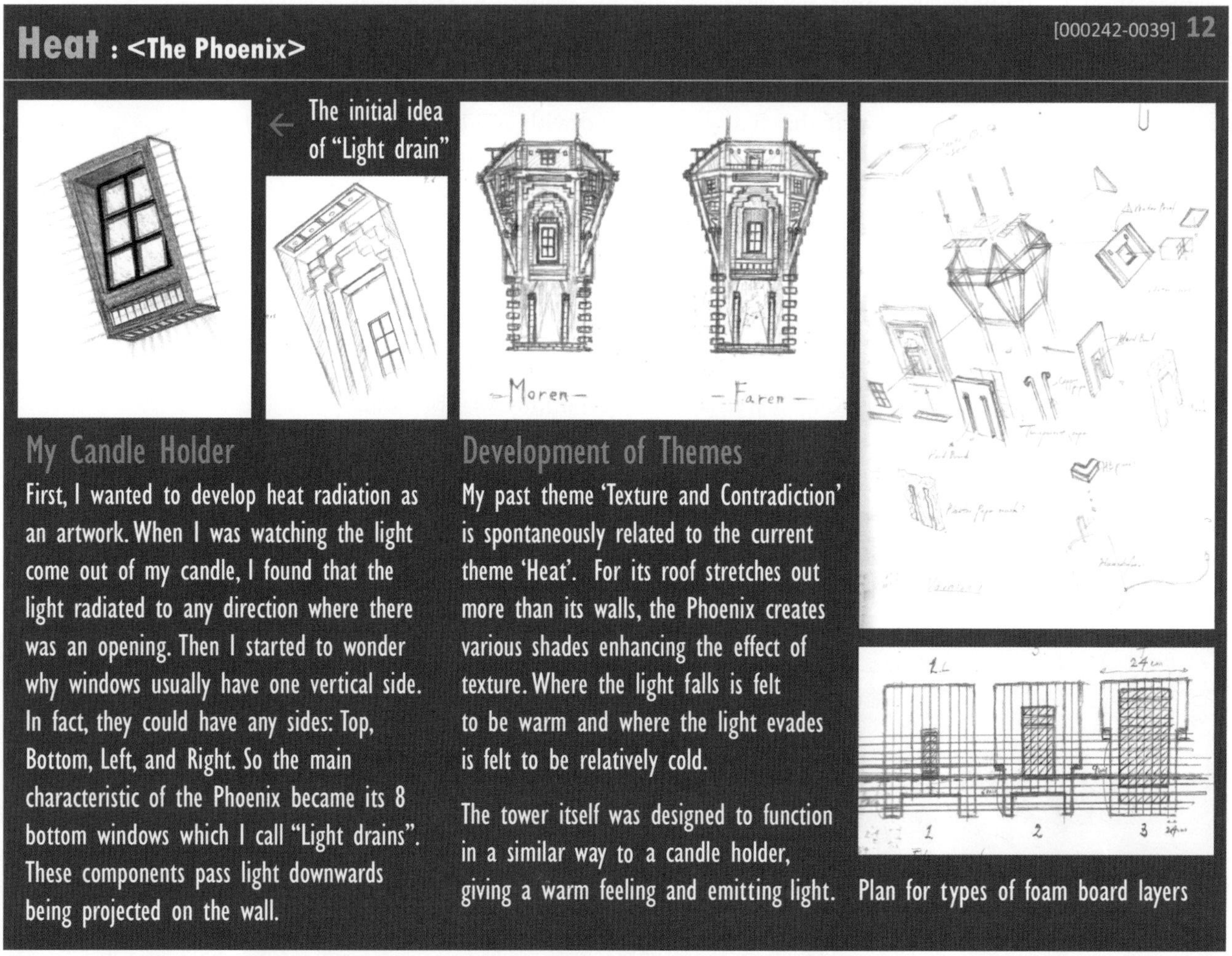

Heat : <The Phoenix>

[000242-0039] 12

The initial idea of "Light drain"

–Moren– –Faren–

My Candle Holder

First, I wanted to develop heat radiation as an artwork. When I was watching the light come out of my candle, I found that the light radiated to any direction where there was an opening. Then I started to wonder why windows usually have one vertical side. In fact, they could have any sides: Top, Bottom, Left, and Right. So the main characteristic of the Phoenix became its 8 bottom windows which I call "Light drains". These components pass light downwards being projected on the wall.

Development of Themes

My past theme 'Texture and Contradiction' is spontaneously related to the current theme 'Heat'. For its roof stretches out more than its walls, the Phoenix creates various shades enhancing the effect of texture. Where the light falls is felt to be warm and where the light evades is felt to be relatively cold.

The tower itself was designed to function in a similar way to a candle holder, giving a warm feeling and emitting light.

Plan for types of foam board layers

Figures 5.05 (left) and 5.06. In these process portfolio screens you can see Wonhee's design process (Figure 5.05) and construction process (Figure 5.06) for his construction piece *The Phoenix*.

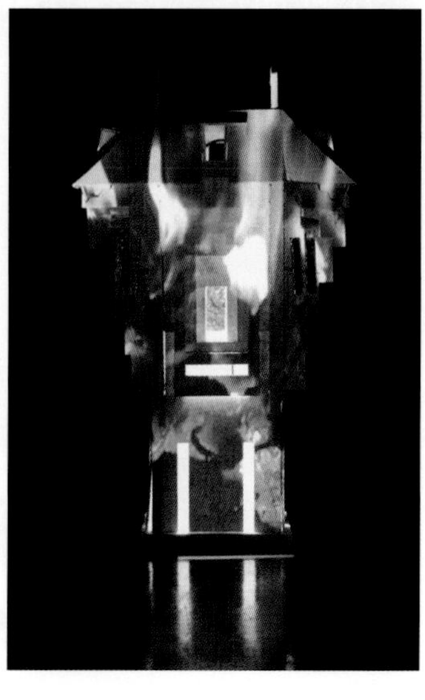

Figures 5.07 (left) and 5.08 (right). Figure 5.07 shows student Wonhee Lee's finished construction of *The Phoenix* illuminated from inside. Figure 5.08 shows the same piece with a video projection of fire.

You can view Wonhee's related exploration of steam in his work *Steamvine* in Chapter 4. This is another great example of a student's art practice being driven by curiosity and cross-curricular investigations.

SPOTLIGHT ON THE STUDENT: WONHEE LEE

Nationality: South Korea
Born: Seoul

Main artistic interests:

- spatial and architectural experience of the audience
- the effect of light on elements
- visualisation of conceptual ideas
- maximised application of physics to art.

Influential artists:

- Mark Rothko
- Hong Se-sop
- Ólafur Eliasson
- Sigalit Landau
- Peter Zumthor

Other subject areas besides science are of course equally worthy of exploration. If there is a subject you are particularly interested in, look for the connections with visual arts. You may find that your artwork takes on a new significance and purpose.

ACTIVITY 5.2: CROSS-POLLINATION

Use something you have learned in another subject area as the concept or the materials for an artwork. For example:

- a biology lesson on photosynthesis
- a chemistry experiment with crystals
- a physics lesson on prisms
- a poem from your English class
- a maths equation.

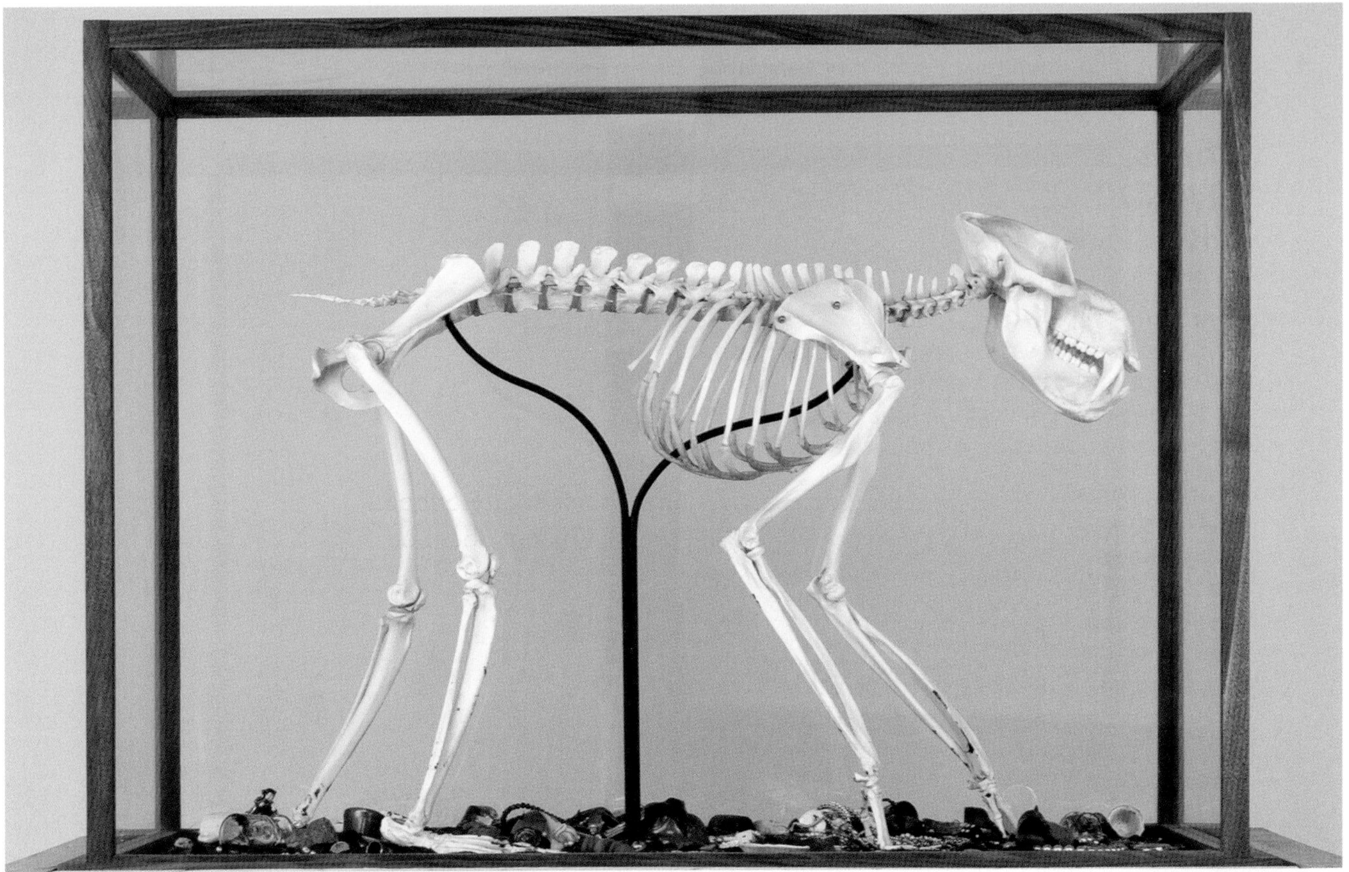

Figure 5.09 *Mandrillus Sphinx*, 2012, by contemporary American artist Marc Dion. Dion's work explores methods of collection and presentation, often employing scientific models to question the way knowledge is constructed.

> The job of an artist is to go against the grain of dominant culture, to challenge perception, prejudice and convention. (Mark Dion)

TOK and art: Methodology

- What similar methods do artists and scientists use to create order (for example, researching, categorising and displaying objects)?
- What are the distinctions between rational (scientific) and irrational (subjective) ways of gathering and organising knowledge?
- Debate this statement: Scientists are looking for answers, artists for more questions.
- The German philosopher Immanuel Kant wrote that: 'Fine art is a way of presenting that is purposive on its own and that furthers, even though without a purpose, the culture of our mental powers to [facilitate] social communication'. What do you think of the idea of art as 'purposiveness' but 'without a purpose'?

5.3 Ethical expression

Art is an area in which freedom of expression reigns. Artists naturally want to explore topics and issues that are exciting and meaningful to them and sometimes this enters into controversial terrain. However, as IB students of a global community, you have a responsibility to engage with sensitive topics in a manner that does not offend others' beliefs or damage the environment.

The *IB DP Visual Arts Guide* states guidelines for sensitive topics as follows:

> Consideration should also be given to the personal, political and spiritual values of others, particularly in relation to race, gender or religious beliefs.
>
> As part of the collective consideration of the school, visual arts students must be supported in maintaining an ethical perspective during their course. Schools must be vigilant in ensuring that work undertaken by the student does not damage the environment, include excessive or gratuitous violence or reference to explicit sexual activity. (*IB DP Visual Arts Guide*, page 9).

It is interesting to note how ethical values change over time. What was controversial in the 20 century may seem quite tame today. Even shock value needs to be seen in a historical perspective.

Figure 5.10: Picasso's painting *Les Demoiselles d'Avignon*, 1907, was considered scandalous at the time it was made, shocking both in content and form. It depicts five prostitutes looking at the viewer in a primitive and confrontational manner and does not follow the rules of perspective and spatial construction that prevailed at the time, instead flattening and fragmenting the picture plane. What was so criticised then was the beginnings of what we now call Cubism.

ACTIVITY 5.3: ART AND ETHICS, A HISTORICAL PERSPECTIVE

Look up some of these famously controversial artworks of the last 150 years, keeping in mind the historical context: when the work was made, and what was acceptable then.

- What ethical values change over time?
- What values do not change?
- Which of these works do you consider to be unethical now and why?

Édouard Manet, *Olympia*, 1863
Marcel Duchamp, *Fountain*, 1917
Piero Manzoni, *Merda d'artista*, 1961
Judy Chicago, *The Dinner Party*, 1979
Marc Quinn, *Self*, 1991–ongoing
Maurizio Cattelan, *La Nona Ora*, 1999

Stelarc, *The Body is Obsolete*, 2013

TOK and art: Art and ethics

- What moral responsibilities does the artist have, or not have? Are they different from any other knower?
- To what extent does the artist have a moral obligation to avoid or confront issues that might shock or be contrary to most people?
- Do you think controversy is important for an artwork to have a strong impact? Why do artists often rely on the shock factor?
- What do we expect from art? Truth? Seduction? Provocation? Beauty?

5.4 Art genres and styles

Becoming familiar with various art **genres** and styles will open up new possibilities for making connections with your own work. As you discover artists and investigate them further, you will be able to identify your influences and sources of inspiration when you write your curatorial rationale (discussed in Chapter 9). This research can also be included in your PP (Chapter 8) and may lead to developing ideas and content for your CS (Chapter 7).

Genre: A category or artistic style that involves a set of characteristics.

Dada: A 20th-century movement in art and literature based on irrationality and the upending of traditional artistic values.

Figure 5.11: Visual journal pages by student Polina Zakharova exploring the significance of Dada, and its application across different media. She looks at the collages of Berlin Dada artist Raoul Hausmann and draws parallels with her own experiments in collage and mixed media.

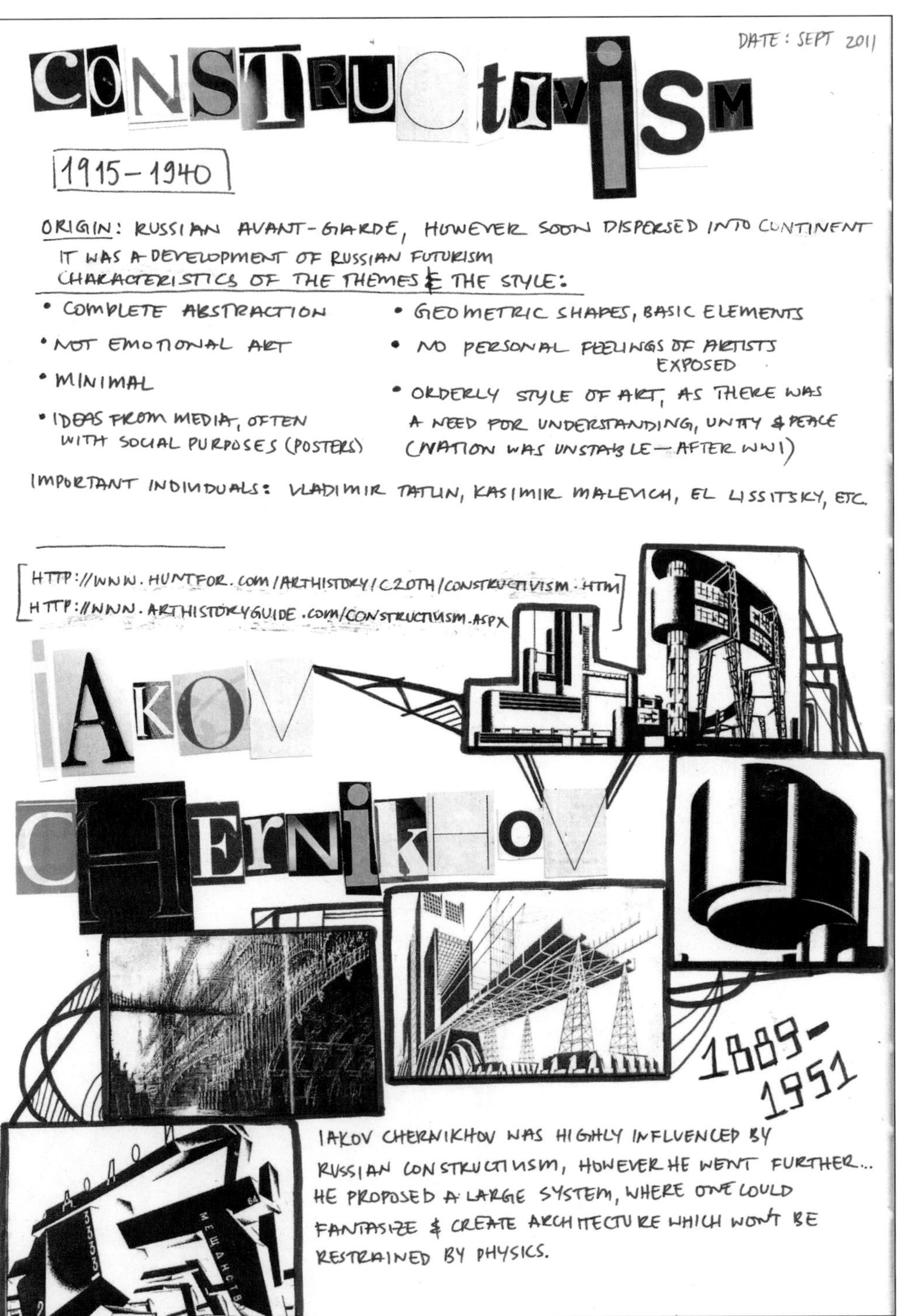

Figure 5.12: Visual journal page by former IB student Anastasia Leonovich, investigating the characteristic themes and styles of Russian Constructivism. This art movement was relevant to her interests in geometric shapes, order, structure and eventually architecture. (Anastasia is now an architect.)

Constructivism: An art style and movement that originated in Russia in the 1920s and has influenced many aspects of modern architecture and design.

ACTIVITY 5.4: ART HISTORY THEMATIC INVESTIGATION

Investigate a broad but recurrent theme from the history of world art that relates to your areas of interest. Find several art works, both familiar and unfamiliar that reflect different approaches to this theme. Be sure to note the name of each artist, the title, source and the general art historical context of the work.

- How have different artists approached this theme?
- How has this theme been represented in three different historical periods?
- How has this theme been represented in three different cultures?
- How can you respond to this in your own work?

THEMES IN ART

- mythology
- self-portraits
- power and status
- paradise and the afterlife
- individuals and society
- conflict and war
- nature and mysticism
- fertility and motherhood
- beliefs and rituals
- order and systems
- tension and motion.

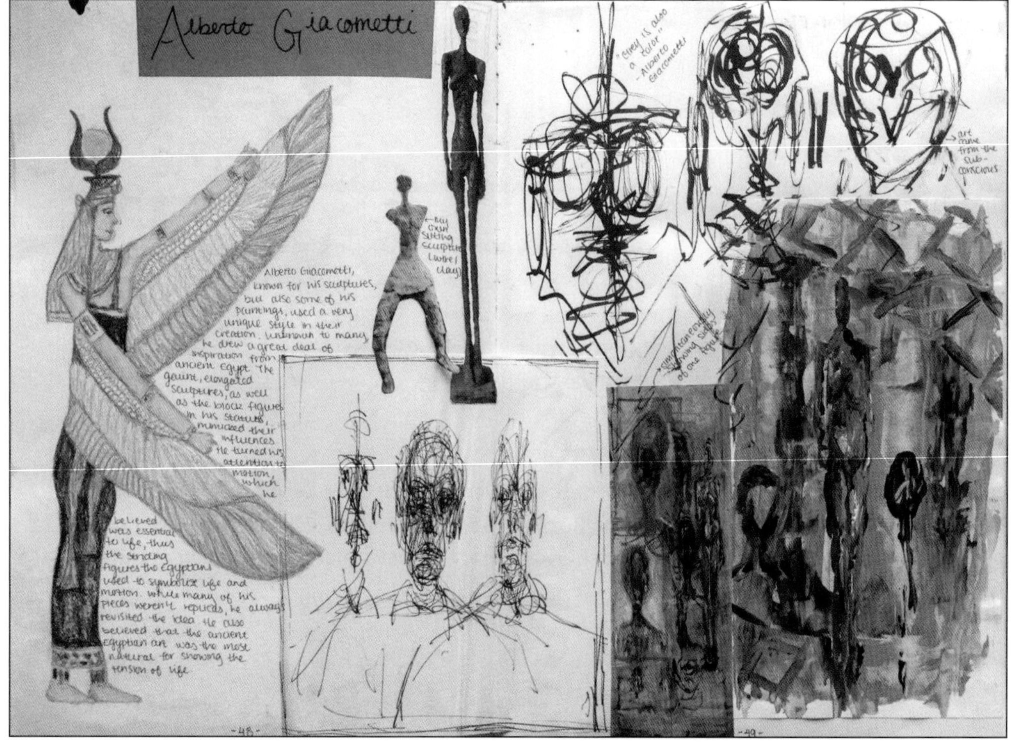

Figure 5.13: In a page from her visual journal, student Ana Grace Rose looks at how tension and motion are addressed in different periods of art history. She makes connections between ancient Egyptian art and the standing sculptures of Alberto Giacometti, and discusses the impact on her own clay figures.

Working in series

Most great artists have areas of focus or recurring motifs in their work which have developed out of abiding interests and attention over a long period of time. There are many fine examples of artists who create series of work around a singular theme.

Choose one from Activities 5.5–5.7 and develop your own series based on area of interest.

ACTIVITY 5.5: CHANGING LIGHT SERIES

Claude Monet studied the changing light in several series of paintings (Rouen Cathedral, the haystacks, the water-lilies).

- Create a series of paintings or photos that record the changing light at different times of day on a building.
- How do time and place influence your subject? Can you compare your series to Monet's series on Rouen Cathedral?

ACTIVITY 5.6: STILL-LIFE VARIATIONS

Giorgio Morandi painted numerous still-life paintings of variations on the same subject: arrangements of bottles!

- Create a collection of objects and set up a still life to draw, paint or photograph.
- Rearrange the objects to create five different compositions.
- Describe one of Giorgio Morandi's still-life compositions in your journal, using **formal analysis** (discussed in Chapter 7).

ACTIVITY 5.7: SELF-TRANSFORMATION SERIES

Cindy Sherman presents herself in various guises and personas as the subject of her photographs.

- Create a series of photographs or drawings in which you transform yourself as the subject.
- Referring to Cindy Sherman's photos compare your work with hers and include your comparison in your visual journal.

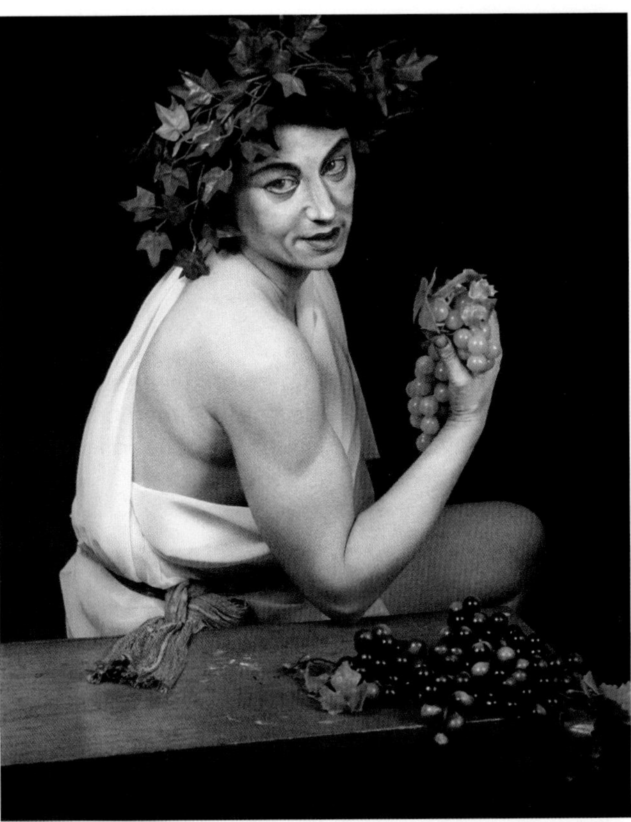

Figure 5.14: Cindy Sherman, *Untitled (#224)*, 1990 (colour photograph; 48 × 38 inches). Cindy Sherman (USA, born 1965) uses herself as the subject of her photographs, staging elaborate scenes with costumes and props. She shifts easily between different roles and personas that range from grotesque to sexy, drawing on images from art history, movies, the internet and popular culture. Her photographs invite the viewer to reflect on representations of identity.

Avant-garde: This French phrase (literally 'front guard') describes art that puts forward new and innovative ideas, and is generally used in reference to early 20th-century modern art.

Artists' manifestos

An art manifesto is a statement of the intentions, opinions, or beliefs of an artist or artistic movement. Manifestos were especially popular during the 20th century among **avant-garde** movements, including Futurism, Surrealism, Dada, Constructivism, Vorticism and De Stijl.

Some 21st-century artist manifestos exist but they tend to be more individual than collective, more ironic than idealistic: a sign of the times?

> I am for all art that takes its form from the lines of life itself, that twists and extends and accumulates and spits and drips, and is heavy and coarse and blunt and sweet and stupid as life itself.
>
> I am for an artist who vanishes, turning up in a white cap painting signs or hallways.
>
> (From *I Am For . . . (Statement,* 1961), Claes Oldenberg, Swedish-American pop artist and sculptor, born 1929)

ACTIVITY 5.8: GROUP ACTIVITY: WRITE AN ART MANIFESTO

In a small group, discuss and design your own art manifesto. Use these questions to guide you.

- What should art be?
- Why is it important to make art?
- What is **not** important?
- What would you like your art to give to the world?
- If you had no limits or constraints of any kind, what kind of art would you make?

5.5 Building a body of work

Now that you have experimented with a range of techniques and art-making forms, identified some key areas of interests and investigated some influential artists, styles and genres, you can begin to think about building a coherent body of work.

ACTIVITY 5.9: CONNECT THE PIECES

Choose three of your own resolved artworks that you think work well together. What are the connecting threads, the invisible and visible links? Remember that to be convincing there must exist a **genuine** common ground. Use the following questions to guide you. Write up your reflection in your visual journal.

- Discuss your choices of materials and techniques.
- Analyse the visual qualities: colour, weight, texture, light, shadow, transparency and so on.
- Discuss ideas or beliefs that underpin your work.
- What are the influences (from other artists, books, pop culture, the media, events, hot topics) that inform your work?

Tip: When creating a body of work for your final exhibition, you are working towards IB DP Visual Arts assessment criterion A, Exhibition: 'a coherent collection of works which fulfil stated artistic intentions and communicate clear thematic or stylistic relationships across individual pieces'.

Throughout your course, reflect on how your studio work, from which you will select and curate your final exhibition, is supported and informed by the other two components, the PP and the CS. Although these three components are assessed individually, they are also very much intertwined, with your artistic interests being the guiding force.

The comparative study

Your CS (discussed in Chapter 7) is a way for you to become familiar with other artists and art genres that may impact significantly on your work. HL students are asked to analyse their own artwork in relation to the artists and art works they have chosen. The CS can be hugely influential for all students in guiding your investigations and giving context to your work.

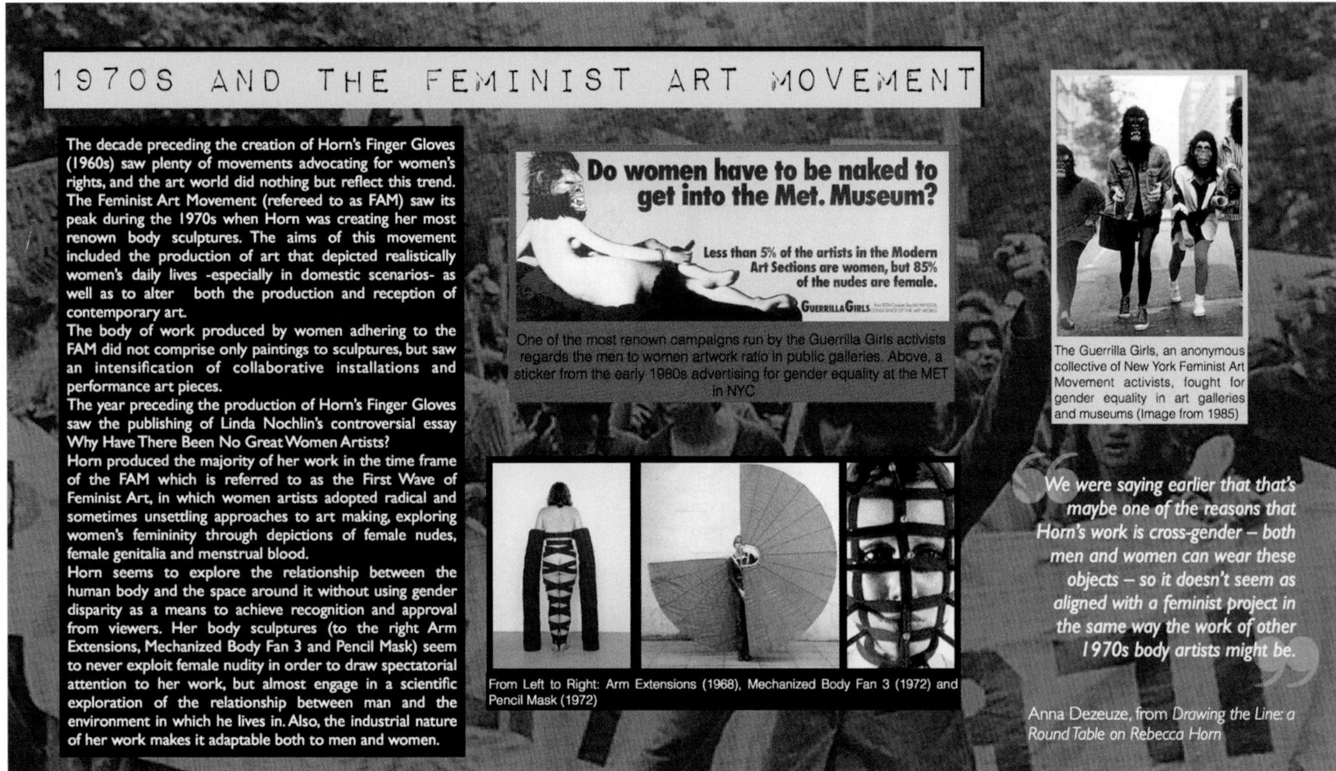

Figure 5.15: Comparative study screen by student Enrico Giori with contextual study of the artist Roni Horn. Enrico deepened his knowledge of the feminist art movement of the 1970s while researching for his CS. This research proved to be a key influence on his developing a body of work around the idea of the stereotype of the housewife. Enrico writes here about the feminist art movement: 'The aims of this movement included the production of art that depicted realistically women's daily lives – especially in domestic scenarios – and altered both the production and reception of contemporary art'.

The process portfolio

Your PP (discussed in Chapter 8) naturally supports and informs your developing studio work, through your exploration of skills, techniques and processes and your critical investigations into artists, artworks, art forms and genres. You reflect in the PP on how your ideas are formed, on how you make independent decisions that support your intentions for your artwork, and on your overall development as an artist.

Tip: When **making connections between other artists and your own developing work**, you are working towards IB DP Visual Arts assessment criterion B, for the PP, critical investigation. 'Students must demonstrate critical investigation of artists, artworks and artistic genres, communicating the student's growing awareness of how this investigation influences and impacts upon their own developing art-making practices and intentions'.

CASE STUDY: ENRICO GIORI

Figure 5.16: Process portfolio screen by Enrico Giori. On this screen Enrico shows the development of his ideas for the diptych *Made in the Shade*, shown in Figure 5.17.

Diptych: A painting or drawing in two parts, usually the same size. It may be one divided image or two closely related images.

Enrico Giori's exploration and elaboration of ideas and process in the PP screen shown in Figure 5.16 lead to the resolved artwork in Figure 5.17, *Made in the Shade*. In the portfolio he discusses his ideas for a piece based on the concept of the housewife and shows how he tried out different variations of scale and media based on a single image:

> Investigating the role of the 1950s homemaker I realised how subservient and oppressed women must have been at that time. I wanted to produce a piece of work which shows the housewife attempting to put an end to this oppressive situation, but ends up being unable to and falls into her old habits. I used the housewife figure drawings I had previously drawn from life. I projected the figure drawing on a 2.5 metre tall sheet of paper stuck to a wall and, using a brush and India ink, I drew the projected image, trying to maintain the spontaneity of the original drawing.

Figure 5.17: *Made in the Shade*, exhibition piece by student Enrico Giori, based on figure drawings from life and reworked in a medium that echoes and reinforces his intentions. His exhibition text for this piece states: '*Made In The Shade* (Diptych), *Sharpie*(c) marker, ink pen, Coloured Pencil and Stitching on Paper mounted on Fabric Samples'. Enrico writes: 'I drew my mother while she performed some of the actions of a typical homemaker, such as loading the washer and hoovering. I deliberately employed a fast and loose drawing style to capture the essence of the moments before my eyes. I then worked on the figure drawings with machine stitching, a stereotypically female craft referenced previously.'

Tip: When **elaborating ideas and concepts** and supporting them with your written rationale you are working towards IB DP Visual Arts assessment criterion C for the exhibition, conceptual qualities: 'effective resolution of imagery, signs and symbols to realise the function, meaning and purpose of the art works, as appropriate to stated intentions'.

In Figure 5.17, *Made in the Shade*, and Figure 5.18, *Bleach Beauty*, Enrico presents work that shows sophisticated application, manipulation, and refinement of skills, with carefully selected media appropriate to his intentions. As a focus Enrico is exploring domesticity and its implications, so it is entirely appropriate that he chose fabric samples, stitching and bleach as materials to communicate the significance of his topic.

Tip: When presenting work with **skilful manipulation of media and techniques**, you are working towards the assessment criterion B for the exhibition, technical competence: 'demonstrate effective application and manipulation of media and materials [and] of the formal qualities'.

Figure 5.18: Exhibition piece by student Enrico Giori. His exhibition text for this piece states: '*Bleach Beauty*, Household Bleach, Beeswax, Black Paper, Self-Made Lightbox'. Enrico writes: 'This piece is painted using bleach on black paper, and finished with beeswax. The use of materials from the domestic environment aims to show the closeness of the woman to the home and her duties. The apron of the woman is embellished with zigzag stitching done with a sewing machine, enhanced by the presence of a LED light box behind the piece, whose light shines through the holes.'

Figure 5.19: ***One Scrub at a Time*** **by student Enrico Giori, a 3D mixed-media piece that combines photographs of glamorous women with objects used for domestic chores. His exhibition text for this piece states: '*One Scrub At A Time Images*, Watercolour, Glue, Sticks, Soap, Clothespins, Doormat, Spray Paint': Enrico writes: 'This installation depicts conflicts between expectations that women are required to fulfil. The doormat, clothes-pegs and soap represent housewives and mothers, whilst the photos of models from fashion magazines represent powerful women. Yellow as a gender-neutral and falsely cheery colour is once again reiterated.**

In this extract from his curatorial rationale (the statement that accompanies the exhibition, discussed in Chapter 9), Enrico discusses some of the major influences on his art:

> I have committed myself to always include a female perspective in all my pieces, and to try and employ art-making techniques which utilise unconventional mediums, such as stitching, embroidery and innovative sculpture forms. Although feminist artists such as Rosler, Rebecca Horn and Cindy Sherman have been inspirational to me in terms of conceptual values, other artists such as Man Ray, Egon Schiele and William Kentridge have impacted my work both conceptually and formally. This has allowed me to develop a drawing and painting style which I hope I can call my own. I have always enjoyed exploring and experimenting with techniques and mediums, mixing and combining to create something personal. For this body of work I have embraced stereotypical female craft forms such as dressmaking, embroidering and stitching and combined these with printing, drawing and painting. Materials have also derived from the domestic environment. Soap bars, vinyl embossed tablecloths used in frottage, fabric and wallpaper from my own designs, combined with traditional charcoal, ink, acrylic and gouache characterise my work. Digital imagery has also played an important role and photography, video and animation allowed me to portray my subject in action, allowing for the smooth development of a storyline.

Popular culture and literature have also influenced my work. 1950s advertisements helped me create a convincing image of housewives, and other sources, such as Lady GaGa's music video Telephone, have conceptually informed my work. I have chosen to connect each of my pieces to a quote from Carol Ann Duffy's The World's Wife, an anthology of feminist poetry that gives voice to all the silenced women who accompanied the most important men of history.'

SPOTLIGHT ON THE STUDENT: ENRICO GIORI

Nationality: Italian
Born: Milan

Main artistic interests:
- process-based and conceptual art
- social commentaries on issues such as gender, expectations and conflicts of interest
- use of humour, irony and satire in artwork
- experimental techniques and printmaking
- links between: philosophy, fashion and culture trends, popular culture (e.g. music videos), literature and poetry.

Influential artists:
- 1970s feminist art movement artists
- William Kentridge
- Carolee Schneemann
- Martha Rosler
- Cindy Sherman
- David Hockney

CASE STUDY: KAREN LAANEM

As we have seen in the work of student Enrico Giori, an area of interest, if well chosen and developed, can be sufficient to generate a whole line of inquiry and a resulting body of work. This work by student Karen Laanem shows another example of how focus, continuity and intentional exploration and development of ideas result in a powerful and coherent body of work. Karen's investigations began with an interest in her family history and developed into a series of painted portraits and photographs of places in her ancestral home in Estonia.

Karen explains how she developed her ideas from a seed of interest to a coherent and resolved body of work that she presented at her IB art show. The passages are extracted from her visual journal and her artist's statement.

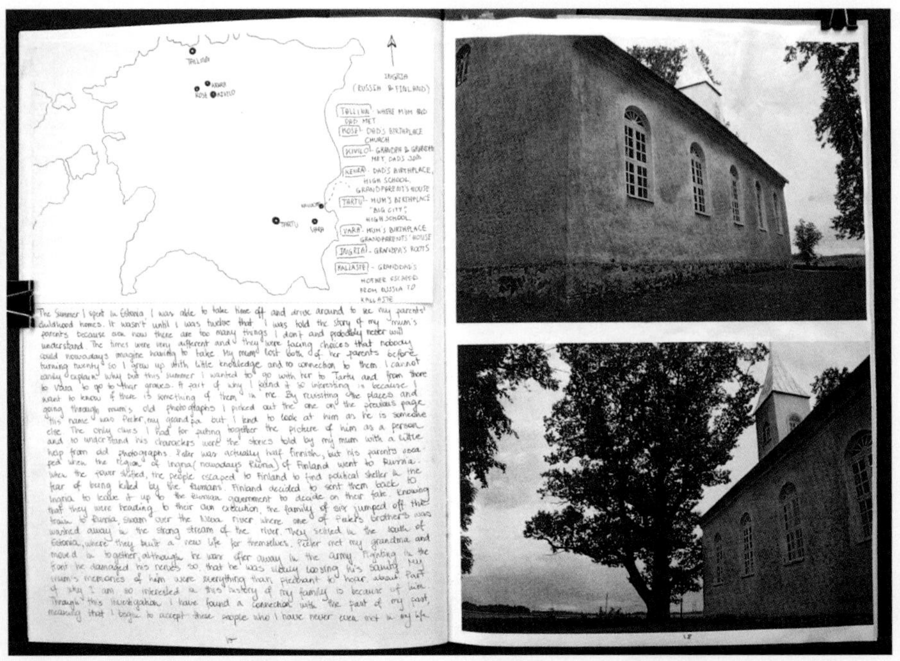

Figure 5.20: Karen visited Estonia and recorded her experiences in her journal with notes, photos and drawings. Karen writes: 'My artwork explores the concepts of time and memory, human experience, loss and pursuit of serenity from realising who I am by exploring where I come from.'

Figure 5.21: *Father* (acrylic painting with lino print) by student Karen Laanem. Karen writes: 'My interest in my family's history began in the summer between the two IB years. Going through old family photo albums, I was looking for the physical similarities I could find with my ancestors. I was drawn to the black-and-white photographs, asking my relatives to tell me stories about those people. My interest developed into a passion, launching a research project that took me to rural parts of Estonia. I visited my ancestors' birthplaces where I took series of photographs . . . to document and to collect evidence . . . '

Figure 5.22 Student work by Karen Laanem, *Grandfather*, acrylic painting. Karen explains: 'I used original family album photographs from the past as a reference in the making of several paintings, including *Grandfather* and *Father*. Influenced by the work of Gerhard Richter, I decided to revivify the presence of those people in reality. Both *Father* and *Grandfather* are painted in acrylic, working directly from old photographs. The original photograph for *Grandfather* can be seen in my journal page, as well as a mosaic of monotype prints made in the process of media exploration.'

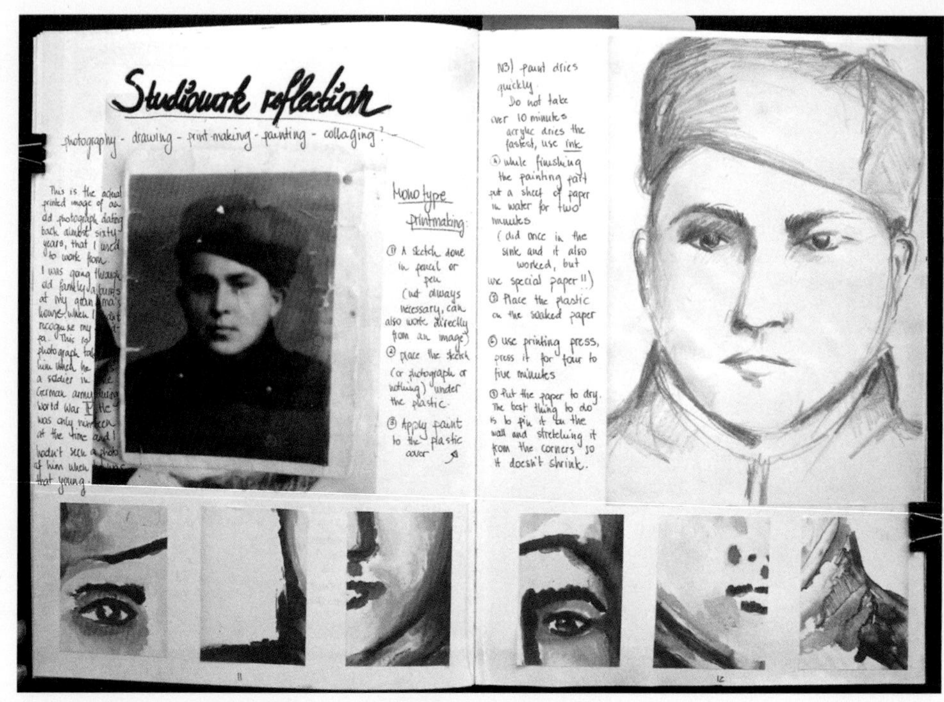

Figure 5.23: In these journal pages, Karen explains the various processes she engaged in when making the portrait of *Grandfather*: photocopy, drawing, monotype printmaking, painting, collaging. The original photograph of her grandfather that she used as her model was taken when he was a soldier in the Second World War, aged only 19.

Figure 5.24: *Daughter* by student Karen Laanem, acrylic painting with lino-printed background pattern. Karen writes about her choice of incorporating printmaking in the backgrounds as appropriate to her intentions of working with memory and impression: 'I was producing linocut designs inspired by the symbolic flower of my homeland. I was interested in the conceptual idea behind printmaking that creates a memory in the form of an imprint from the actual carving . . . I decided to combine the two media (print and paint) and produce a unique pattern for each of the three portraits *Father*, *Daughter* and *Grandfather*.'

Figure 5.25: ***Linda*****, photograph by student Karen Laanem. Karen says: 'This photograph of an old woman records surfaces and textures as well as a portrait of a person and a place. The reflecting glass window in the linear wooden wall contrasts with the flowery textile and the cut grass. I leave my photographs uncropped, true to what I saw and experienced in those places.'**

Besides making paintings, and prints, Karen took black-and-white photographs of people and places when she was conducting her research. She writes about her relationship with photography as a medium and how it relates to memory:

> A photograph is a selective fragment of reality, yet once taken, becomes the representation of the past. In a way, this makes photographers able to write history by sharing their personal selection with the rest of the world. My work, however, does not try to write history, but rather tell the story that has already been written about the people and places I saw. To simplify and take away the completeness of these records I use black and white photography. Not only does black and white photography change our perception of surfaces, but by stripping away the colour it also allows the viewer a more ambiguous interpretation of the work.

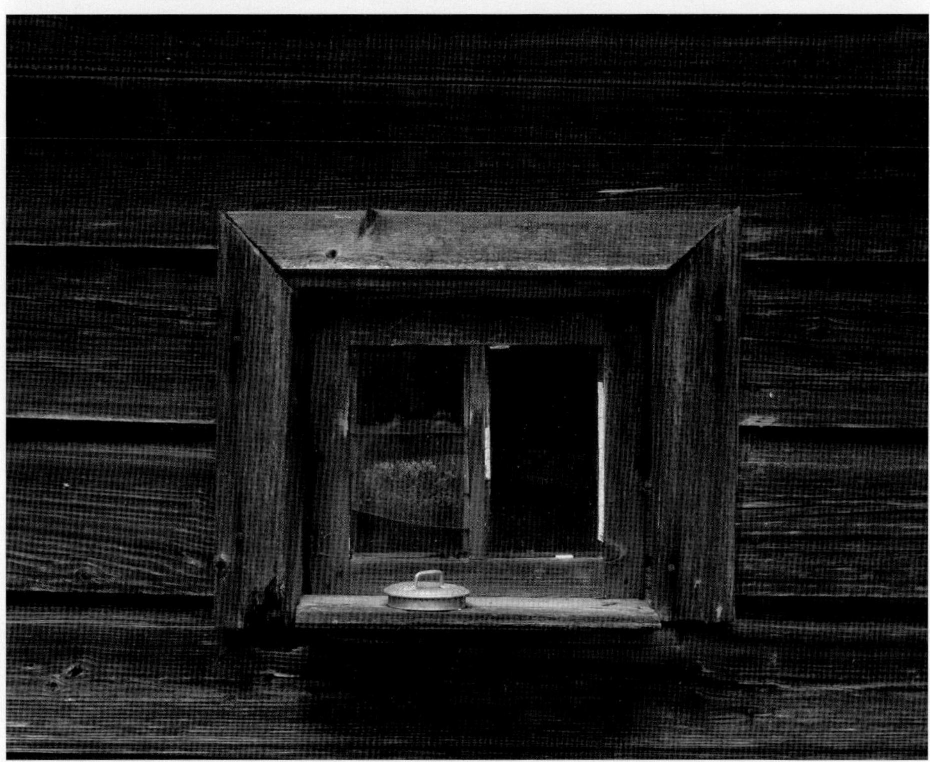

Figure 5.26: Photograph by Karen Laanem.

> A photograph is a secret about a secret. The more it tells you the less you know. (Diane Arbus)

Karen writes:

Each of the photographs I chose to include in my exhibition tell a story from the past. A collapsed roof of a house that was once called home, but was then forsaken to conceal a tragedy. A broken kitchen window, that served as an escape route in the middle of a night to a rebellious teenager. A grandmother visiting the birthplace of her departed husband to tell the story of [the] two of them meeting for the first time. A lace-curtained window protecting the love and warmth of one family's values from the destructive reality of the outside world.

Each of these photographs carries a meaning of its own, but together [they] form a collective memory of my family's history. It can be regarded as both a visual documentary or my personal perception of the past, but either way it unfolds important aspects of my work as an artist and of my self-discovery as a family member.

Finally, the ambiguity in my work relates to my fascination with history and quest for exploring the past. Quoting one of my favourite photographers, Diane Arbus: 'A photograph is a secret about a secret. The more it tells you the less you know.'

Summary

In this chapter you have considered the importance of identifying areas of interest to develop focus and continuity. You have looked at ways of finding focus, through making cross-curricular connections and looking at artists, and through exploring styles and genres from art history. You have investigated what is meant by ethical values in art and how these change over time, and what moral responsibilities the artist might have.

You have seen examples of how three students developed focused, intentional bodies of work around ideas and investigations they have identified as being meaningful.

Chapter 6 Curating and presenting

Introduction

Curating is part of your experience as an art student. In this chapter you will look at the role of the curator and at what curatorial practice means.

You will consider the role of the artist and of the audience, exploring the relationship between maker and viewer.

You will reflect on how methods of display and presentation impact and communicate meaning through your own experiments with different methods of display. You will explore the approaches of artists who collect and document in their work. You will consider originality and the role of appropriation in art practice and what this means for an IB student.

The many activities in this chapter are aimed at developing your curatorial thinking skills and awareness of the artists' relationship with the viewer, and towards formulating an informed response to the art you encounter.

Figure 6.01: In a group exhibition such as this, each artist works with a portion of the space, whether on the wall, the floor (or the ceiling!), curating her own work in relation to the rest of the show.

Curate: From the Latin *curare*, meaning 'take care of'. Curatorial practice is to oversee and care for a collection.

LEARNING OBJECTIVES

- Explore the meaning of curatorial practice and the role of the curator.
- Consider the relationship between the artist and the audience, and the viewers' experience.
- Become aware of methods of display and how these communicate meaning.
- Reflect on originality and appropriation in art and what this means for the student.
- Develop an informed response to the art you encounter.

6.1 What is curatorial practice?

Curatorial practice regards how art is presented and communicated to an audience. A curator is often the mediator between the artist and the viewer. The curator selects and organises the work in such a way that the audience is guided through a particular viewing experience.

As an art student you are both an artist and a curator. You are making your own artwork, learning how to articulate it, how to present it, and how to place it in context with other artwork. As you develop the ability to respond thoughtfully to the art you encounter, you will also become more discerning regarding your own artwork and how it communicates with a potential audience.

- You create a body of work.
- You make a careful selection of resolved pieces that work well together.
- You design a method of display for showing the work.
- You consider the viewers' role in looking at the work.
- You write a curatorial rationale that supports your decisions about how you present your work.

Tip: Primary sources, such as an interview with an artist or curator, are highly recommended as resources for your CS (discussed in Chapter 7).

ACTIVITY 6.1: WHAT IS THE ROLE OF A CURATOR?

Look up an exhibition you have seen and liked and find out about the curator.

- Why is the role of the curator so important?
- What kind of knowledge does a curator need?
- How are the artworks presented? Chronologically? Thematically? By materials? By size and format?
- How would you redesign this show? Can you think of alternative modes of presentation?

ACTIVITY 6.2: INTERVIEW AN ARTIST

Curators need artists, so let's begin by going directly to the source. Find out about an artist working in your community and arrange a studio visit if possible. You can also conduct an interview by email but a studio visit is far more effective. Do some research before your interview, familiarise yourself with the artist's work and have a list of questions ready.

Start your interview with some general questions and then add some of your own that are specific to that artist's work:

- What are you currently working on?
- What is your preferred medium?
- What is your favourite art tool?
- Do you have a piece you are especially proud of?
- How do you know when a work is finished?
- How do you select work for exhibitions?
- Who are the artists and thinkers who influence you?
- What are you looking at or thinking about these days for ideas?
- What mistakes have you made and what have you learned from them?
- How did you start making art?
- Why do you make art?
- What advice would you give to an art student?

Interview with sculptor Tim de Christopher

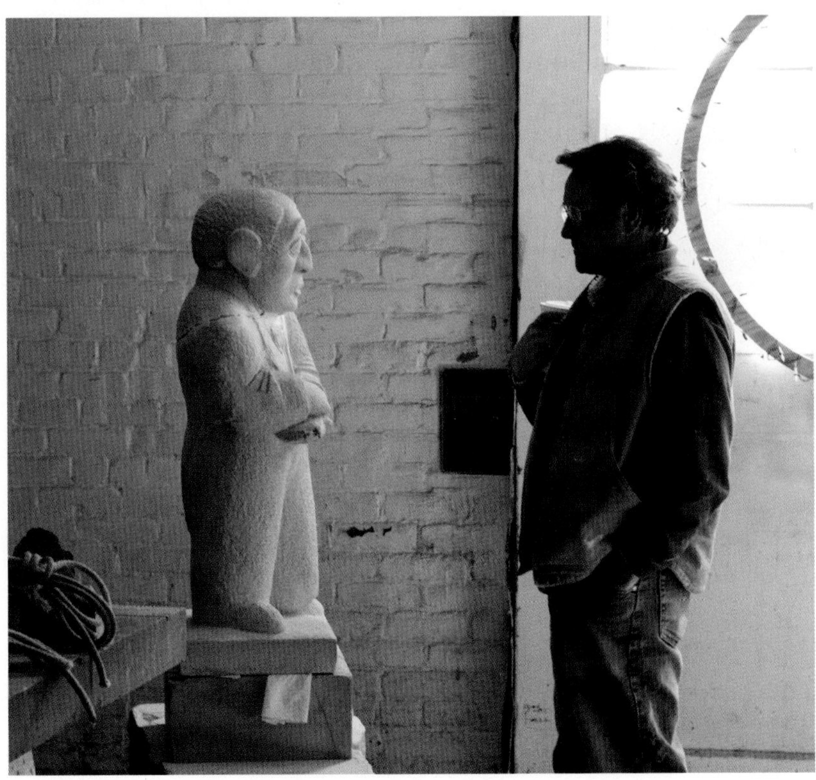

Figure 6.02: American sculptor Tim de Christopher and one of his pieces. Tim says: 'The sculpture is a figure, unnamed, but generally referred to as "the Mason". Yes, his head was broken off, he was broken in my studio and badly repaired, but I sort of like him.'

What are you currently working on?
I'm currently working on a large relief panel which will be a narrative scene depicting the story of Ariadne and the Minotaur, but expressed in the contemporary idiom of an urban landscape based on mythological characters, for example Zeus's Menswear, Minotaur's 24-hour Diner, etc.

Figure 6.03: *Fruit of Our Labours*, by sculptor Tim de Christopher. Tim says: 'This installation is about our labours through life, our legacies and the artefacts that we collect and produce and leave behind . . . like archaeological remains.'

What is your preferred medium?
I typically work in stone, mainly Indiana limestone, sometimes combined with wood and steel.

What is your favourite art tool?
I am a sculptor. It takes many, many tools, and many trades, to make my work. They are all important and all necessary, but stone-working tools predominate.

Who are the artists and thinkers who influence you?
Ancient artists, medieval artists, some 'outsider' artists like Achilles Rizzoli, some modern artists and even one or two (famous) contemporary artists.

What are you looking at or thinking about these days for ideas?
These days I am looking at things Greek, from classical works to modern art, I am especially looking at Picasso's *Minotaurs*.

What mistakes have you made and what have you learned from them?
I have made just about every mistake in the book, but the big mistakes are the mistakes of judgement, which are generally the hardest ones. It is important to learn what you can and be willing to learn from your mistakes. I have learned that much, but am still guilty of making them from time to time.

How did you start making art?
I have been making things, making 'art', all my life. I was raised in a household of art and design. It is an inherited affliction.

Why do you make art?
I make art because it is what I do best and at this point I do not want to do anything else, and I have tried over and over to do something else, but it has never worked for me.

What advice would you give to an art student?
Be careful what you wish for and do good work.

Developing discernment

The first stage of curating an exhibition is selecting the work. As artist and curator you will be selecting a **coherent** body of work and presenting it for your final exhibition (discussed in Chapter 9). Selecting work involves the ability to be discerning and exercise good judgement. As you develop a **discerning eye** and the ability to view work critically, you can apply this to both your own work and that of other artists. The activities in this section will encourage you to reflect on how you make these value judgements.

Coherence: The quality of forming a unified and consistent whole. (For your final exhibition this means that the artworks are relevant and work together as a unified body of work.)

Discerning eye: To discern is to exercise good judgement and understanding, to be discriminating.

ACTIVITY 6.3: EXERCISING JUDGEMENT

- Compare two artworks by the same artist, one that you deem successful, one less so, and explain your reasoning in both cases.
- Select one of your own pieces that you feel is successfully resolved and explain why.
- Identify one of your own pieces that you feel is not successful and explain why.

ACTIVITY 6.4: JUSTIFYING CHOICES

- Find reproductions of ten artworks by an artist whose work interests you.
- Select only four artworks that you think go together.
- Justify why you chose these works and not the others. What are your criteria for selecting them?

I wish I could change my mind as easily as my socks. But then I don't change socks so easily. (Francesca Woodman)

ACTIVITY 6.5: ARTICULATING AN OPINION

It is important to be able to explain why you like or dislike an artwork, but your value judgement should be supported by an informed and considered opinion.

- Make a presentation on an artist's work that you really don't like.
- Do your research first: historical context, art movements, influences.
- Discover how context informs the appreciation of an artwork.
- Explain why you dislike the work using **art subject-specific vocabulary**.

Class critiques and self-evaluations

A class critique is a group conversation, the purpose of which is to give feedback on student work in progress. A critique is a valuable opportunity for learning to present work, discuss intentions and articulate connections and can be of great value in helping you to view your work more critically. It is not an exam, but it is often used as an informal way for a teacher to check on your progress.

Self-evaluations are when you reflect on your own progress, including the difficulties and challenges faced. You consider the valued feedback you have received from teachers and peers and your response to it.

ACTIVITY 6.6: REVIEW YOUR WORK

Choose a piece of your work, and use these questions as a basis for a group critique or a written self-reflection in your visual journal:

- What do you feel is working well? Why?
- What are you experiencing difficulty with? Why?
- What sort of challenges are you setting for yourself?
- What have you discovered about working with these materials?
- How did that happen?
- Where did you get that idea?
- What does this mean to you?
- Where do you think this is going next?
- What ideas are you thinking about?
- What artists are you looking at?
- What interests you in this work?
- What aspect of this work do you want to emphasise?

Writing and reading on art

Curatorial practice includes writing about the art works in an exhibition or collection, including wall texts, exhibition texts, catalogue introductions, press releases, articles and books. Throughout the course you will engage in writing about art, when analysing and comparing art works in your comparative study (discussed in Chapter 7) and when reflecting on your own work and your curatorial decisions in your curatorial rationale (discussed in Chapter 9).

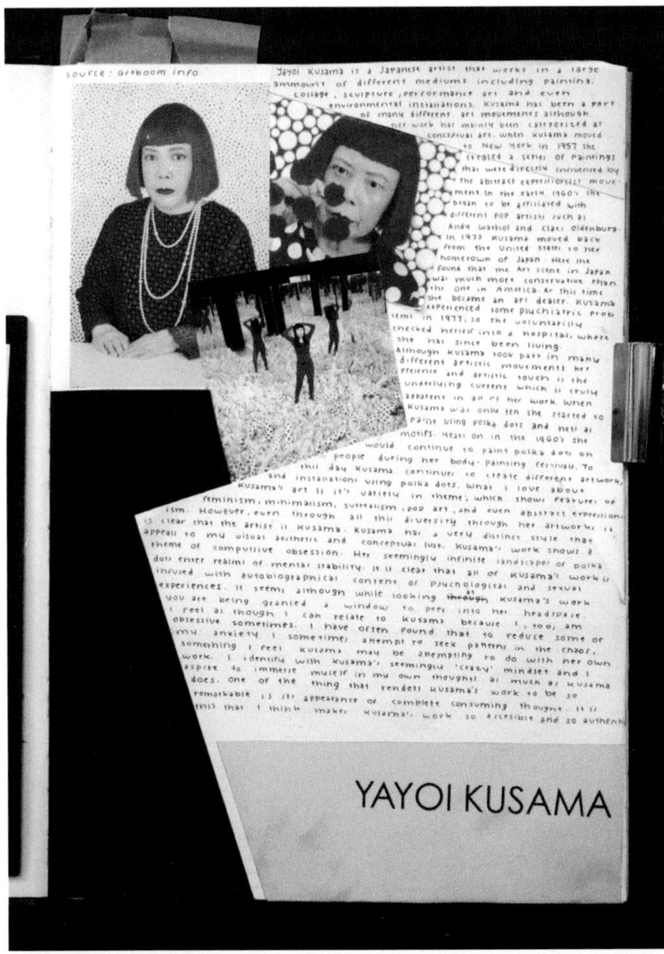

Figure 6.04: Visual journal page by student Lavinia Fasano, with her elegantly designed response to an exhibition by Japanese artist Yayoi Kusama. Lavinia writes: 'Kusama's seemingly infinite landscapes of polka dots are a window into her headspace of compulsive obsession . . . I identify with Kusama's seemingly crazy mindset and aspire to immerse myself in my thoughts as much as she does [in hers].'

To gain familiarity and ease with writing about art it is helpful to read critical essays, reflective commentaries, exhibition catalogues, online articles and books that offer examples of visual analysis and subject specific language. Exploring these secondary sources is an important part of your ongoing research and will also help you to build specialist art vocabulary.

ACTIVITY 6.7: READING ART TEXT

In the extract below, Dawn Ades describes the physical properties of Joseph Cornell's *Untitled (Forgotten Game),* with visual analysis of its formal qualities (materials, textures, colours, even sound), and discusses its *function and* purpose, with references to other artworks, symbols and stories.

- Read the extract.
- Underline and look up any unfamiliar art vocabulary.
- What other artists are referenced in the text?
- What symbols are present in this piece?
- What do you think are the artist's intentions in making this work?
- Is this writing descriptive or interpretive, or both?

As is often the case with Cornell's work, the active involvement of the spectator is invited. This box is not a purely visual game; it also moves and makes sounds. . . . Five rows of six circular holes each are cut into the wood front of the box, which is painted an ivory white and weathered to look like a neglected birdhouse. Cornell devised various ways of purposefully aging surfaces, and the flaking of the paint here, like the cracked glass, is intentional. The holes are smallest at the beginning of each slope and increase in size, as it were, in pace with the growing noise of the ball gathering speed as it descends each ramp in turn.

Sounds are essential to this box: both the rumbling of the rolling ball and the periodic tinkling of the bells. Writing about this work, Diane Waldman recalled Max Ernst quoting Leonardo da Vinci, 'like the tinkling of a bell, which makes one hear that which one imagines' . . . In this box, Cornell used sound as vividly as he did visual and kinetic elements to invoke memory. (Dawn Ades)

Tip: Any chance you get to increase your specialist art vocabulary and refine your understanding of art terminology will help you in meeting the subject-specific language criteria (E) in both the CS and the PP.

Figure 6.05 *Untitled (Forgotten Game)*,1949, a mixed-media box construction by self-taught American artist Joseph Cornell. Cornell was influenced by the Surrealist concept of irrational juxtaposition (see Chapter 1). He worked independently with found objects, cut-outs, photographs and collage, to create many of his characteristic box assemblages. He was also an experimental filmmaker, using collage and montage techniques.

6.2 Artist and audience

Art's more interesting if you look at it. (Ruth Franklin)

Through curatorial practice, you are bringing in a new awareness of the relationship between artist and audience. Developing this awareness is fundamental preparation for curating your own show for the final exhibition (discussed in Chapter 9).

Whenever you visit an exhibition, observe how the physical space, the **methods of display**, the lighting, and the way work is grouped or separated influence your experience of the art. The activities in this section will help you to develop your understanding of the relationship between artist and audience.

Museums and galleries

Visiting art galleries and museums is a great way to learn about artists, form your own ideas, and enrich your understanding of curatorial practice.

Bring a camera, your visual journal, and drawing or writing materials to the exhibition. Do a preliminary wander through the exhibit, then go back to the beginning and walk through again, stopping to really look at a few key works. Make visual **annotations** in your visual arts journal (see Activity 6.9).

ACTIVITY 6.8: BEFORE YOU GO

Familiarise yourself with what you are going to see. If the venue is a museum it will have a website with images, information, biographies and so on.

- What is the title of the show?
- What are the key themes, styles, artists?
- What is the cultural context and background?

Art's whatever you choose to frame. (Fleur Adcock.) Do you agree?

Methods of display: How an artwork is put on view, placed, hung, lit, arranged and presented to the viewer.

Annotation: An explanatory note or comment added to a drawing or diagram.

Tip: Keep a record of information and evidence of exhibitions seen. Documentation might include brochures, images, websites, personal photos, drawings and notes. Include your critical reflections, visual note-taking and drawings in your visual journal. These pages may add value to your PP and the CS.

Tip: A portable sketchbook that fits easily in your bag or pocket is good to have on hand when you find yourself wanting to make a note or a quick sketch. This can be considered part of your visual journal.

Thumbnail sketch: A small, rough sketch that records only the essential information. Making thumbnail sketches is a good way of working out ideas and trying compositional variations.

Tip: Visual annotations made on site when looking at art works may be incorporated into your PP or your CS.

ACTIVITY 6.9: VISUAL NOTE-TAKING

Small **thumbnail sketches** record the artwork and serve as a memory aid. The aim is not to make an exact copy but to register an image on the page and in your mind. Once you have drawn it you won't forget it! Visual annotation helps you remember ideas and makes good material for the process portfolio.

- Make drawings in front of an artwork that you see for yourself; don't rely on second-hand sources (reproductions).
- Sketch the physical space of the exhibition, an overview of the exhibition plan, or even an architectural study of the building.
- Make annotations in your visual journal to accompany the sketches.

Figure 6.06: Work by student Isobel Glover, with notes and watercolour sketches she made during a visit to a Matisse exhibition. Isobel used a small notebook to record her experiences while she was travelling.

ACTIVITY 6.10: POST-VISIT REFLECTION

Use your visual journal to reflect on the exhibition and your personal response to the work encountered.

- What was the most interesting thing about this show (e.g. how it was curated, the space, themes addressed, individual artists)?
- Did you especially like or dislike some work? Explain why, using subject-specific art language.
- Were there any themes, ideas or materials that you are exploring in your studio work or that you'd like to try out?
- Include plenty of images, photos, drawings and graphic notes, as well as written content; make the pages lively and visually interesting. Make sure you acknowledge your sources.

Figure 6.07: Visual journal pages by student Ewa Nizalowska, recording a visit to the Albertina Museum in Vienna where she was struck by the work of Norwegian artist Edvard Munch. She experimented with drawing in Munch's style and in doing so became aware of the 'hasty uneven lines' he used.

Visual response to work encountered

When you visit exhibitions and look at other artists' work you may identify areas of particular interest or relevance to your own art practice. It might have to do with the meaning and content of the work, the style, or the presentation format. Just as you have formulated a written response to the work, you could also attempt a visual response. This is not a visual annotation (as in Activity 6.9) but your personal interpretation. How is being inspired by another artist different from copying? (Later in this chapter, section 6.4, 'Originality and appropriation', takes a closer look at this topic.)

Contemporary art galleries

Contemporary art galleries can present ideal opportunities for observing different methods of display, including site-specific (discussed in Chapter 3), digital and interactive works. Use the following guiding questions for an on-site reflection:

- What different methods of display can you observe? How is art hung, placed, lit, spaced and otherwise displayed?
- Do you see any shows that explore a theme or thread? Describe how the work is related through exploration of ideas. Describe how work is related through visual connections.
- Is your experience as the viewer influenced by the way the work is presented?
- Do you see any site-specific art, made in response to the location? How is it specific to the site?
- Are there any occasions in which you are drawn in to participate or interact with the work?

Beyond the art museum

Art museums are not the only places for looking at exhibitions. Find out about what your local community offers: are there other kinds of museums or cultural places you could visit to investigate cultural connections? Non-art collections often provide excellent opportunities for looking at methods of display, and for drawing both natural and manmade objects:

- natural history museums
- science museums
- maritime museums
- archaeology museums
- ethnography museums
- specialist museums, e.g. a dolls' house museum, a house of historical interest
- botanical gardens.

Artefact: An object intentionally made by human hands, typically of cultural or historical interest.

ACTIVITY 6.11: A TALKING ARTEFACT

Choose an **artefact** from an archaeology or ethnography collection, or, alternatively, a personal object that is meaningful to you.

- Why have you chosen this artefact?
- What is the story of this artefact?
- Why is this artefact of importance?
- How is an artefact different from an artwork?
- Make a drawing to accompany your responses.

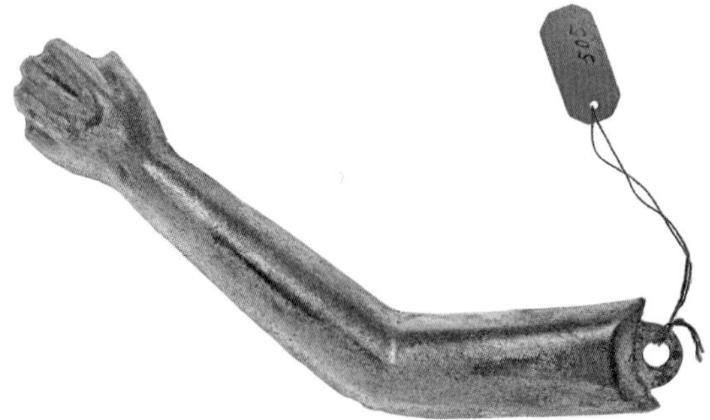

Figure 6.08: This artefact is a Roman Catholic ex-voto that dates from the French colonisation of Algeria. These are symbols of devotion and are used to seek miracles or gratitude. This limb is made of cast metal and has a hole from which it may be hung. This might be a prayer for healing or an expression of thanks.

Ex-voto: An offering given in order to fulfill a vow or to give thanks for a blessing.

Informed response: In the context of the IB, this is your own individual response to artworks you see, informed by knowledge and experience.

Knowledge and the viewer

How does knowledge affect your understanding and appreciation of art? What is meant by an **informed response**?

When looking at work by other artists, be curious about the artist's intentions. What are the strategies the artist (or the curator) uses to communicate with the viewer? Consider methods of display used and how meaning is communicated or impacted through the presentation of the work.

ACTIVITY 6.12: INTUITIVE RESPONSE TO ARTWORK ENCOUNTERED

This activity asks you to consider the impact of information (knowledge) on your understanding of art. At an art exhibition, look carefully at the work *before* reading any of the supporting material or wall texts. Make notes of your intuitive response to the work. Go back and read the supporting material and look at the work a second time.

- How is your experience of the work different after gaining some background information?
- Do you enjoy it more (or less) when equipped with knowledge?
- Record your before and after response in your visual journal.

Figure 6.09: Seeing art for yourself is entirely different from looking at images on a screen or in a book. Things like scale can only be experienced directly in front of the work. In this image an IB art student looks at large-scale work by Valery Koshlyakov at the Venice Biennale.

Engaging with an audience

What makes an exhibition engaging and why are audiences drawn to certain exhibitions? Although a multisensory art installation may be more immediately seductive, many older, more traditional art forms or lesser-known museum collections, things that don't change with the current trends, are valuable sources of inspiration and can be filled with surprising discoveries. What draws **you** in as a viewer?

- What makes an interesting viewer experience?
- Does art have to 'knock you out' to be worthy of attention?
- Can old art and new be exhibited together? What happens when they are?
- What stays with you of the art you have seen? What fades rapidly?
- Does being connected digitally enhance your experience?

Scale: Scale and proportion in art are concerned with size. Scale generally refers to the size of an artwork in relation to the world around it (miniature, small scale, full scale (life-size) or large scale).

ACTIVITY 6.13: EXHIBITION WALL TEXTS

Collect examples of exhibition wall texts from shows you've visited or viewed online. Wall texts in museums are similar to the exhibition texts that you write for your **resolved work** in that they provide the viewer with additional information about the work.

- What information does a text give you besides the title of the work?
- How does it guide the viewer in looking at the work?

Resolved work: An art piece that has reached a stage of completion where no further changes are necessary.

Tip: Write your own text each time you finish a studio piece. This will be useful when you assemble your portfolio for your final exhibition (Chapter 9), where a brief exhibition text is required for each piece you present.

Sun Rising Over Ocean (polyptych)
Linocut print, acrylic, marker, tracing paper
90 x 66 cm
This piece is the most representative of my work because it incorporates elements of design, Japanese motifs, and mixed media. I made this piece before I formally studied Hokusai, However, this work was inspired by his renowned piece, *The Great Wave* that I had seen in images. The backgrounds of the series vary greatly, ranging from colored markers and tracing paper to plain white. Through these, I wanted to emphasise the idea of process as each one progressed into a more complex piece.

Figure 6.10: Exhibition text by student Alyssa Spaeth. Alyssa's series of prints is accompanied by an explanatory exhibition text, stating title, medium, size and a brief description of her intentions.

TOK and art: Viewer response

- Is it important for a work of art to be seen by an audience or not?
- Does the viewer need to have knowledge of art history in order to understand the artwork? Should art be 'accessible' to those without this knowledge?
- How has the role of the audience's response to art changed from the Renaissance to today?
- What knowledge of art can be gained by focusing on the viewers' response?
- Can it be argued that art exists only when there is an audience? Does this depend on the artwork?
- What is the role of the critic in judgement of the worth of art?
- Are any of the following sufficient indicators of the value of a work: its popularity, its commercial value in the market, its universality in its appeal beyond its cultural boundaries, and/or its longevity?

ACTIVITY 6.14: CURATING AN IMAGINARY EXHIBITION

This comprehensive activity, which addresses multiple aspects of curatorial practice, can be done individually or in small groups. Record everything in your visual journal or save as a digital document; you may be able to use parts of this later for your PP.

a) Choose a focus topic

Choose a theme for your virtual exhibition and find at least five art works from different cultural contexts that address this topic. You can include artists from different time periods as well as cultures in your virtual exhibition. Look at what kind of shows are on at major museums to get a sense of how curators approach thematic exhibitions (for example, Figure 6.11 refers to a thematic exhibition featuring artworks from different cultural backgrounds that addressed a common theme).

b) Design the exhibition

- Print or sketch images of all of the works you want to include in your show. (For a rich visual effect, try mixing photos and drawings.)
- Write an exhibition text for each piece (a short descriptive text).
- How do the pieces relate to each other? What are the connections?
- Consider the sequencing of the words and the relationships between them – how would you organise this show so that you are directing the viewer's experience?
- Design the layout of the exhibition – what kind of space do you envision?
- Give your exhibition an appropriate and memorable title.

c) Write an introduction

This could be the introduction to an exhibition catalogue. Explain the concept behind the show, why you choose the works you did, their connections, and the different contexts the work comes from. Describe the exhibition space and what the viewer's role might be. This is good practice for your curatorial rationale (discussed in Chapter 9).

d) Make a presentation

Create a presentation, slideshow or other type of visual presentation of the work you have selected and present it to your class.

e) Studio work

Add one more piece to the show – but this one isn't virtual: it's real, and made by you! Make a piece that fits well with the other works in the virtual exhibition, sharing similar concerns in subject matter or in visual approaches, or both.

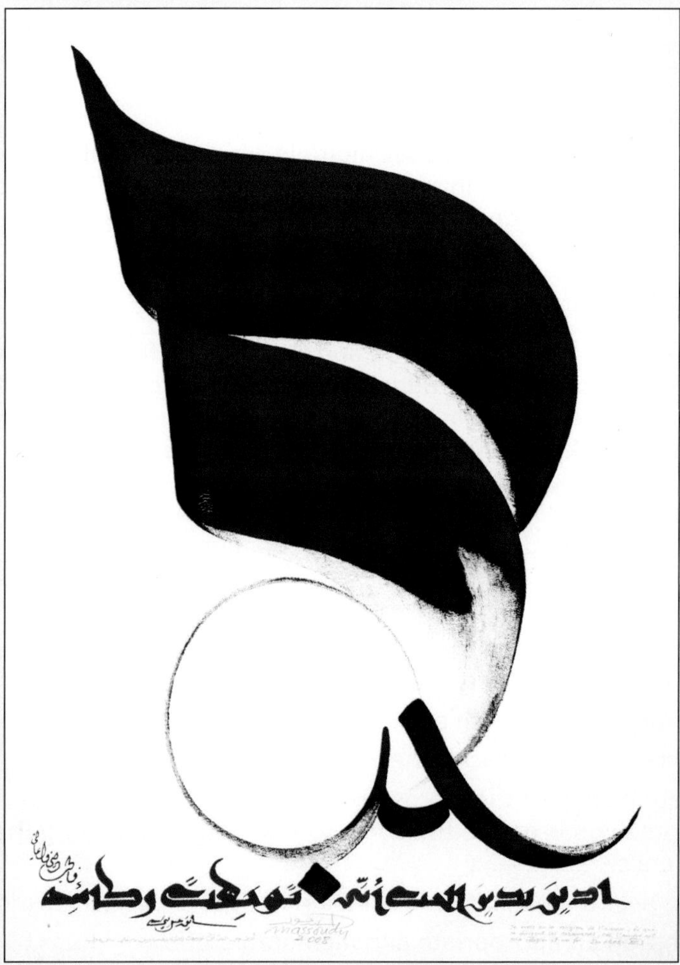

Figure 6.11 Exhibition poster. An example of a thematic exhibition is *Word into Art*, at the British Museum in London, 2006. This show brought together the work of contemporary artists from the Middle East and North Africa. All the works in this exhibition shared an interest in the written word: script, calligraphy, letters and languages.

6.3 Methods of display

How you present art work contributes significantly to its meaning. In this section we will look at methods of display and how they impact the viewer's experience.

Figure 6.12: At La Vigna Art Studios students use materials found outdoors to create a temporary artwork. These sculptural forms are made from pine cones and red clay and arranged on a fallen tree trunk. The natural environment became part of the display and an integral part of the work.

ACTIVITY 6.15: DISPLAYING YOUR WORK

This activity will help you think about different ways of displaying your work for your final exhibition. For each method of display, photograph the results and compare them.

- How does display impact the viewer experience of the artwork?
- How does display impact the meaning or message communicated?
- Which method is most effective? Why?

a) 2D methods of display

Make a selection of four to six of your two-dimensional artworks. Try at least three different methods of displaying these pieces, such as:

- on the wall in a row at eye level
- on the wall in a square formation
- on the wall at floor level
- on the wall upside down
- arranged flat on a table
- illuminated with spotlights in a dark room.

Plinth: A rectangular block or slab, usually stone, serving as a base for a sculpture.

b) 3D methods of display

Make a selection of three to five three-dimensional art works. Try different methods of displaying these pieces using a variety of supports, **plinths**, surfaces, backgrounds and lighting.

c) Digital methods of display

Make a small selection of artworks that include lens-based, electronic or screen-based art forms.

- Design at least two different methods of displaying the work: investigate uses of lighting, blackout curtains, monitors and projections.

Figure 6.13: Student Erika Murakawa tries different methods of display for her *Peace Project: 1000 Cranes*, observing the effects of hanging, piling and arranging, and how people would interact with the space. Erika writes: 'This piece was inspired by the story of a young girl who died from the effects of radiation after the bomb was dropped on Hiroshima. I created 1000 white origami cranes as a symbol of peace. I wanted to commemorate the people who suffered and died from this violence. Traditionally, Japanese believe that a thousand cranes will bring happiness and peace.'

ACTIVITY 6.16: TARGETING AN AUDIENCE

Curate a mini exhibition in your school, targeting a specific audience. How would you curate a show differently according to the audience? Here are a few target audiences to try:

- primary school students
- teaching staff
- parents.

ACTIVITY 6.17: IMPROMPTU CURATING

This activity is intended to reveal how presentation and display change the way we see things. You don't need any special materials, just whatever you have available. Work in small groups.

- Empty out your personal belongings from your bag onto the table and select and choose objects that work together visually or thematically
- Use objects or furniture present in the room, rearranging or assembling them into a new configuration
- Write a short rationale that explains the reasoning behind your choices
- Give your display a title
- Present your display and the short rationale to the class
- Reflect on your impromptu curation:
    - How does limiting the materials available impact your thinking?
    - What have you learned about making connections?
    - What makes an effective presentation?
    - What methods of display would you like to try if you could?

Collecting and displaying as an art practice

Artists are naturally hunters and gatherers of visual material so it makes sense that collecting plays a role in many contemporary artists' practices. Some artists make work around pre-existing collections and others use very personal, individual collections. Collections may derive from the natural world, the home and the domestic sphere, or salvaged material from junkyards, flea markets and recycling centres. For some artists it is the methodology of collecting that is important to their practice.

Figure 6.14: Detail of the installation *Waste not Want not* by Chinese artist Song Dong. The artist has used the entire contents of his mother's house in Beijing as his primary material. The contents of the house are categorised, collated and organised into displays like the bundles of fabric shown in this photo.

ACTIVITY 6.18: ARTISTS WORKING WITH COLLECTIONS

For any artist working with collections, presentation and display are key factors. Strategies for displaying a collection vary according to the artist's intention and what she wishes to communicate.

- Look up one of these artists who use collecting and documenting as part of their practice:
  - Song Dong
  - Mark Dion
  - Susan Hiller
  - Joseph Cornell
  - Sophie Calle
  - Annette Messager
  - Mike Kelley.
- What methods of presentation and display does your chosen artist use?
- How does this artist's methods of display communicate meaning and affect the viewer's understanding of the work?

ACTIVITY 6.19: YOUR PERSONAL COLLECTION

Over the course of several days or weeks, assemble a collection of objects that form a document, a visual record, or a tribute to someone or something important to you. The presentation format is as important as the collection itself. Format creates meaning; create your display with intentionality.

How will you present the collection?

- Choose a container or a method of display for your objects.
- Make the method of display an important part of the work.
- Write a statement of intent to accompany the work. (This is good preparation for writing your curatorial rationale, discussed in Chapter 9).

6.4 Originality and appropriation

When we look at works of art, we are often reminded of things we have seen before. Artists frequently reference the past and other artists' work, revisiting themes, styles and imagery, and using traditional methods to realise new ideas.

Originality is a topic that fascinates us all, one that we aspire to and seek out; we are always looking for **the real thing**. But what does it really mean to be original?

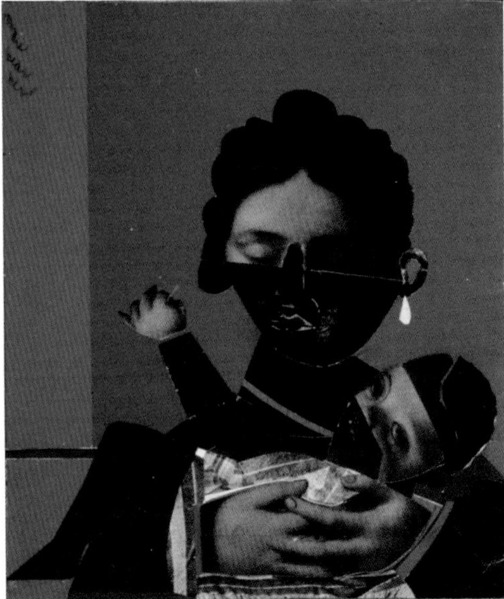

Figure 6.15 (left): Cimabue, *Madonna and Child*, 1285 (tempera and gold leaf on wood panel). Figure 6.16 (right): Romare Bearden, *Mother and Child*, 1971 (collage of magazines and coloured cut paper). Bearden has taken the iconography, the formal composition and the tenderness of this classical subject and made his own homage to the love between mother and child. What are the similarities and the differences between these two artworks?

The idea or the thing?

Marcel Duchamp, the great prankster, inventor of the ready-made (see Chapter 1), changed the course of art history by proposing that art could be an **idea** rather than a thing. Duchamp rejected the assumption that art must be made by the skilled hand of an individual craftsman and argued that a work of art should be primarily about the artist's idea, or **concept**, not the object itself, which is basically the premise behind conceptual art.

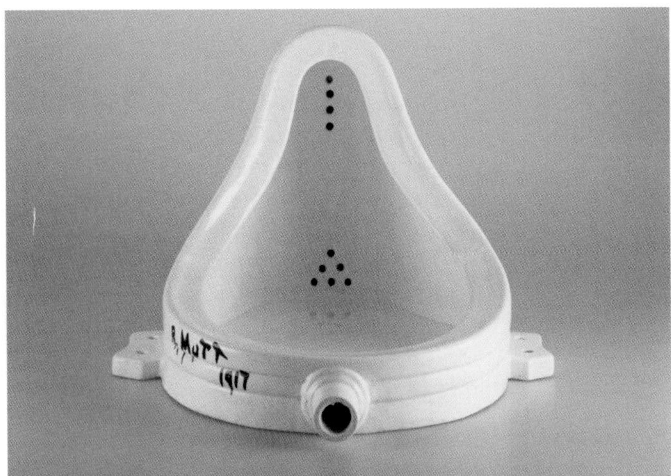

Figure 6.17: *Fountain* is one of Duchamp's early ready-mades, a porcelain urinal which he signed 'R. Mutt'. The 'original' was lost but Duchamp issued 12 official replicas in 1964, which are in museum collections around the world. The original was a mass-produced plumbing fixture and the 12 replicas were crafted ceramic sculptures based on the Alfred Stieglitz photo of the original.

What did Jean-Luc Godard mean when he said: 'It's not where you take things from – it's where you take them to'?

TOK and art: What does it mean to be original?

- Can ideas be owned?
- Does a signature make a work of art?
- Is the idea or the thing the original?
- Does a work of art become less valuable when it is infinitely reproducible?

Appropriation: Intentional borrowing. Appropriation in art and art history refers to the practice of artists taking a pre-existing image from another context – art history, advertising, the media – and creating a new image or object by combining or transforming the original.

Cubism: Style of modern art in which an object or person is shown as a set of geometric shapes and as if seen from many different angles at the same time.

Fine art: Drawings, paintings and sculptures that are admired for their beauty and have no practical use.

Pop art: type of modern art that started in the 1960s and uses images and objects from everyday life.

Appropriation

Many contemporary artists work with **appropriation** using a variety of media and sophisticated technology (see Jeff Koons, Figure 6.18), but it is not an exclusively contemporary trend. Duchamp was using appropriation in his ready-mades (see also Chapter 1), **Cubism** made use of appropriation in collage, and **pop artists** like Andy Warhol and Roy Lichtenstein (Figures 6.20 and 6.22) appropriated images from consumer products, advertising, comics and **fine art**.

Figure 6.18: From the *Popeye* series, by Jeff Koons, 2002. Koons has appropriated a familiar cartoon character for his neo-pop sculpture. The figure is a stainless steel reproduction of a mass-market PVC Popeye figurine.

ACTIVITY 6.20: ARTISTS REVISITING ARTISTS

Choose one of the examples of artists revisiting past artworks (either Figures 6.19 and 6.20, or Figures 6.21 and 6.22) and answer the questions below in your visual journal. Be sure to include the images for reference, and to cite your sources.

- What significant changes has the second artist made to the first image?
- How do the composition, colours and techniques differ?
- How has the context of the artwork changed?
- Does it communicate a different message or meaning?
- Is this appropriation or interpretation?

Figure 6.19: Leonardo da Vinci, *Annunciation*, circa 1472–75 (oil and tempera on panel). This Italian Renaissance painting shows the moment in the bible when the angel Gabriel tells the Virgin Mary that she will bear the Son of God.

Renaissance: The period of growth of interest and activity in the areas of art, literature and ideas in Europe during the 15th and 16th centuries.

Figure 6.20: Andy Warhol, *Leonardo's Annunciation 1472*, 1984 (print edition). Warhol explicitly references Leonardo's painting in the title of his work. This is one of a series of silkscreen prints in different colour schemes. How has Warhol changed the mood and the meaning of Leonardo's *Annunciation*?

Figure 6.21 (left): Henri Matisse, *Goldfish*, 1911. Figure 6.22 (right): Roy Lichtenstein, *Still Life with Goldfish*, 1972. American Pop artist Roy Lichtenstein revisited well-known paintings by Matisse, Monet, Van Gogh and Cézanne in his signature pixilated, graphic style. In Figure 6.22 Lichtenstein pays homage to Matisse's painting. What other objects does he introduce into the picture and why?

ARTISTS REVISITING ARTISTS

Picasso reinterpreting Velázquez's *Las Meninas*

Richard Diebenkorn revisits Matisse's *Windows*

Bill Viola's video transcription of Hieronymous Bosch's painting *Christ Mocked*

Versions of Leonardo's *Mona Lisa*, by Duchamp, Botero or Warhol.

Tracy Emin's response to Frida Kahlo's self-portrait

Ingres's *Odalisque*, and Lalla Essaydi's *Les Femmes du Maroc: La Grande Odalisque*

Velázquez's *Portrait of Pope Innocent X*, and Francis Bacon's response to it.

They always say time changes things, but you actually have to change them yourself. (Andy Warhol)

Immature poets imitate; mature poets steal. (TS Eliot)

ACTIVITY 6.21: APPROPRIATE AN ADVERTISEMENT

Explore the concept of appropriation through digital manipulation.

- Choose an image from advertising that appeals to you.
- Import it into Photoshop, Brushes, or other image-manipulating software.
- Reconstruct the ad by zooming in, cropping, layering, changing the text, changing the colours, or subtracting from or adding to it.
- By altering the ad, give it a different meaning altogether.

Tip: When your work has been clearly inspired by another artist make sure you acknowledge this, clearly citing the sources of your influence.

TOK and art: Appropriation

- How has technology blurred the boundaries of appropriation?
- When is appropriation of another artist's work homage and when is it plagiarism?
- Can recycled and re-uploaded images be considered original work?
- Can you maintain ownership of an idea when it is in the public domain?
- Find an example of 'acceptable' and 'unacceptable' artistic appropriation.

Originality in IB DP Visual Arts

The importance of the process and the making of the work is an essential part of IB DP Visual Arts. All of the work that you submit for assessment must be entirely made **by you**. If you have designed a wearable piece of art, for example, but had it made by someone else, you may only present the plans and designs as your own work, not the finished product. If you are using found objects to create a new artwork, the resulting combination of objects can be considered an original art piece.

If using appropriation, parody, reference or homage to other artists works in your own work be aware of copyright laws and make sure you always indicate your sources clearly and explicitly. Some images, even when altered significantly, may still be in breach of copyright.

> The reproduction of another artist's work either as a process for developing and honing skills, or to create another image through parody or pastiche has a long history in Western art, but presents significant challenges in the context of a university matriculation course where students are asked to declare that the work that they submit is their own ...
>
> Where students choose to explore appropriation, pastiche, parody, détournement or homage in their art-making practices, teachers need to counsel them to choose imagery that comes from creative commons or public domain sources, or otherwise formal permission is sought. It is essential that the source of any original imagery is correctly attributed in their visual arts journal and in the accompanying exhibition text of any work submitted. (From IB advice on appropriation in art-making, given in the IBO's *Academic Honesty in Visual Arts*, online curriculum centre.)

Collaborative work

Figure 6.23: Student Collaborative Mural at La Vigna Art Studios, Pisa. A collaborative piece like this wall *sgraffito* comprises distinct elements, so that an individual can take ownership of a specific part within the work.

Tip: The final assessment is always an individual one so if you work on a collaborative project, make sure you can clearly show your individual contribution. Document the development of the project thoroughly in your process portfolio.

'. . . internally assessed work must be entirely [the students'] own. Where collaboration between students is permitted, it must be clear to all students what the difference is between collaboration and collusion.' (*IB DP Visual Arts Guide, page 49*)

Collaborative art practices involve two or more artists sharing ownership for the process and the resulting art works. Students who are interested in collaborations should explore artists who work collaboratively and how these partnerships evolve. It can be a very exciting way of working, but also very challenging and not suited to all personalities. Many collaborative teams tend to work with installation and performance rather than the more intimate areas of art-making more suited to individuals. (Chapter 3 looks at the site-specific collaborative practice of Christo and Jeanne-Claude.)

Contemporary artists like Jeff Koons or Takashi Murakami have huge production studios full of assistants executing the work according to instructions. Damien Hirst employs many young artists to paint the dots on his famous dot paintings. Andy Warhol ran an art factory. Even Michelangelo mixed paints in the workshop of Ghirlandaio! Although artists who have reached a certain level of fame and fortune may have assistants who do many of the tasks for them, this doesn't apply to you. As an IB DP Visual Arts student you must make your work yourself.

Summary

In this chapter you have learned to look at art with a discerning eye, seeing connections and relationships among other artists' works and within your own work. You have seen how presentation impacts meaning, and experimented with creating and curating displays. You have considered yourself as the viewer as well as the artist, and seen how, as a student artist, you are both the maker **and** the curator of your own work. You have explored the concept of originality and appropriation and asked the question: What does it mean to be original as an artist, as an IB student?

Chapter 7

The comparative study

Introduction

This chapter looks at the requirements of the comparative study (CS) and its role in the course. You will compare and contrast artworks from different cultural backgrounds, considering different modes of analysis and making connections between the chosen works. You will learn how to identify and reference sources and use subject-specific art language when you analyse artworks. You will also begin to see your own developing art practice in relation to the artists you study, and consider how this impacts your work.

LEARNING OBJECTIVES

- Become familiar with the requirements of the CS.
- Analyse, interpret and evaluate artworks.
- Identify sources and use an academic referencing system.
- Use subject-specific language to discuss art.
- Compare and make connections between artworks from different cultural contexts.
- Consider how to structure and present your CS.
- See your own developing art practice in relation to other artists and art history (HL).

7.1 What is the comparative study?

Context: The circumstances that surround an event or an idea and help it to be understood.

The CS is an independent critical comparison of at least three works by at least two different artists from different cultural **contexts** that you have chosen for their relevance and personal interest.

You will use research and personal reflection to analyse and interpret these art works. This will help you to develop informed ways of looking at the work of other artists and understand how critical investigation underpins the art-making process. For HL students this is a chance to make important connections with your own art-making practice and think about how theory is related to practice.

How is the comparative study assessed?

The CS is one of the three assessed components of the course. The final version, which comprises 20% of your overall IB DP Visual Arts grade, is submitted as a digital file and assessed on screen. Although there is no prescribed format or word count there is a specified number of screens for SL and HL.

> You are just as qualified as any expert to make a judgement and have a feeling or a response to any work of art. (Bill Viola)

The formal requirements of the comparative study task

SL students: 10–15 screens
HL students: 10–15 screens, plus 3–5 screens in which you analyse your own artwork in relation to the artists and artworks you have chosen.

The CS is assessed according to a set of criteria that address key areas of learning: critical thinking skills and the ability to analyse, interpret, evaluate and compare, using art language, research and personal insight. (A detailed discussion of the assessment criteria with tables and descriptors can be found in Chapter 10.)

The assessment criteria for the comparative study

A Identification and analysis of formal qualities........................... 6 points
B Analysis and understanding of function and purpose............ 6 points
C Analysis and evaluation of cultural significance....................... 6 points
D Making comparisons and connections.................... 6 points
E Presentation and subject specific language........................... 6 Points
F (HL ONLY) Making connections to own art-making practice ....12 points

7.2 Analyse, interpret, evaluate, compare

Developing your skills in research, analysis, interpretation, evaluation and comparison is a key learning objective for this component of the course, as is developing your understanding of art terminology. Research and analysis will help you to develop an informed response to the artwork you encounter. Gaining knowledge and understanding will change the way you look at an artwork as you discover more about the artist's intentions and the context in which the work was made.

This section helps you to identify and understand the analytical and interpretive skills you need for your CS. Developing these skills will help you meet the assessment objectives for the CS (described in Chapter 10).

Analysis of formal qualities

When analysing an artwork in any media you can begin by describing the formal, visual aspects of the work. This is essentially describing what you see. Describe the visual structure of the image in detail, referring to the **formal elements of art** and design: line, shape, size, space, colour, texture, value and so on. You can also describe the medium and the materials used, and discuss how it was made (is it a painting, a light projection, a knitted sock . . .?)

The terms used to describe the formal qualities of art are important vocabulary for an art student. If you are able to identify these elements you will be better equipped to discuss a work of art (your own or someone else's).

Formal elements of art: The 'formal' qualities or elements of art do not mean that it is fancy, elegant or conventional. 'Formal' refers to the form, as in the formal elements, such as line, shape, colour, space, size, texture, value, pattern . . .

Formal qualities are not entirely separate from one another and can be considered holistically (as a whole). Analysis will also vary depending on the medium of the artwork. When you are analysing a painting, the formal qualities are not the same as when you are analysing a moving image, a sculpture or an installation. Every medium has its specific language and visual elements.

Tip: When describing the formal qualities of an artwork, use subject-specific language whenever possible.

When analysing non-traditional art forms, try to address the most relevant formal qualities. The whole notion of formal elements in the 21st century is changing and you may need to find new vocabulary altogether!

STUDENT EXAMPLE: TALIA STERN

Formal Analysis of Velasquez

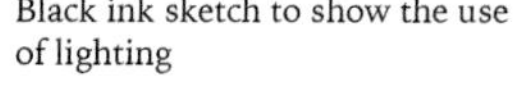

Black ink sketch to show the use of lighting

Layout sketch. The child is centralized, creating a symmetry in the painting, however the canvas destabilises this.

Use of Red:
Velasquez also uses hints of red in order to draw the public's eye across the canvas. Velasquez only uses very little red on some of character's outfits which create this effect of balance.

Use of Light:
The source of light in this painting is coming from the window to the right. It seems to be directly hitting the canvas, which is then reflected on the figures in the centre of the painting, especially the "Infante". Through the use of the color palette of her light dress and fair hair creates luminous effect and making her standout from the crowd.

Structure:
We can divide this painting into this grid which allows us to organize the different figures separately which was very commonly done at the time. This allows us to see that Velasquez played close attention to the balance of the painting. There are 6 planes which also help in creating this balance:

1. the canvas being painted, the dog, the midget and the child to the right
2. The princess with her maids
3. Velasquez
4. The Man and Woman in the dark
5. The mirror with the royal couple and the paintings
6. The mysterious man in the doorway

The family situation in this painting reflects the the social identity maintained in public. The fact that the royal couple, parents of the little girl, aren't present in this painting apart from their vague reflection looming over the little girl's head hints at the distanced relationship. There is first of all a lack of privacy and intimacy, as the little girl is posing, not only for Velasquez but for her parents as well. Her entourage is crowding her and fill the bottom half of the canvas completely, created an effect of claustrophobia. The princess' maids are bending down to her level, creating a triangular shape in the painting which emphasises a certain hierarchy or power. She gives an air of superiority.

Figure 7.01: Screen from comparative study (SL), by student Talia Stern. Here Talia analyses the formal qualities in Velázquez's painting, considering colour, light, and compositional structure.

SPOTLIGHT ON THE STUDENT: TALIA STERN

Nationality: French/American.
Born: Paris

Main artistic interests:
- music's relationship with colour, shape and form
- expression of synesthesia
- human psychology conveyed through use of space.

Influential artists:
- Wassily Kandinsky
- Sonia Delaunay
- Alfred Hitchcock
- Edward Hopper
- Paul Klee.

ACTIVITY 7.1: FORMAL AND CONCEPTUAL COMPARISONS

- Choose two artworks that clearly have visual, formal qualities in common.
- Compare them in terms of their formal qualities.
- Choose a third artwork that doesn't necessarily share formal qualities with the first two, but does address similar **concepts**.
- Compare the third artwork with the other two, this time comparing ideas and concepts.

Conceptual: Conceptual qualities in art refer to the idea or concept behind the work rather than the actual product.

Interpreting function and purpose

Examining the function and purpose of an object means asking the question, 'What is it made for?'

Some artworks have a very clear purpose: a designed object such as a chair or a vessel has a practical function as well as a decorative function. You have probably seen many examples of art with a religious purpose, or a narrative purpose (telling a story, as in history painting), or art that has a mainly personal, expressive function. Some art functions as a status symbol, conferring power or wealth to the owner; some work is created with the intent to shock or disturb. Function and purpose may be more relevant when discussing certain artworks (e.g. religious, ceremonial, commemorative, propaganda) and less with others.

Some of the functions of art

(A single artwork may have more than one!)

- Expressive – expresses the artists' feelings.
- Descriptive – records the likeness of a place or person or other subject.
- Conceptual –the idea or concept behind the work is more important than the object.
- Practical function – has a practical use, such as clothing, vessels, furniture, a building.
- Religious – tells a religious story or is an object of devotion.
- Historical narrative function – tells a story of an event in history.
- Commemorative – made to honour someone (like a statue of a famous person).
- Political function – serves a political purpose, such as propaganda.
- Symbolic – symbolises certain beliefs or ideas without representing them.
- Decorative – used to adorn the body, a room, a building and so on.
- Ritual – used as part of a ritual or ceremony, or has magical powers.
- Shock – intended to shock or upset the viewer

ACTIVITY 7.2: WHAT'S MY FUNCTION?

Find examples of five artworks with different functions. You might want to refer to the list or add more functions to it.

TOK and art: Function of art

- Are there common standards by which we can judge art from different cultures?
- How do you decide what is good and bad art?
- How does knowledge influence understanding of art?
- What role does emotional response play in looking at art?
- Does all art have a social function?
- Does all art have an expressive function?
- Does all art have a function?

Figure 7.02: Rachel Whiteread, *House*, 1993. This temporary public sculpture was a concrete cast of the inside of a house scheduled for demolition in a neighbourhood in east London. *House* remained in place for eleven weeks, and was then demolished to make way for the rest of the development.

ACTIVITY 7.3: WHY WAS IT MADE?

Discuss the function and purpose of Rachel Whiteread's public sculpture *House* (Figure 7.2).

- What do you think the artist's intentions were in making this?
- Who was it made for?
- What would you say were the function and purpose of *House*?
- Can an artwork have more than one function?
- Is function always functional?

Evaluation of cultural significance

For the CS you are asked to choose artworks from different cultural contexts for comparison. A cultural context is the background from which an artwork emerges, the place and time and the causes and conditions that have helped shape the work. Different cultural contexts might mean the artwork comes from different geographical or cultural backgrounds, or different periods in history. (Chapter 3 explores the definition of culture in greater depth.) When you evaluate the cultural significance of an artwork you are asking: Where was it made? When was it made? What is the background from which this artwork emerged: the cultural, social, political, historical and personal influences that shaped it?

Arthur Bispo do Rosário (1911-1989)

Rosario is a Brazilian outsider artist, who initially served in the Brazilian Navy, and was an amateur boxer. His life took a turn when he began having hallucinations in 1938 and one day went up to a group of monks to state that he was sent by God for a mission on Earth. This eventually resulted in him becoming diagnosed with schizophrenia in 1939 and becoming a patient for a total of 50 years at the Colônia Juliano Moreira, a mental institution in Rio de Janeiro. There, in an attic, Rosario created over 800 works that he never sold, demonstrating that he never made art to make money (Phaidon, 2012). Confined from mainstream society and forcefully put in the institution, art was arguably his way of remaining sane and expressing his thoughts. He has been compared to Andy Warhol for the way he recycles found objects in his works, although both individuals come from entirely contrasting backgrounds (social elite/impoverished). "*He used art as a way to turn confinement into freedom,*" said Raquel Fernandes, director of the Bispo do Rosario Museum of Contemporary Art (AP. 2015)

Art Brut (Outsider Art):
This term was coined by French artist Jean Dubuffet, who was greatly influenced by the book "Art of the Mentally Ill" by phsiciatist Hans Prinzhorn. He used this term to label art that was created outside the boundaries of official culture, such as works created by insane-asylum patients. The themes presented in these works often convey perplexing mental states and imaginative worlds (Fadul, 2014). It is sometimes referred to by the term *raw art*, which I believe brings forth the nature of the artists who do not make art for the money, but purely for creative expression.

Artist's Works

"Rede de arrastão" / "Piston", Arthur Bispo do Rosário, n/a, Mixed media, n/a

"Manto da Apresentação", Arthur Bispo do Rosário, n/a, woven yarn, 118. 5 x 141 x 20 cm

"Confetes", Arthur Bispo do Rosário, n/a, plastic, wood, paper, 113 x 46 x 13 cm

Figure 7.03: Comparative study screen (HL) by student Sari Imai. Sari analyses the cultural significance of the Brazilian artist Arthur Bispo do Rosário, in the context of Outsider Art: 'Confined from mainstream society and put in an institution, art was arguably his way of remaining sane and expressing his thoughts. He has been compared to Andy Warhol for the way he recycles found objects in his works, although both individuals come from contrasting backgrounds (social elite/impoverished). "He used contemporary art as a way to turn confinement into freedom," said Raquel Fernandes, director of the Bispo do Rosário Museum of Contemporary Art (AP: 2015)".'

Conceptual and material significance

As discussed in Chapter 4, the materials an artist uses can be closely linked to the cultural significance of the work. They may also contribute to conceptual meaning – the message that the work communicates.

As you have seen, cultural context isn't only related to place. The weavings in Figures 7.4 and 7.5 are both from Ghana but come from different historical contexts and reflect different cultural content. Both tapestries present colourful, abstract patterns. However, they are not limited to a decorative function.

ACTIVITY 7.4: EXPLORING CONTEXT

Often the meaning and significance of a work of art are deeply tied to context. Choose an artwork and respond to the questions.

- What was happening in the world at the time this piece was made?
- What cultural, religious or political beliefs influence this work?
- What personal experiences may have influenced it?
- What other artists and cultural movements were at the forefront at this time?

Figure 7.04: 19th-century traditional Ghanaian double-weave *kente* cloth (cotton, silk), Ewe peoples. *Kente* cloths are colourful, patterned ceremonial cloths traditionally woven by hand. Small strips of cloth are first woven, then arranged and sewn together to create a colourful, abstract pattern. The function and purpose are not purely decorative. They are also symbolic of prestige and high social status and imbued with the history, philosophy and belief systems of the people – far more than pretty pieces of cloth.

Figure 7.05: Detail of Rikki Wemega-Kwawu, *Kente for the Space Age*, 2007. This weaving by the contemporary Ghanaian artist is made of pre-paid phone cards, a commonplace object recycled from popular culture that carries its own implications and symbols from contemporary urban African life.

ACTIVITY 7.5: INTERPRETING CULTURAL SIGNIFICANCE

What conceptual meaning is communicated through the materials? How is this different in these two artworks? Reread the captions to Figures 7.4 and 7.5 and discuss each artwork. Use the questions to guide you:

- What does it mean? Does it contain symbols? Does it tell a story?
- Why did the artist create this artwork? Does it have a specific purpose or role (e.g. religious, political, practical)?
- What was the context in which the work was made? What was going on in that place and time?
- What were the social and historical factors that might have influenced the work (e.g. war, technology, pop culture)?
- What audience was the work intended for?
- What kind of relationship with the 'viewer' do you think the artist desired?
- What conceptual meaning is communicated through the materials?

Comparing and contrasting

In any comparison, it is essential to discuss the similarities and the differences. After establishing the common ground in the artworks you are looking at (perhaps a similar subject matter or shared formal qualities), you can discuss the ways in which the works are different.

7.3 Research and resources

Before you compile your CS you will need to find appropriate resources and do some preliminary research on the artworks you have chosen to compare. If you select artworks that have readily available background information (i.e. published material), it will be much easier to gather information and compile a bibliography. Museums and galleries are a good place to start if you aren't sure about the suitability of your sources.

Primary and secondary sources

You are strongly recommended to see at least one of the artworks yourself in a museum, gallery or artist's studio: artwork seen first-hand would be considered a **primary source**. When this is not possible, try to find good-quality reproductions. Art books and exhibition catalogues usually have better-quality reproductions than the small low-resolution images found on the internet, and can be extremely useful in conducting research.

ACTIVITY 7.6: COMPARE AND CONTRAST TWO ARTWORKS

Choose artists whose work addresses content or style related to what you are developing in your own work. Your teacher may be able to suggest appropriate works or it could be an artist you are already researching for your CS.

Discuss the two artworks using these guidelines:

- Compare and contrast the formal qualities.
- Compare and contrast the function and purpose.
- Compare and contrast the cultural similarities and differences.
- Express your own critical interpretation of the significance of the work based on your research.

Primary source: In the context of art, a primary source is an original document, creative work, artefact or relic, not interpreted by a third party. When you interview an artist or visit an exhibition or studio and experience the work directly, this is considered a primary source.

ACTIVITY 7.7: FIND A PRIMARY SOURCE

Visit a gallery, museum or studio, interview an artist, or identify some public art in your community. Document your source with photos and notes in your journal.

When using the internet as a research tool, identify the reliability of the website and the author. Many art institutions, museums, universities and established contemporary artists have websites with educational forums and are a reliable source of information.

Referencing

As an IB student you must always acknowledge all the sources you have used in any work submitted for assessment. Give the source details of all the images, text extracts and quotes you refer to in your work, including work or ideas of another artist, person or source that you have paraphrased or summarised.You may choose the referencing style you prefer or the one used by your school, but it is important to be consistent throughout.

Sources include (but are not limited to) images, books and websites. Here are some other sources you might want to reference in your bibliography:

- participation in practical workshops
- exhibitions and exhibition catalogues
- filmed interviews with visual arts professionals
- lectures and lecture notes
- audio recordings and soundtracks
- newspaper articles and magazines
- online groups and forums
- feedback and advice from others
- films, and television and radio programmes.

Tip: You are required to submit the bibliography **(list of sources) for your CS as a separate document**. As soon as you know you would like to refer to an image or text, collect the reference information in a Word document. Doing this will save you a lot of time later when you compile your bibliography.

Citing sources

When citing images the recommended format is: **Artist / Title / Date / Media / Source.**

When citing texts, present in the following order: **Author / Title / Publisher / Date / Page or Website**

If citing work you found on the internet, you must cite the artist and the details of the work, not just the URL where you found it! Include the date you accessed the page, along with the URL.

For example, the recommended format for citing Figure 7.06 would be ***Diego Velasquez/ Las Meninas/1656/ Oil on canvas 318 x 108.7 inches/Museo del Prado, Madrid***

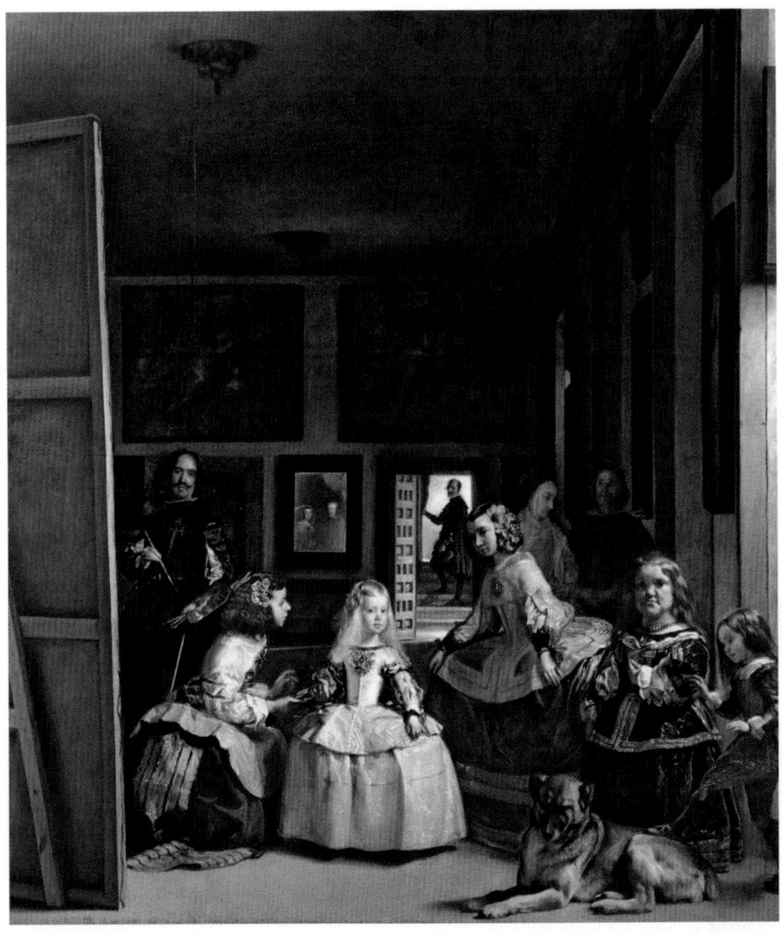

Figure 7.06: Diego Velázquez, *Las Meninas*, 1656 (oil on canvas, 318 × 108.7 inches), Museo del Prado, Madrid.

Subject-specific language

Although the CS is not assessed on the quality of your grammar, it is important to write clearly and coherently, using appropriate art terminology and vocabulary. Subject-specific language **is** an assessed criteria, so try to use the correct art language whenever possible. This can be language describing visual qualities, as in 'contrasting dark tones', or more technical terms, as in '*intaglio* printmaking' (see 'Printmaking terms', in Chapter 4).

ACTIVITY 7.8: USING SUBJECT-SPECIFIC LANGUAGE TO DESCRIBE AN ARTWORK

You can do this activity in your visual journal.

- Choose one artwork to describe.
- Describe the formal qualities using subject-specific language.
- Describe the techniques and materials using subject-specific language.
- Describe the function and purpose of the work and what it communicates to the viewer using subject-specific language.

Include an image of the work and cite your sources.

Tip: Your teacher can review the first draft of your CS and make suggestions for improvement. Make sure you show your first draft to your teacher in plenty of time for you to review their comments and write your draft for submission! Remember that your final draft must be **entirely your own work.**

Artwork #1: "Blackbird"

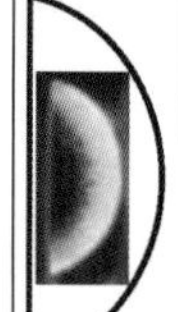

FORM & COMPOSITION

- square piece that has unity (all aspects link to the same theme of African-American discrimination)
  - small scale: viewer must go up close to see the photograph, small objects, and understand the narrative behind the assemblage, further creating a more intimate and personal atmosphere between the work (Saar herself) and the viewer
- mostly consisting of straight lines, with occasional curves (e.g watermelon and bird)
- objects neatly placed in separate compartments - fairly symmetrical (photograph: top centre, watermelons and alphabet blocks: one on each side)
- focal points: photograph, metal piece with "blackbird"⟹most important elements
- work is clearly divided into the top-half (photograph) and the bottom-half (objects)
  - allows the artist to maximise space for the photo

line of symmetry

"Blackbird", Betye Saar, 2002, Mixed media on vintage blackboard, (included base): 59 x 59 x 6 cm, Michael Rosenfeld Gallery

- Saar did not paint any of the objects, they are all in their found state⟹not artificial and creates a genuine and amicable atmosphere
- 3 main colours present (light browns, reds and dark teal)
  - subtle brown of wood that is a tertiary colour, allows the objects to stand out (e.g. red watermelons and the blackbirds)
- most vibrant shade is the red
- otherwise, mainly neutral tones
- faded sepia photograph and paint on the wooden objects contribute to the nostalgic atmosphere that the assemblage evokes
  - audience is immediately able to recognise that the piece is referring to the past

Colour Scheme

MATERIALS

"Blackbird" is part of a collection of works that Saar did following her great-aunt's death; many of which use objects that previously belonged to her. This piece uses both familial and thrifted objects that each use symbolism (discussed further in slide 13).

Theme: **education**

- vintage blackboard that acts as the base of the piece
- photograph of Saar's great-aunt's class
- wooden alphabet blocks

Alphabet block

Theme: **black segregation**

- wooden watermelons
- wooden blackbirds

CREATIVE PROCESS

Saar's creative process is lengthily as she "*takes time in collecting things and putting things together.*" At the same time, her assemblages are never thoroughly planned; she begins by putting various objects together "*until something clicks and things seem to fit together*".

Sometimes, she "*picks up a photograph and works with it, until the piece dictates what it's going to be.*"

***citations in italic: UCLA Department of Art Lectures | Betye Saar, 2014**

Figure 7.07: Comparative study screen by student Sari Imai. In this example, Sari analyses an artwork, *Blackbird* by Betye Saar. Sari uses subject-specific language when discussing the composition ('line of symmetry'), when analysing the colour scheme ('subtle brown of wood is a tertiary colour . . . Otherwise mainly neutral tones'). She also supports and enhances her analysis with quotes from the artist on her creative process.

Tip: Pay attention to the spelling of artists' names and of subject-specific terms.

Quotes

You may use quotes to support your comparison if they are relevant and properly referenced. A quote from an artist can give us insight into what they were thinking about, their working process and how they want the work to be perceived.

ACTIVITY 7.9: FIND A SIGNIFICANT QUOTE

Find a quote from an artist whose work you are discussing in your CS.

- How does the quote support or explain the artist's work or working methods?
- How does it reflect the cultural and historical context the artist is working in?
- How does it further your understanding of their artwork?

7.4 Choosing artworks and artists

Choose your artworks for the CS, bearing in mind the availability of appropriate resources (as discussed in section 7.3), the marking criteria (detailed in Chapter 10) and the requirements of the task:

- You must select a minimum of three artworks by at least two different artists. You may include more pieces if you wish, but try to keep it manageable.
- The artists or artworks should come from different cultural or historical contexts (as discussed in section 7.2, 'Evaluation of cultural significance').
- The artworks can be in any fine or applied art media including painting, drawing, sculpture, print, photography, textiles, installation, new media, architecture, artefacts and designed objects.

Reflect on what is meaningful to you and choose artworks that you would like to learn more about. You can compare anything, but it will only have convincing strength if there is solid ground for comparison, either formally or conceptually, or both. You might select works that address a particular theme, or investigate key works in art history. Your choice of artworks might be inspired by a TOK question like the ones you find throughout this book.

HL students should investigate artists or artworks that are clearly related to their own artistic interests:

- What are you working on in the studio?
- What techniques and media you are exploring?
- What ideas and themes interest you?
- What exhibitions have you seen lately?

Student examples

In this section we look at how three students chose their artworks for the CS and what they say about their choices.

STUDENT EXAMPLE: TALIA STERN (SL)

Introduction

For my comparative study, I have decided to look at these three artworks as they have similar contextual elements despite their considerably different time period. With two paintings one from the 17th century and the other 20th century and one photograph of the 21st century, I will be able to analyze how each artists uses stylistic features to shape meaning.

Diego Velázquez (1599-1660)
Las Meninas
1656, oil on canvas 318 in x 108.7 in
Museo de Prado, Madrid

Max Beckmann (1884-1950)
Family Picture
1920, oil on canvas 65.1 x 100.9 cm
2015 Artists Rights Society (ARS), New York / VG Bild-Kunst, Bonn

Gregory Crewdson (1962-)
Untitled (Sunday Roast)
from the series 'Beneath the Roses'
2005 Digital carbon print144.8 x 223.5 cm
Gregory Crewdson, Courtesy Gagosian Gallery, New York© Gregory Crewdson, 2010

I will be looking at family relationships created by the artist through various methods such as the use of space, as well as color and shapes. These three pieces each bring up a different look at the psychology of family dynamics influenced by culture and time. This allows for an interesting comparison as the artist's background, style and time period all differ from one another, yet one can still find similarities between them.

Figure 7.08: First screen of comparative study by SL student Talia Stern (you will recall Talia's work from Figure 7.01). Talia chose to compare artworks that explore the psychology of family dynamics, making meaningful connections between these three artists from different cultural and temporal contexts.

Talia chose artworks by three artists from different backgrounds, analysing how each one depicts family dynamics through pictorial means:

- Diego Velázquez (1599–1660), *Las Meninas*
- Max Beckmann (1884–1950), *Family Picture*
- Gregory Crewdson (1962–), *Untitled (Sunday Roast)*

STUDENT EXAMPLE: SARI IMAI (HL)

Introduction to Pieces

"**Blackbird**", Betye Saar, 2002, Mixed media on vintage blackboard, (included base): 23.25 x 23.25 x 2.25 inch, Michael Rosenfeld Gallery

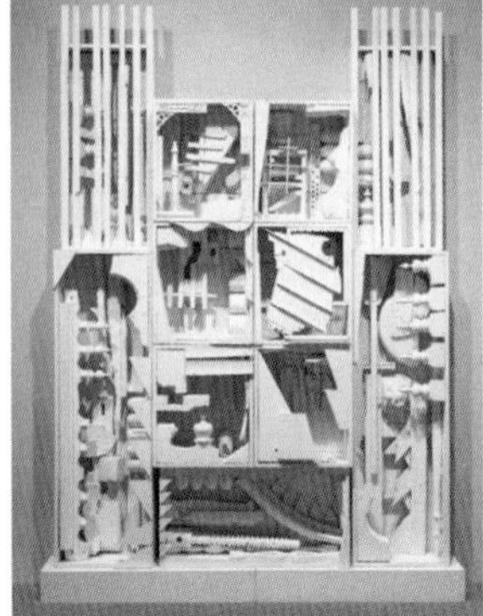

"**Dawn's Wedding Chapel II**", Louise Nevelson, 1959, Painted wood, (included base): 294.3 x 212.1 x 26.7 cm, Whitney Museum of American Art

"**Sandálias e peneiras**", Arthur Bispo do Rosario, N/A, wood, rubber, wire, cardboard , 110 x 80 x 24 cm

After Betye Saar's father died in 1931, she and her mother moved in with her great-aunt Hattie. As a child she "*loved looking through [her] great-aunt Hattie's album filled with photographs of family and friends from Kansas City, Missouri.*" As her aunt and mother "*exchanged stories and memories of their shared past*", she realised that "*every picture tells a story*" (Tomlinson, 2006). "Blackbird" is one of the many pieces that Saar created after her great-aunt died in 1975.

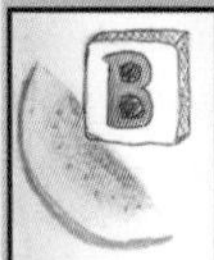

Although Nevelson was Jewish, she was greatly interested in all religions, and in particular, how they "*gave [her] some measure of peace between the storms*". (Nevelson, n/d) The reference to Christianity in this piece can be seen through its title, "Dawn's Wedding Chapel". This is one of the 11 wooden assemblages that are part of Nevelson's first white installation (previously she solely used black paint).

Arthur Bispo do Rosario did not consider himself an artist, but rather a messenger sent from the Heavens. He was never taught how to paint nor sculpt, and created pieces for himself, rather than for an audience. "Sandálias e peneiras" is one of the 822 works that he created in preparation for his Judgement Day and is a very personal piece. Unlike most of his works, which are heavily centred around embroidery, Rosario reutilises objects from his close environment to recreate his life in a visual form.

Figure 7.09: CS screen by student Sari Imai showing introduction of artworks.

Sari writes: Sari chose to look at assemblage sculpture, as it related to her own artwork, examining the work of three artists from different cultural backgrounds.

- Betye Saar
- Louise Nevelson
- Arthur Bispo do Rosário

For my assemblage series *Monochromatic Me*, I looked at three different artists; two of which are contemporary American assemblage artists that were influenced by contrasting cultures (African-American and Jewish), and the third who is considered to be an outsider artist originating from Brazil.

My theme deals with humans and their attachment to objects, more specifically looking at personal objects and their various forms, textures and memories that they contain. The works of these artists greatly influenced the development of my work, as they use found objects whose auras that they once evoked are transformed once assembled to together.

I chose these artists as I was particularly interested in exploring how the objects that each artist has used bring forth parts of their identity, their culture and their nation's history.

STUDENT EXAMPLE: MILA GAJIĆ (HL)

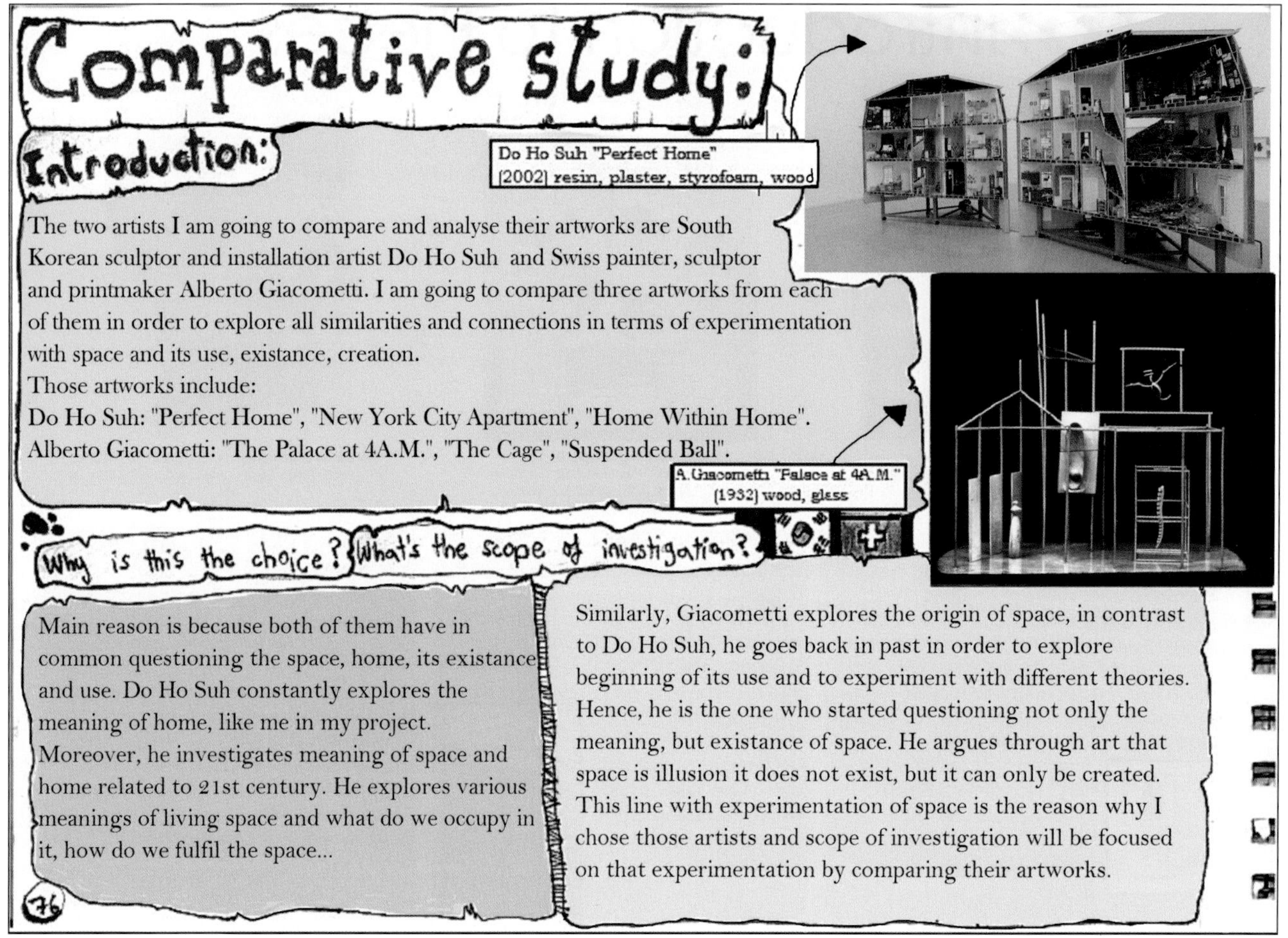

Comparative study:
Introduction:
Do Ho Suh "Perfect Home"
(2002) resin, plaster, styrofoam, wood
The two artists I am going to compare and analyse their artworks are South Korean sculptor and installation artist Do Ho Suh and Swiss painter, sculptor and printmaker Alberto Giacometti. I am going to compare three artworks from each of them in order to explore all similarities and connections in terms of experimentation with space and its use, existance, creation.
Those artworks include:
Do Ho Suh: "Perfect Home", "New York City Apartment", "Home Within Home".
Alberto Giacometti: "The Palace at 4A.M.", "The Cage", "Suspended Ball".
A. Giacometti "Palace at 4A.M."
(1932) wood, glass
Why is this the choice?
What's the scope of investigation?
Main reason is because both of them have in common questioning the space, home, its existance and use. Do Ho Suh constantly explores the meaning of home, like me in my project. Moreover, he investigates meaning of space and home related to 21st century. He explores various meanings of living space and what do we occupy in it, how do we fulfil the space...
Similarly, Giacometti explores the origin of space, in contrast to Do Ho Suh, he goes back in past in order to explore beginning of its use and to experiment with different theories. Hence, he is the one who started questioning not only the meaning, but existance of space. He argues through art that space is illusion it does not exist, but it can only be created. This line with experimentation of space is the reason why I chose those artists and scope of investigation will be focused on that experimentation by comparing their artworks.
76

Figure 7.10: CS screen by student Mila Gajić introducing the artists and the scope of the investigation.

Mila chose to focus on two artists from different cultural and historical backgrounds for her CS. She analyses three artworks by each artist that explore the idea of space and home, and their existence in physical reality and in the mind. This research was very relevant to her own developing sculptures of houses, which you can see in the case study at the end of this chapter.

- Do Ho Suh: *Perfect Home*, *New York City Apartment*, *Home within Home*
- Alberto Giacometti: *The Palace at 4 a.m.*, *The Cage* and *Suspended Ball.*

7.5 Structuring and presenting your comparative study

How you structure your CS is up to you as long as it is clear and coherent and addresses the assessment criteria.

Venn diagrams and other graphic organisers can be useful in your planning stages and may be incorporated into the presentation.

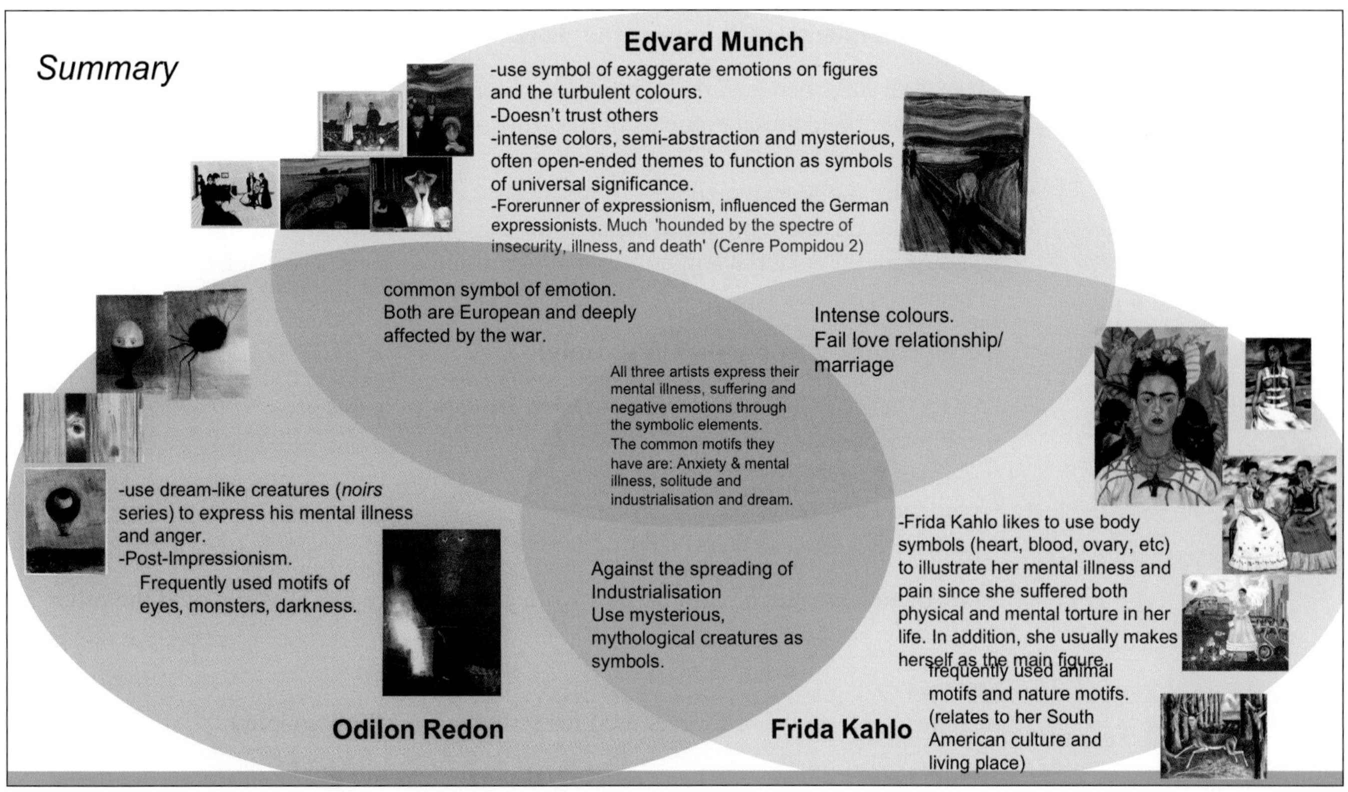

Summary
Edvard Munch
-use symbol of exaggerate emotions on figures and the turbulent colours.
-Doesn't trust others
-intense colors, semi-abstraction and mysterious, often open-ended themes to function as symbols of universal significance.
-Forerunner of expressionism, influenced the German expressionists. Much 'hounded by the spectre of insecurity, illness, and death' (Cenre Pompidou 2)
common symbol of emotion. Both are European and deeply affected by the war.
Intense colours. Fail love relationship/ marriage
All three artists express their mental illness, suffering and negative emotions through the symbolic elements. The common motifs they have are: Anxiety & mental illness, solitude and industrialisation and dream.
-use dream-like creatures (noirs series) to express his mental illness and anger.
-Post-Impressionism.
Frequently used motifs of eyes, monsters, darkness.
Against the spreading of Industrialisation
Use mysterious, mythological creatures as symbols.
-Frida Kahlo likes to use body symbols (heart, blood, ovary, etc) to illustrate her mental illness and pain since she suffered both physical and mental torture in her life. In addition, she usually makes herself as the main figure.
frequently used animal motifs and nature motifs. (relates to her South American culture and living place)
Odilon Redon
Frida Kahlo

Figure 7.11: Comparative study screen by student Daimei Wu. On this screen Daimei uses a Venn diagram to compare three artists, evidencing their shared characteristics. (See Figure 7.14 For Daimei's studio work, inspired by her study of Frida Kahlo.)

Optional framework for structuring the comparative study

Introduction

- Introduce area of interest and any common theme or concepts that underpin the comparison.

The artworks and their context

Identify and discuss the selected art works in terms of their

- cultural and historical context
- formal qualities
- function and purpose
- cultural, material and conceptual significance.

Making connections between the works

Make clear links between the artworks. You could:

- compare the cultural contexts of the work - how are they shaped by their culture and time?
- compare the formal qualities - how are they similar? How do they differ?
- compare the content, motifs, signs, symbols - how is meaning communicated?
- compare the material and conceptual significance - how is this related to cultural context?

Connections with own art (HL only)

Reflect on the relationship with your own artwork in terms of:

- cultural context
- formal qualities
- function and purpose
- materials, conceptual and cultural significance.

Note: Include images of your own artwork and reference just as you would the other works: title, medium, size, date.

Sources

Include a separate list of sources used for investigation (Bibliography).

Presentation

Your presentation should be visually engaging, interesting to look at and easy to read. The CS is not an essay. It is a visual presentation that balances written and visual content; it can include journal pages, handwriting, drawings, diagrams, photos and text.

You can develop your investigation in a Word document or in your visual journal, collecting images and background information on artists and adding your interpretations, evaluations and visual analysis. To create your digital presentation you can assemble your pages on paper, photograph/scan and add text or design elements digitally, or work directly on screen: this is a matter of personal preference.

A visually engaging presentation includes a variety of interesting visual approaches and is clear and easy for the person reading it to follow. Some suggestions to keep in mind:

- Pay attention to design, balancing visual and written content.
- Use clear, good-quality photos, and detailed close-ups.

- Include your own drawings or extracts from your visual journal.
- Label all images and include full references on separate source page.
- Label your own work clearly as such.
- Use subject-specific art language accurately and appropriately.
- Use sub-headers to help clarify content, such as 'Function and purpose'.

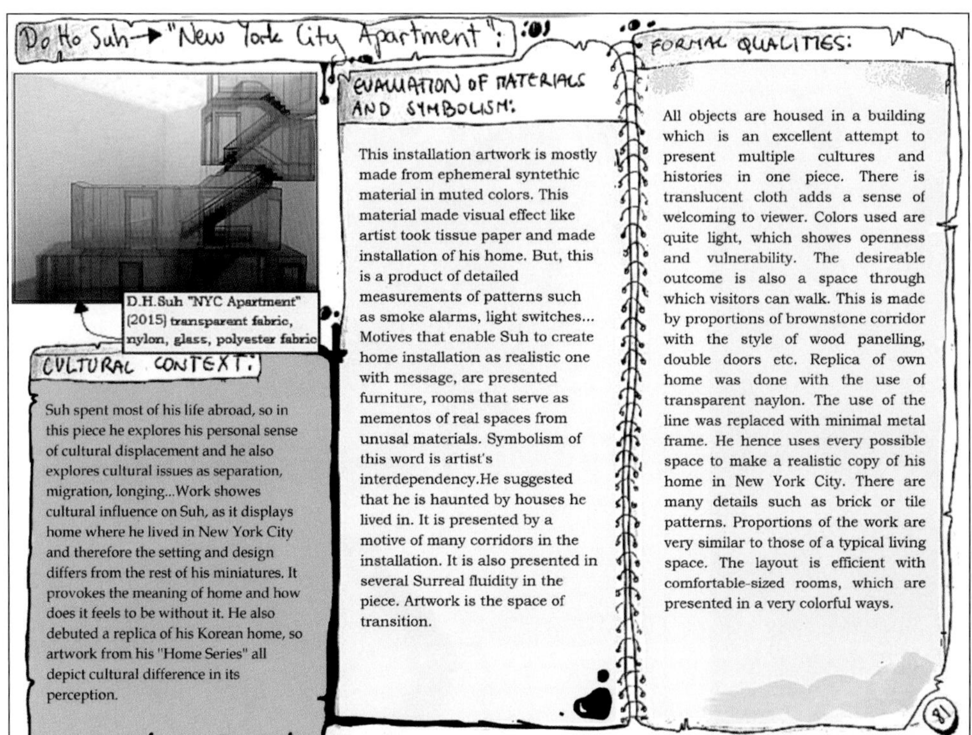

Figure 7.12: CS screen by student Mila Gajić. Mila takes an unusual visual approach, composing her CS as if it were a sketchbook, using a hand-drawn layout but keeping the text clear and legible. She also makes use of sub-headers to tell us what she is addressing in her analysis.

Tip: Tips on presentation

You can use a slide presentation software such as Microsoft's PowerPoint®, Apple's Keynote® or Prezi Pro™ and convert the document to a portable document file (PDF) for electronic submission.

Don't use animations within slides or animated transitions between slides; this information will not translate when the file is converted to a PDF.

Resize images for your presentation to a maximum height or width of 1500 pixels, optimised for web and devices. This will significantly reduce the overall size of your file, without compromising the image quality when viewed on a screen.

Be consistent in your design scheme and stick with one or two fonts throughout. Avoid narrow, decorative or cursive fonts and make sure text is high contrast to background for easy visibility. Keep slide backgrounds simple and consistent throughout.

Wherever possible, use visuals and graphics in preference to lengthy text.

The CS will be viewed on screen so a landscape (horizontal) format is preferable.

7.6 Making connections to your own art

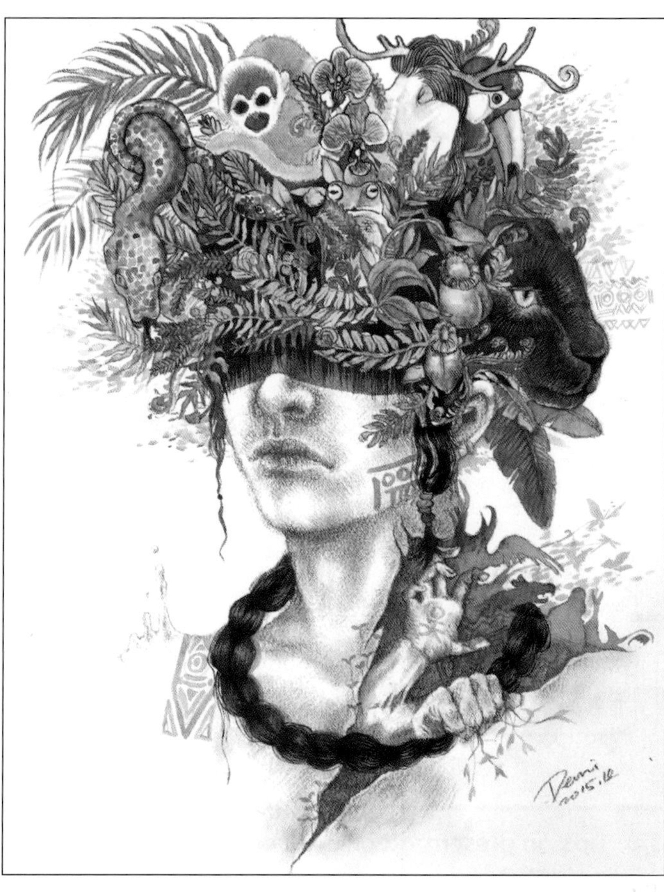

Figures 7.13 (left): Frida Kahlo, *Self-Portrait with Thorn Necklace and Hummingbird*, 1940 (oil on canvas). Figure 7.14 (right): *Human Nature* by student Daimei Wu (watercolour and pencil). Frida Kahlo was one of the artists that Daimei researched for her CS, which consequently inspired Daimei's self-portrait. Although Daimei's work is not a direct copy, it is clearly a homage to the artist.

Tip: The CS enhances your understanding of art and helps to give context to your own work.

Making connections between your own developing art practice and the work of other artists is an important part of your developmental process. This enables you to place yourself in a wider context and may also help you to identify the techniques, styles and thematic content you want to develop in your own work. You might apply some of the techniques or styles of a given artist in your own work, but when borrowing directly from another's ideas be sure to acknowledge your sources of inspiration.

ACTIVITY 7.10: CONTEXTUALISING YOUR ARTWORK

This is an opportunity to reflect on your own development and place yourself in context within a broader field of art-making practice.

- Who are the artists who have helped form you?
- Who do you consider to be your 'creative ancestors'? Look back in time at art history: who are those influential figures whose work you loved even as a child, or maybe a friend or teacher who has influenced you?
- Make a mind-map that shows the artists and thinkers who have impacted your development as an artist.

You have to look back to connect the dots.
(Steve Jobs)

Figure 7.15: Mind-map by the author, of the artists who have influenced her painting. It includes notes about the aspect of the work that was influential, such as 'mineral colours', 'simplification of form' or 'elements of surprise'.

HL students are required to add 3–5 screens that make connections between aspects of their own work and the artworks analysed in the CS. SL students will also benefit from reflecting on these connections, although they will not include this in the CS presentation. The activities and reflections in this section are for any student wishing to explore their own developing artwork in relation to other artists' work.

ACTIVITY 7.11: MEANINGFUL CONNECTIONS

Consider the development of your own art in relation to the artworks you have chosen for your CS.

- Can you make meaningful connections between your work and the artworks you have chosen?
- Are the connections conceptual or formal, or both?
- Has this work influenced you directly and if so, how?

Tip: Remember that in your CS it is not your artworks that are being assessed, but your ability to make informed and meaningful connections with one or more of the selected works.

STUDENT EXAMPLE: SARI IMAI

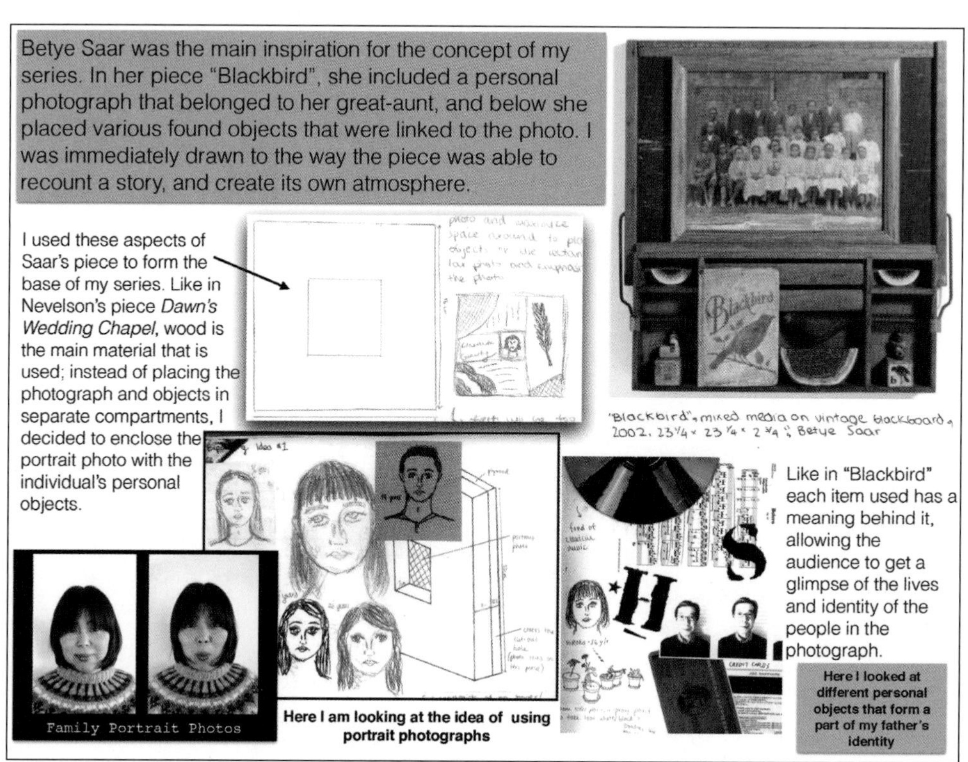

Betye Saar was the main inspiration for the concept of my series. In her piece "Blackbird", she included a personal photograph that belonged to her great-aunt, and below she placed various found objects that were linked to the photo. I was immediately drawn to the way the piece was able to recount a story, and create its own atmosphere.
I used these aspects of Saar's piece to form the base of my series. Like in Nevelson's piece Dawn's Wedding Chapel, wood is the main material that is used; instead of placing the photograph and objects in separate compartments, I decided to enclose the portrait photo with the individual's personal objects.
"Blackbird", mixed media on vintage blackboard, 2002, 23¼ × 23¼ × 2¾", Betye Saar
Like in "Blackbird" each item used has a meaning behind it, allowing the audience to get a glimpse of the lives and identity of the people in the photograph.
Family Portrait Photos
Here I am looking at the idea of using portrait photographs
Here I looked at different personal objects that form a part of my father's identity

Figure 7.16: In this comparative study screen HL student Sari Imai discusses how Betye Saar's piece *Blackbird* (Figure 7.07) was a major influence on her own work.

SPOTLIGHT ON THE STUDENT: SARI IMAI

Nationality: Japanese
Born: Neuilly sur Seine, France

Main artistic interests:

- an individual's sentimental attachment to objects
- 3D work utilising found objects
- evoking a personal and intimate atmosphere.

Influential artists:

- Louise Nevelson
- Betye Saar
- Robert Gober
- Robert Rauschenberg
- Francisco de Zurbarán.

CASE STUDY: MILA GAJIĆ

The experience of the CS as a tool for learning to investigate, analyse and interpret art can have a profound impact on a student's developing work when the artworks for comparison are chosen wisely. In the case of Mila, an HL student, her aptly chosen exploration of two artists' work led her to reflect on the concepts that would form the basis of her studio work for her exhibition.

SPOTLIGHT ON THE STUDENT: MILA GAJIĆ

Nationality: Bosnia-Herzegovina
Born: Gradiška

Main artistic interests:

- relationship between figure and space
- exploring the concept of space
- interior design
- the human figure
- miniature.

Influential artists:

- Charles Matton
- Alberto Giacometti
- Do Ho Suh
- OKO

You have already seen some of student Mila Gajićs work for her CS (Figures 7.10 and 7.12) in which she explores the idea of space and home both materially and symbolically, in the work of Korean artist Do Ho Suh and Swiss artist Alberto Giacometti. The relationship between these artists' work and Mila's own developing work is significant: the connections include formal qualities, cultural and contextual references and conceptual meaning.

Figure 7.17: Korean artist Do Ho Suh's sculptural installation *Perfect Home*, 2003, was made out of translucent nylon, life size and complete with the furnishings of the interior of a home. Although the scale is much larger than Mila was able to work in, the attention to detail and the intimate feeling of the space were strong influences on Mila's work.

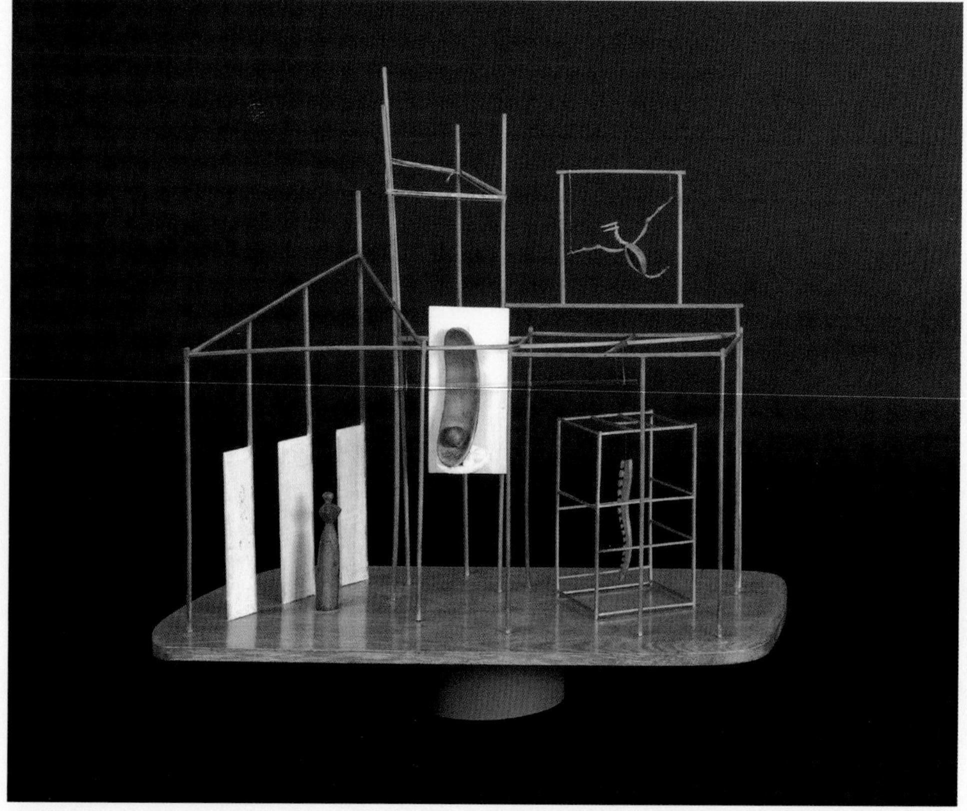

Figure 7.18: Alberto Giacometti, *The Palace at 4 a.m.*, 1932 (sculpture made of wood, glass, wire and string), MOMA. The building is like a delicate cage or a drawing in three dimensions. There are enigmatic figures in the space, but they exist in separate zones, perhaps dreaming. Giacometti influenced how Mila thought about space and the presence or absence of the figure in her own work.

In these extracts from her CS and exhibition text, Mila writes about the focus of her investigations for her work, and how the artists she studied laid the foundation for the main ideas that she explored in her own artwork.

I use different materials to question the meaning and value of home and possible uses of space. I'm exploring abstraction with miniatures, interior design and sculpture under the influence of artists from different cultures, such as Charles Matton, Alberto Giacometti, Do Ho Suh.

My ideas didn't come by pure observation of surroundings but with personal experience. Since I left home to study away, I often felt like I don't have place to settle down. Sometimes I would question where do I belong or I'd feel like I'm constantly on the road. This experience influenced my art and the main connection between all of my artworks is space, meaning, value of home and the role or absence of the figure.

Most of my works present rooms where people are absent, which leaves space for viewers to recognise their own meaningful place inside or ideally to use imagination and invent it, since I also question imagination as potential space.

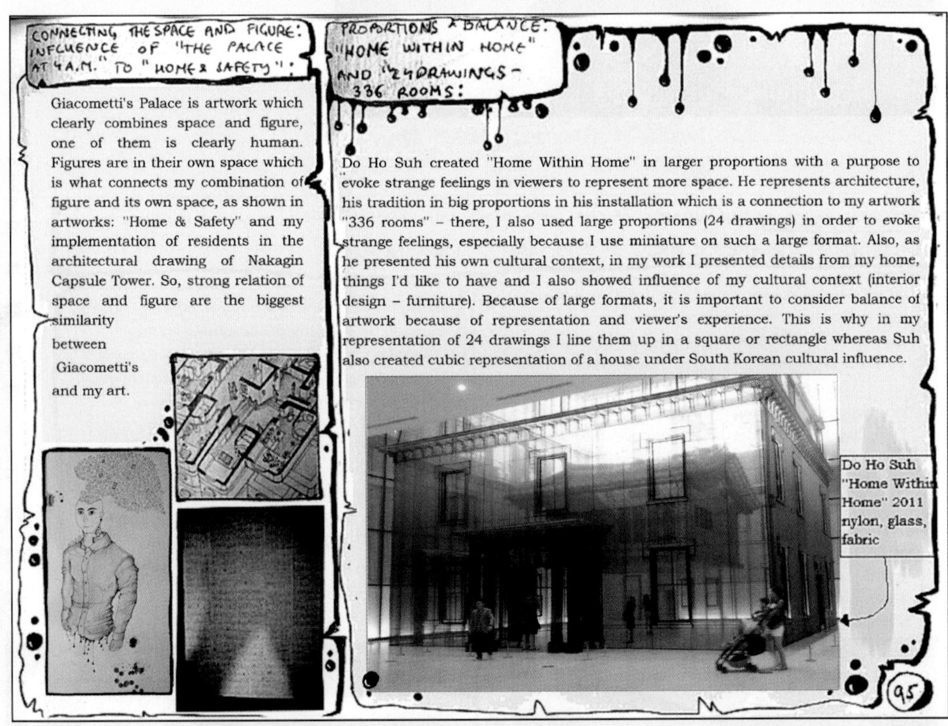

Figure 7.19: Screen 20 of Mila Gajićs comparative study. Here she explains the profound impact of the artists she researched for her CS, Do Ho Suh and Alberto Giacometti, on her own art work.

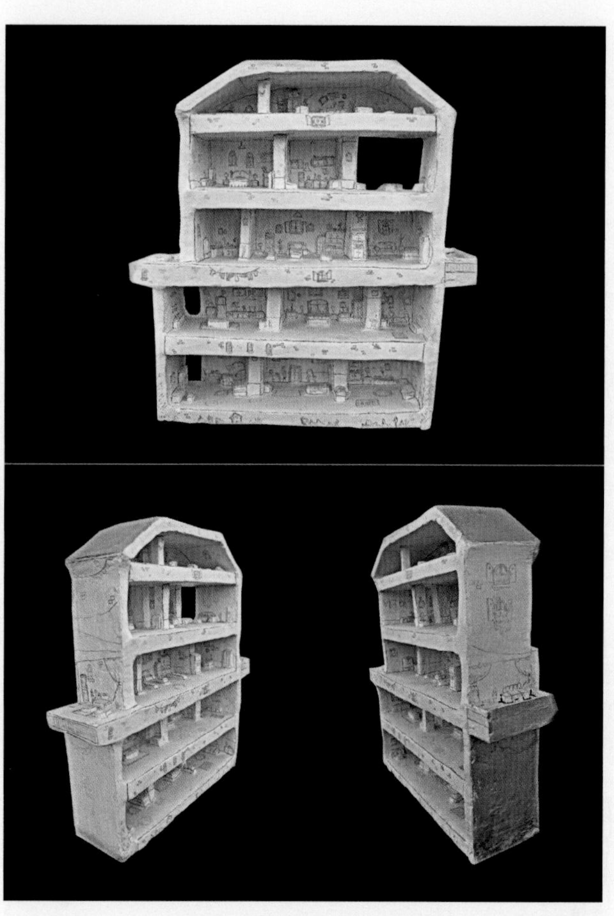

Figure 7.20: Mila Gajić, sculptures of house, mixed media, seen from three different viewpoints. Mila writes: 'I was so inspired by the way this artist (Do Ho Suh) represents home as empty rooms without people. I made four sculptures that depict miniature living spaces, and I also created "empty" rooms absent of people. In his installations everything is usually one colour – mine are all white. He inspired me to think about the meaning of home to me and implement personal content in my work.'

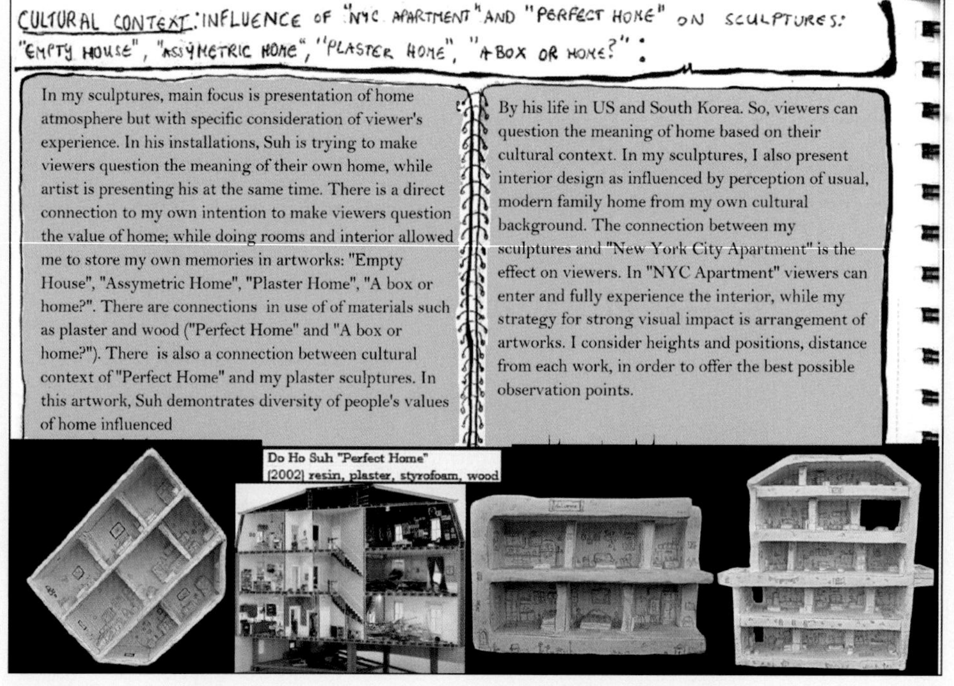

CULTURAL CONTEXT: INFLUENCE OF "NYC APARTMENT" AND "PERFECT HOME" ON SCULPTURES: "EMPTY HOUSE", "ASSYMETRIC HOME", "PLASTER HOME", "A BOX OR HOME?":

In my sculptures, main focus is presentation of home atmosphere but with specific consideration of viewer's experience. In his installations, Suh is trying to make viewers question the meaning of their own home, while artist is presenting his at the same time. There is a direct connection to my own intention to make viewers question the value of home; while doing rooms and interior allowed me to store my own memories in artworks: "Empty House", "Assymetric Home", "Plaster Home", "A box or home?". There are connections in use of of materials such as plaster and wood ("Perfect Home" and "A box or home?"). There is also a connection between cultural context of "Perfect Home" and my plaster sculptures. In this artwork, Suh demontrates diversity of people's values of home influenced

By his life in US and South Korea. So, viewers can question the meaning of home based on their cultural context. In my sculptures, I also present interior design as influenced by perception of usual, modern family home from my own cultural background. The connection between my sculptures and "New York City Apartment" is the effect on viewers. In "NYC Apartment" viewers can enter and fully experience the interior, while my strategy for strong visual impact is arrangement of artworks. I consider heights and positions, distance from each work, in order to offer the best possible observation points.

Figure 7.21: Here Mila discusses the contextual influences of the artists she studied on her own sculptures of houses: 'Do Ho Suh demonstrates the diversity of how people value home, influenced by his life in both US and Korea. In my sculptures I present my interiors as modern family homes influenced by my own cultural background.'

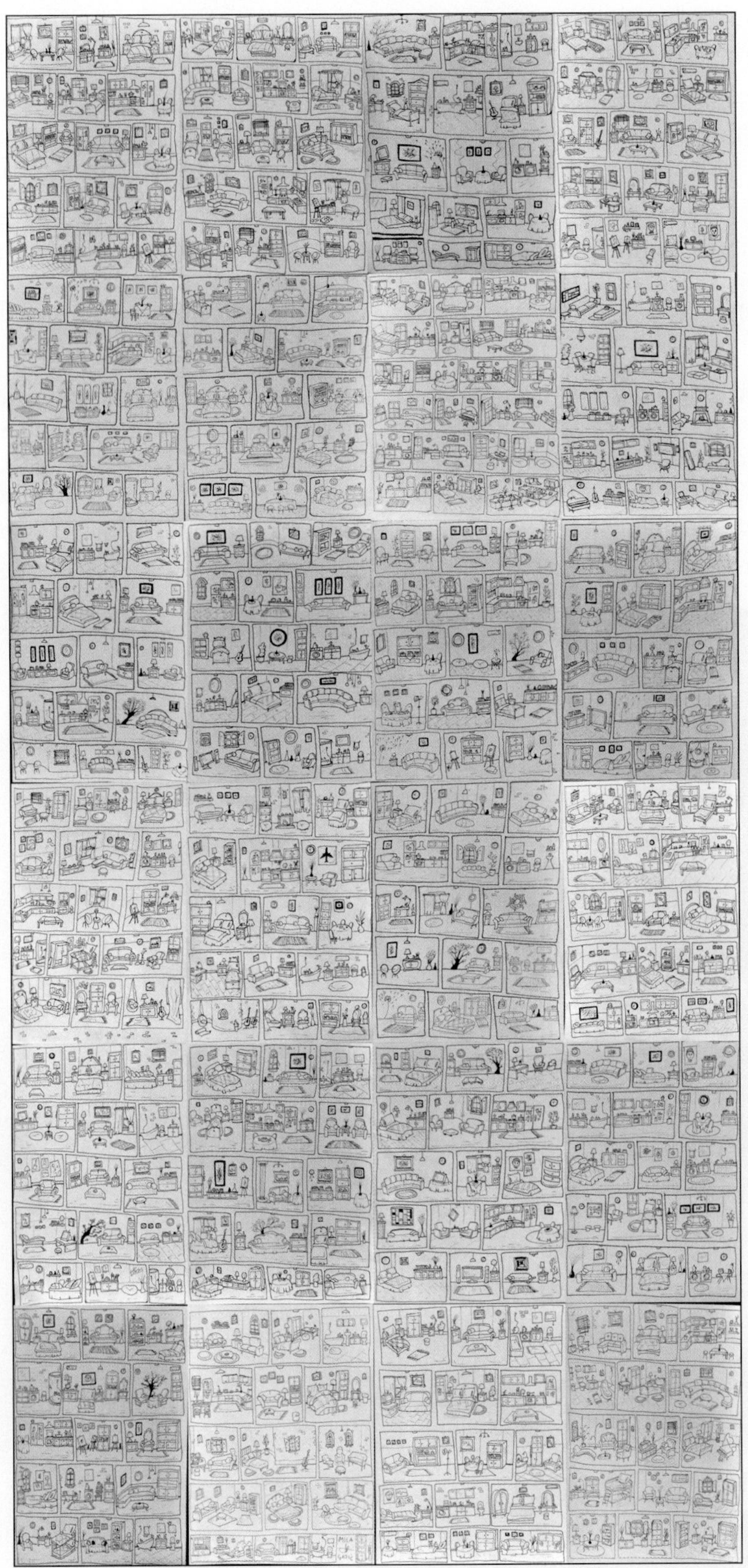

Figure 7.22: *336 Rooms* by student Mila Gajić (composite pencil drawing on 24 pieces of paper). Mila explains: 'For the drawing 336 rooms I made 24 drawings, using miniature within a large format to evoke strange feelings. [Do Suh] presents things from his own culture in *Home within Home*, in my work I present things from my home, things I'd like to have and from my cultural background.'

Mila writes about her desire for the viewer to explore their own concept of home and comfort:

> Creating this project helped me to answer many questions I had about myself, regarding my 'comfort zone'. Although I created spaces which I cannot use for living, it proved to me that imagination and art fulfill powerful needs.
>
> Sometimes our physical surroundings can be boring and mind can be the only "safe" place we can escape to. we can create our own world which is always there whether we are in our home town or far away.'
>
> Even though my main question for viewers is about their perception of home and its value, I want people at some point to recognise themselves and ideally, I want them to create their own comfort zone which doesn't have to be physical, to explore the untouchable. Through art, I learned that it's good to have [our] own abstract world, but we should never completely move there.

Figure 7.23: *House 2* (drawing on wooden boxes), by student Mila Gajić. Mila writes: 'I was influenced by his [Alberto Giacometti's] bronze sculptures and how he uses the figure to question the concept of space. I asked myself, what is it that makes a space whole, complete, and is it really empty without people? He inspired me to use figures in some of my project, to explore the concept of space with and without figures.'

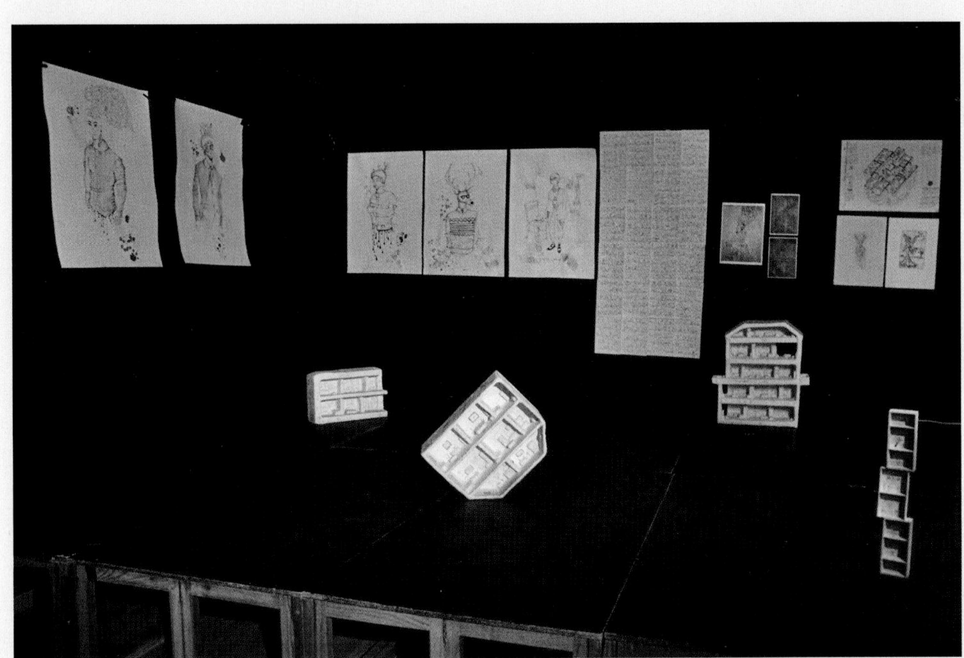

Figure 7.24: Exhibition overview, Mila Gajić. Mila decided to show her (mostly white) work against a black background to create contrast. She says that black and white allow- the viewer to superimpose their own meaning of home on the uncoloured sculptures of houses.

Summary

In this chapter you have looked at the requirements of the CS component of the course and developed skills that will be useful when working on your own CS. You have applied different strategies for comparing artworks, using formal analysis, considering cultural context, function and purpose, material and conceptual significance, and made meaningful connections between artworks.

Now that you have completed this chapter you should be familiar with the requirements regarding citing sources and using subject-specific language.

You have seen some examples of how different students have approached the task and how they make connections with their own artwork, and begun to consider your own developing artwork in a wider context.

Chapter 8

The process portfolio

Introduction

This chapter looks at the requirements of the process portfolio (PP), in which you document the development of your IB art practice throughout the course.

You will become familiar with the IB DP Visual Arts art-making forms table and the assessment requirements of the PP task. You will consider how to compile and present your portfolio, looking at ways of documenting work and assembling screens.

You will investigate the art-making process by looking at other artists' methods and reflecting on your own processes and development. The chapter includes examples that address the assessed criteria and activities to help you identify the most appropriate material from your own art-making processes and reflections.

LEARNING OBJECTIVES

- Become familiar with the requirements of the PP.
- Collect and present evidence of:
  - your skills and knowledge with a range of techniques, materials and processes
  - your investigation into artists, artworks and ideas
  - how you make artistic decisions that reflect your intentions
  - your own development, reviewing and refining your work
  - how you reflect on the art-making process – your own and the processes of other artists.

8.1 What is the process portfolio?

The PP is one of the three assessed components of the IB DP Visual Arts course. It is a collection of evidence of your **development** as an artist, not the finished work (that will go in your exhibition, as discussed in Chapter 9). For your PP you compile and collate carefully selected materials that document the development of your art-making practice and processes.

The PP shows your engagement with art-making practice, critical practice and conceptual practice. You complete it towards the end of the course, compiling and submitting it electronically.

How is the process portfolio assessed?

The PP is assessed according to a set of criteria that are addressed throughout this chapter. It is submitted for final assessment as a digital document and constitutes 40% of the final overall mark. (A detailed discussion of the assessment criteria with tables and descriptors can be found in Chapter 10.)

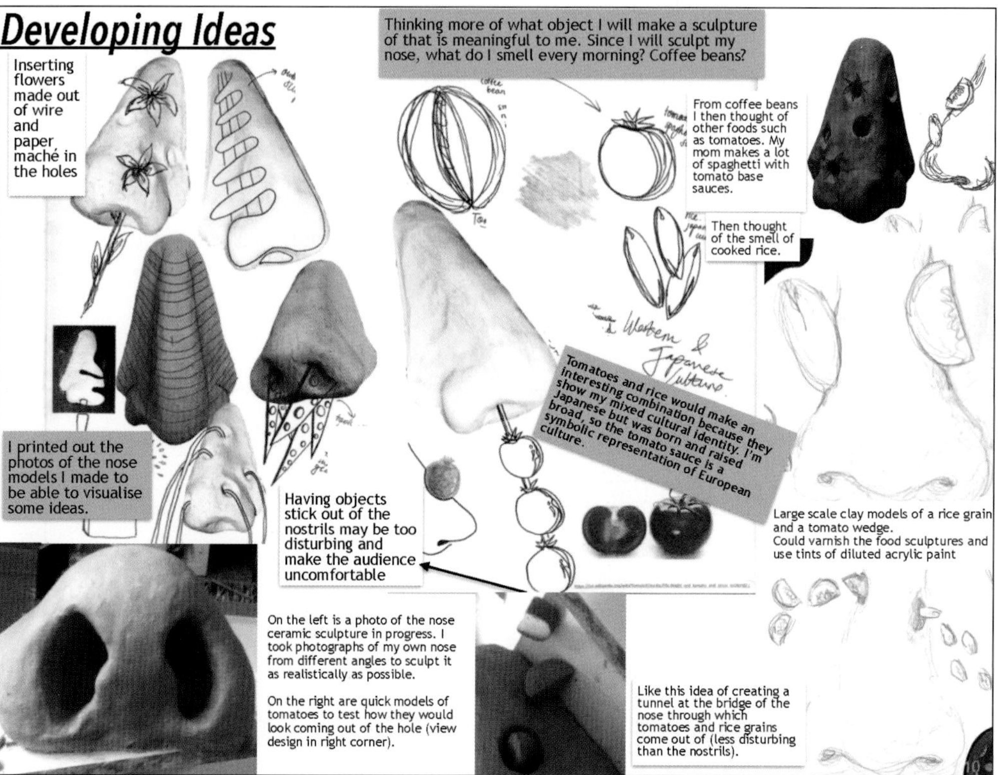

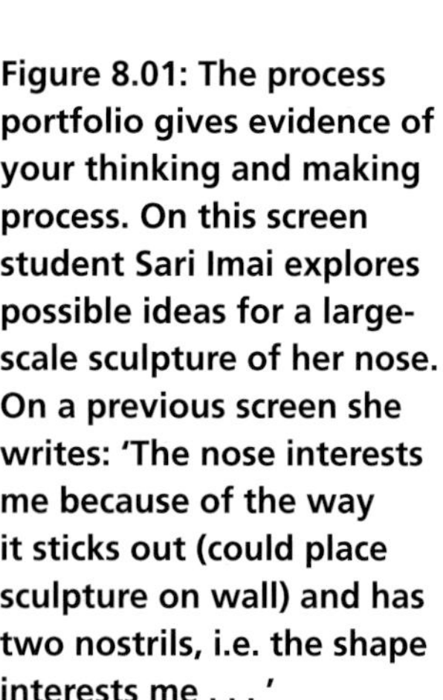

Figure 8.01: The process portfolio gives evidence of your thinking and making process. On this screen student Sari Imai explores possible ideas for a large-scale sculpture of her nose. On a previous screen she writes: 'The nose interests me because of the way it sticks out (could place sculpture on wall) and has two nostrils, i.e. the shape interests me . . . '

The formal requirements of the process portfolio task

SL students: students submit 9–18 screens that give evidence of your experimentation, exploration, manipulation and refinement of a variety of art-making activities. The submitted work should address at least **two** art-making forms, from separate columns of the art-making forms table.

HL students: 13–25 screens that give evidence of your experimentation, exploration, manipulation and refinement of a variety of art-making activities. The submitted work should address at least **three** art-making forms, from at least two columns of the art-making forms table (see below).

The assessment criteria for the process portfolio

A	Skills, techniques and processes	12 marks
B	Critical investigation	6 marks
C	Communicating ideas and intentions	6 marks
D	Reviewing, refining, and reflecting	6 marks
E	Presentation and subject specific language	4 marks

The art-making forms table

In order to encourage ample experimentation with a range of techniques and media, there is a minimum requirement regarding art-making forms to be addressed in your PP (see previous section listing the formal requirements of the task). All of the art-making experiences that you engage in throughout the course are potential material for your PP.

The art-making forms table divides art-making forms into three main categories: 2D, 3D and lens-based, electronic and screen-based art forms. The art-making forms table shown here is not a definitive list but an open-ended and ongoing invitation to experiment widely. (Chapter 4 looks at different art-making forms with a range of examples of student work.)

The art-making forms table

Two-dimensional forms	Three-dimensional forms	Lens-based, electronic and screen-based forms
• drawing • painting • printmaking • graphics	• sculpture • designed objects • site specific/ephemeral • textiles	• time-based and sequential art • lens media • Lens-less photography • digital/screen based

In order to meet the art-making forms requirements an HL student who chooses (for example) to explore painting, printmaking and sculpture has already met the distribution requirements. An SL student who explores drawing and video has already met the requirements.

8.2 Documenting process

Art resides in the quality of doing; process is not magic. (Charles Eames)

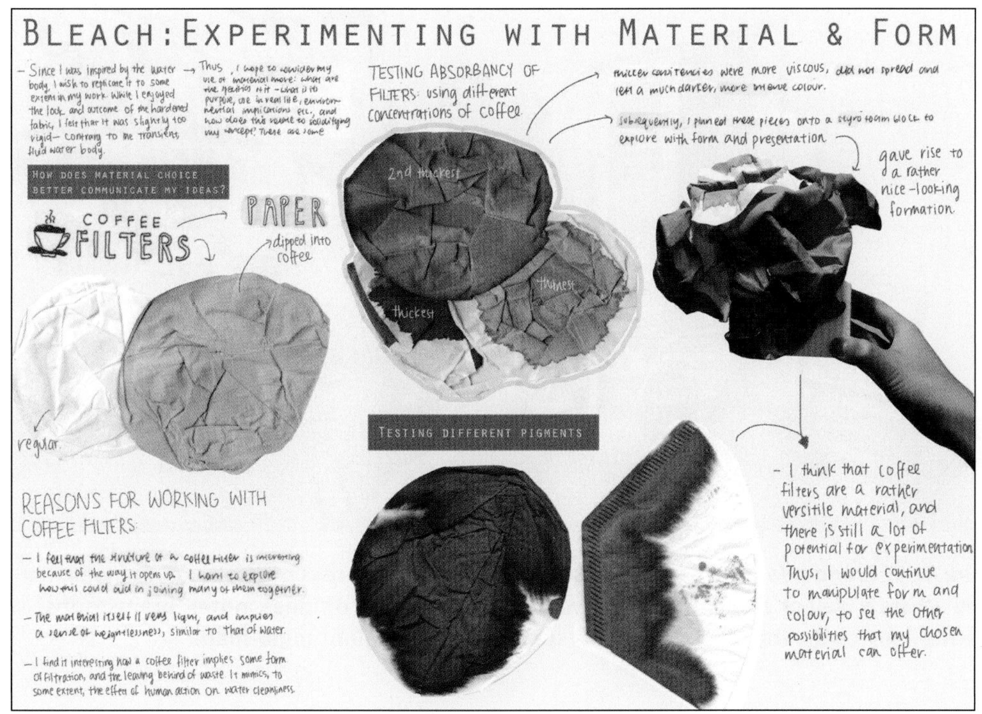

Figure 8.02: In this process portfolio screen student Natasha Koh experiments with bleach and coffee in different concentrations and configurations, testing pigments and materials. The portfolio can include experiments that don't necessarily lead to resolved artworks, but are part of your exploration. Natasha writes: 'The structure of a coffee filter is interesting because of the way it opens up, I want to explore how this aids in joining many of them together . . . and a coffee filter implies some form of filtration, the leaving behind of waste.'

The PP places the emphasis on the **processes** of art-making, including the process of critical and conceptual thinking, rather than on the final result. Your resolved work, on the other hand, can become part of your final curated exhibition (discussed in Chapter 9).

As a student of art, it is crucial to experiment freely, try out new and unusual approaches, and to risk making things that aren't necessarily **nice** or **pretty**. Learn from your mishaps: you might discover more exciting possibilities than you had previously imagined. Making art is a continuously changing and evolving process, so, with the emphasis on the journey of discovery rather than the destination, record what happens along the way.

Recording the development of your work

Keep a record of the development of all your artwork, the changes, the failures, the whole messy process. The visual journal is a good place for making notes of your ideas and how they evolve but you should also get in the habit of photographing your work at different stages of development. Taking pictures is still only one way of documenting process – you can use thumbnail sketches, screenshots, video stills, recordings, annotated drawings, anything that is part of your process.

Keep a process folder

Keep a loose folder, drawer or box for all your 'process documentation' – this will be valuable material when it comes time to assemble your PP presentation. You can also keep a digital file with similar contents to draw upon when compiling your screens.

ACTIVITY 8.1: CREATE A MOOD BOARD

Dedicate a bulletin board, a wall, or a corner to your process notes, images and sources. Like police in a detective movie, spread your evidence out so you can see everything at once. If you can't keep stuff up on the wall for any length of time, photograph the whole wall for your portfolio. Things you might put on your board include:

- postcards
- photos
- clippings from magazines and newspapers
- articles
- quotes
- sketches
- dreams
- brainstorms
- souvenirs.

Figure 8.03: *Grande dame* artist Louise Bourgeois has her process portfolio on the wall. For some artists a wall or a bulletin board works as a repository of ideas, notes, brainstorms, sketches, postcards: the creative process spread out like a giant mind-map.

ACTIVITY 8.2: DESIGN A SCREEN SHOWING THE DEVELOPMENT OF A PIECE

Document the development of a process-oriented studio work. Take photos and record each step of the process over a period of time. Compose a portfolio screen from journal pages or sketches and text that demonstrate and explain the process from start to finish. Include work-in-progress photos.

- What technique and medium have you chosen and why?
- What technical challenges did you face?
- How do your choices of materials and technique support your intentions?

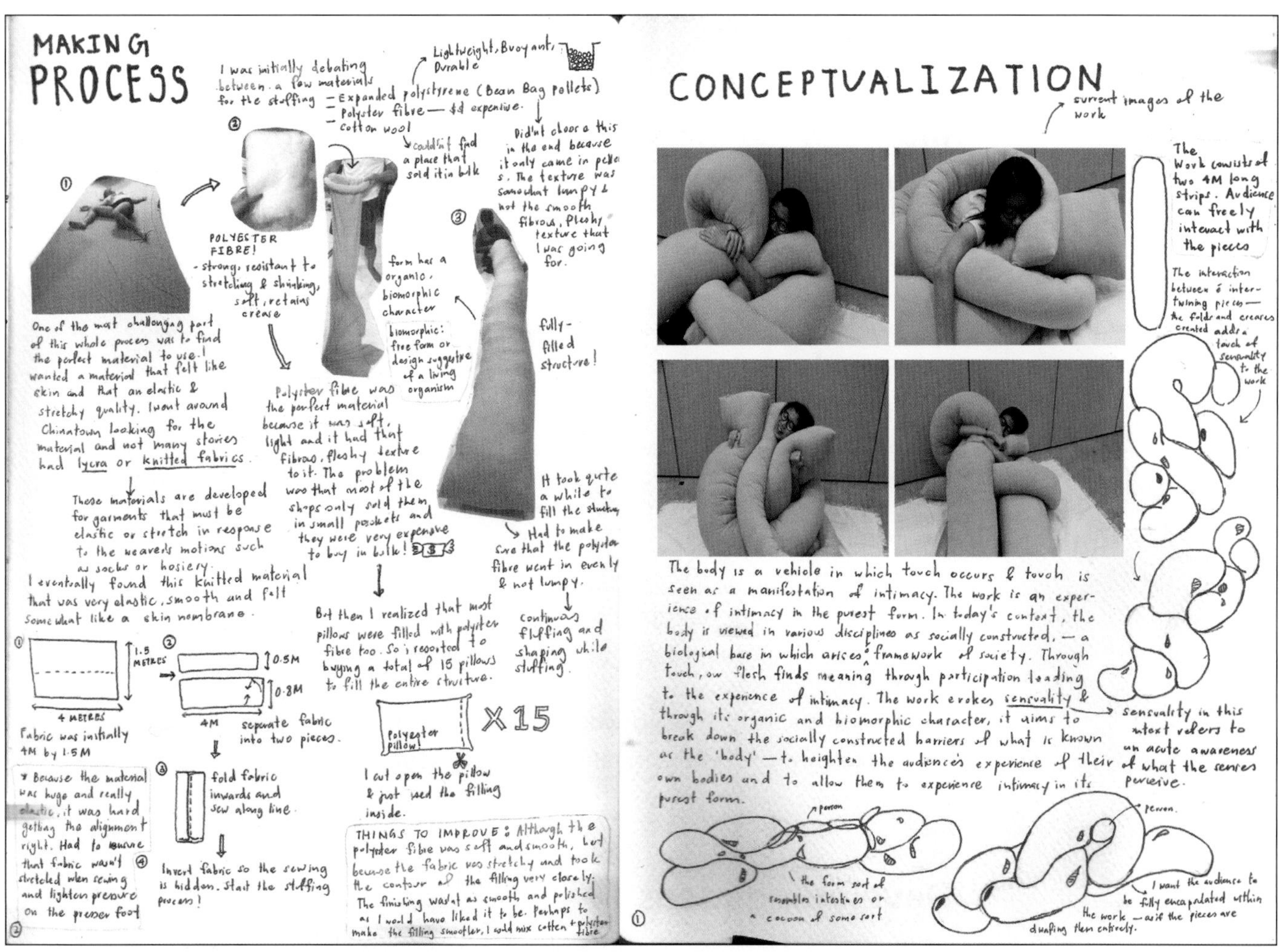

Figure 8.04: Screen 5 of student Beverly Chew's process portfolio. Beverly shows us the making of a work in progress, documenting the various developmental stages with annotated sketches and photos in her visual journal. She explains the material and technical processes (including cutting open 15 pillows and stuffing and sewing four metres of knitted elastic fabric) and reflects on how the work communicates her intentions (creating an experience of bodily intimacy for a participative audience).

8.3 Artists on process

For me, drawing is an inquiry, a way of finding out – the first thing that I discover is that I do not know. (Bridget Riley)

Your PP is a documentation of both your **making process** and your **thinking process**. What triggers an idea for an artwork? How does an idea develop into artwork? What medium best suits your idea? What stages does the work go through before finding its resolved form? Thinking is of course a part of this process, but thinking in art happens mainly through the vehicle of the medium and the physical process of making.

It is very helpful to observe how other artists develop ideas through material (making) and conceptual (thinking) processes. Of course you should look at the work of contemporary artists, but don't be afraid to learn from the past. Look at the 'Old Masters': there is much to be gained from them in both knowledge and technique. Whenever possible go see actual artwork yourself, in museums and galleries, in studios, not just on the internet. The physical presence of a work tells us much more about process than a photograph of it.

ACTIVITY 8.3: DESIGN A PORTFOLIO SCREEN THAT INVESTIGATES YOUR INFLUENCES

Choose an artist whose work has directly inspired you. Design a screen for your process portfolio that shows clear connections between their work and your own practice. Consider any formal, stylistic influences and material and conceptual influences.

- Demonstrate, using visual examples, how the artists' way of working has influenced your handling of techniques and materials.
- Discuss the influence of the artists' ideas and subject matter on your own thinking process.
- Discuss the way in which your work differs from this artist.
- Make sure you reference all images and sources.

Developing ideas

Edward Hopper is famous for his intimate, realistic scenes of everyday life in America in the first half of the 20th century: sunlit buildings, empty streets, cafes, gas stations, people alone or together in rooms, everything rigorously structured and illuminated with strong directional light and rich, dark colours. He painted the inner life of the human being through quiet, atmospheric depictions of outer life. Hopper's moody, set-like paintings have inspired many filmmakers, musicians and animations.

Figure 8.05: Edward Hopper, *Room in New York*, 1932 (oil on canvas). Here Hopper gives us insight into how his ideas were formed and developed, recounting how an idea for this painting arose from his experience of his surroundings: 'The idea had been in my mind a long time before I painted it. It was suggested by glimpses of lighted interiors seen as I walked along city streets at night, probably near the district where I live (Washington Square) although it's no particular street or house, but is really a synthesis of many impressions.' (From: *Edward Hopper* by Gail Levin)

ACTIVITY 8.4: VISUAL ANALYSIS OF A PAINTING

This activity uses the same approach to analysis as you do in your CS (discussed in Chapter 7) but is also relevant to criterion B, critical investigation, in the PP.

Analyse *Room in New York* or another painting by Edward Hopper. Include an annotated image (photo or drawing) in your journal.

- **Formal elements:** Describe the use of line, form, space, composition and colour in this painting.
- **Cultural context:** Where and when was it made? Find out the background around this artwork: cultural, social, political, historical, personal.
- **Interpretation:** Include discussion of subject, meaning, mood and the artist's intention.

Contemporary practices

There are many diverse approaches to artistic process these days, often referred to as 'practice'. Developing an awareness of other artists' working methods will help you to reflect on your own way of working. Some artists are more studio-based, whereas others have a practice that extends well beyond the studio walls, or that may have social, community or environmental aspects.

Australian artist Fiona Hall has a wide-ranging and diverse artistic practice: she transforms the ordinary into the extraordinary, using everyday materials like money, recycled cans and bottles, and household products. From these banal materials she crafts wondrous objects that explore the complex and fraught relationship between humans and nature.

Her creative process involves many stages of thinking and making:

- researching a topic of particular significance
- collecting materials
- imagining, designing
- making and refining
- creating further meaning through methods of presentation and display.

Figure 8.06: Fiona Hall, *Tender*, 2003 (US dollars, wire, vitrines). Fiona Hall's collection of delicate birds' nests in all shapes and sizes are constructed from finely shredded American dollar bills. The title of the work refers to 'this note is legal tender' which is the official stamp on each banknote, linking money and capitalism to the undermining of the earth's fragile ecosystems.

ACTIVITY 8.5: ENVIRONMENTAL RESPONSE

Identify a key issue in the relationship between humans and the natural world, something that you think needs attention in our world today.

- Research this topic and collect information from a range of sources.
- Collect found or recycled materials that are relevant to the issue.
- Experiment with making something both playful and serious.
- Document the whole process for your PP.

ACTIVITY 8.6: OBSERVING AN ARTIST'S PROCESS

When visiting an exhibition, observe the work closely and answer the following questions in your journal. This information, with images, can be used to compose a PP screen.

- What materials are used?
- What techniques are used?
- What is the scale of the work?
- Was this work made in the studio?
- Is the work part of a series?
- Do you think the work took a long time to make?
- Did it involve collaboration with others?

Shifting disciplines

Many contemporary artists are working across a range of media, shifting between or combining fine art, traditional craft and new media technology, creating **hybrid** works that defy categorisation.

Hybrid: A hybrid artwork is made up of elements from different origins, crossing boundaries between art and science, art and social research and so on.

Figure 8.07: Mat Collishaw, still from *Retrospectre*, 2010 (mixed-medium video installation, five-minute loop), BFI. Mat Collishaw's assemblage *Retrospectre* offers contemporary visual content in an old-fashioned framework. The structure consists of a collection of antique frames, windows, doors and part of an altarpiece, fitted with mirrored glass. Mysterious, beautiful and sometimes brutal video imagery are projected from behind onto the mirrors for a ghostly effect.

Contemporary **YBA** artist Mat Collishaw uses a range of media and processes, including sculpture, video, photography and new technology. He explores society's darker side, from 'death row' to child prostitution. The imagery he constructs from these horrific and morbid subjects is opulent, romantic and seductive, causing us to reflect on how we respond to visual material, regardless of content.

> I'll take lots of pictures of the kind of things that I'm interested in and print them all out, and then put them up here; and then the project kind of slowly starts taking some kind of form, and then I'll start making something and printing the pictures out and putting them up here too so I can reflect on them.
>
> A lot of the work I'm taking is from nature. Even if I'm working on things on computer programmes, which is a lot, generally it all comes back to actually studying nature. So I'll have things like this little bat here, which got quite a freakish look to it. Again, I might be taking something like the translucency of the wing, or the way that the feathers actually meet the wing there.
>
> These are all bits of junk – old cameras and just funny little optical toys. I get bored very easily, so I like to be shifting disciplines, and often I have, like, two, three or four different things going on at the same time. So I've been making a 3D picture while making some wax models, while I'm doing some painting, and making a film – something that you see in one process, you might be able to use in a different one. I don't particularly just want to get locked into one way of making things. I find it too dull. (Mat Collishaw.)

YBA: The Young British Artists were a group of art students who graduated from Goldsmiths, University of London in the late 1980s, and became influential in shaping an entrepreneurial approach to art marketing and branding in the 1990s. (Notorious YBAs include Damien Hirst, whose work showed dead animals preserved in formaldehyde, and Tracey Emin, who presented her own unmade bed in an artwork.)

TOK and art: The process versus the product

- When looking at art do you need to see the hand of the creator?
- Do you admire artworks for how they're made or the final result?
- Does knowing about how an artwork was made change the way you think about it?

ACTIVITY 8.7: OUTSIDE THE COMFORT ZONE

Take an idea you have previously explored and revisit it using a different medium or by radically changing the scale.

- Work bigger than you normally would (or much smaller).
- Use a combination of techniques and media that you have never tried.
- Make something unlike what you usually make.

8.4 Compiling your process portfolio

The portfolio is submitted as a digital document (PDF – portable digital file) and assessed on screen. You can create your presentation using the digital platform of your choice and convert it to a PDF. Your presentation should have a balance of visual and written content, but there is no specified word count, just a required number of **screens** per level (see table in 8.1).

Tip: You might want to scan your journal pages and work on your PP development throughout the course, not just towards the end.

Some pages may be complete as they are and ready to use as a PP screen (as in Beverly Chew's work shown in Figure 8.04). With others, you may prefer to select and edit parts of several journal pages, adding text on screen.

Selecting material

Pages from your visual arts journal can be selected, edited and included in your PP as well as pages from other sketchbooks and notebooks, loose drawings, folios, media experiments, documentation of development of work, digital images, screen shots, contact sheets, video and moving image stills, and images of unresolved and resolved work that are not included in the final exhibition.

Figure 8.08: Student Enrico Giori's work table. Enrico is in the process of assembling a process portfolio screen. On the table we can see Enrico's visual journal and other drawings and images that he is using to compile his digital presentation.

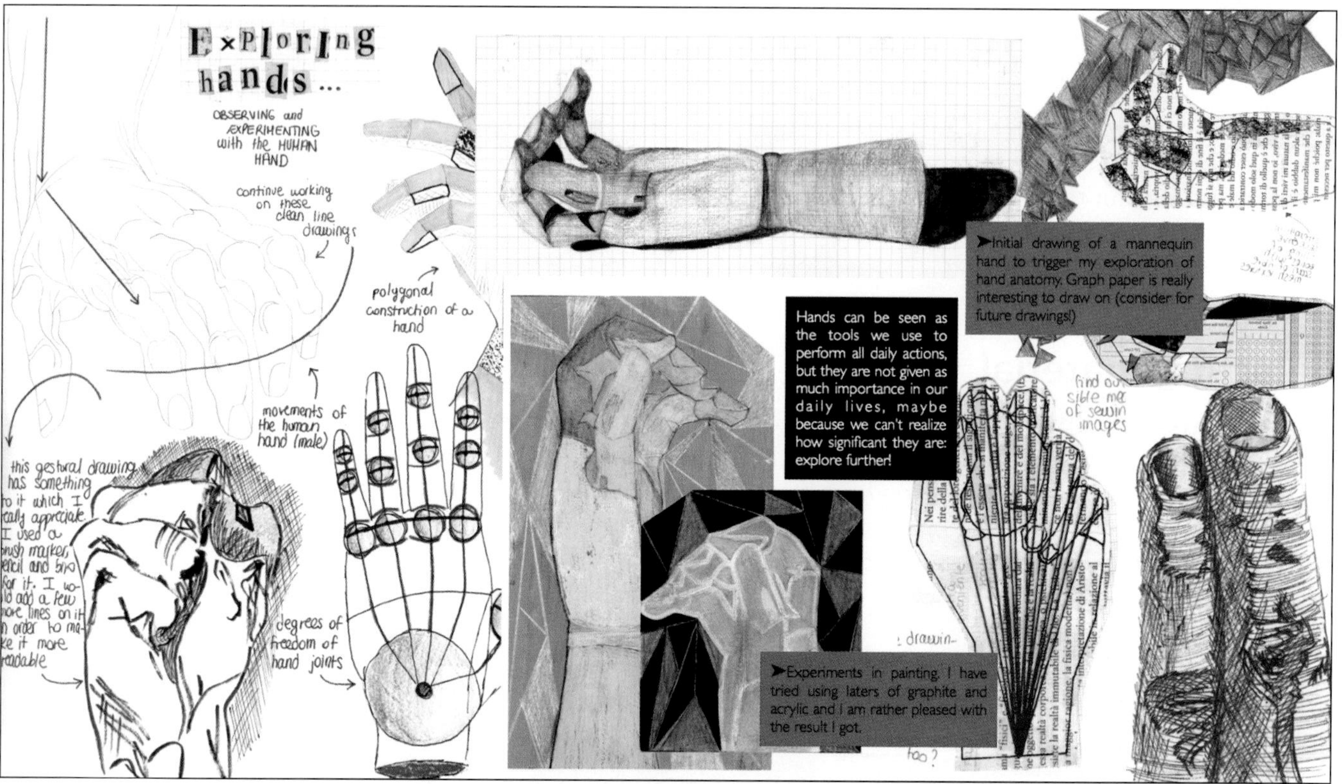

Figure 8.09: Process portfolio screen by student Enrico Giori. Enrico composed this screen as a digital collage from different visual journal pages and added text boxes to clarify his intentions. One of the advantages of composing this way is that you can manipulate the scale of individual drawings, adjusting images to fit the screen and the overall graphic layout.

Tip: A landscape (horizontal) format will maximise on screen viewing.

Composing screens

You may lay out your 'screens' on a large paper, like a collage, then scan, or you may prefer to compose directly on screen, or use a combination of both approaches.

Any combination of scanned journal pages or partial pages, photos, images, digital drawings, text, handwritten and or typed is acceptable.

> I think the process portfolio is really exciting for showcasing how a variety of materials/ideas are explored. I see it like a type of digital collage allowing students to use multiple types of files to show evidence of their studio process. I think it is quite natural for students to design these screens. (IB DP Visual Arts teacher)

ACTIVITY 8.8: DIGITAL COLLAGE SCREEN

Design a PP screen by cutting and pasting isolated images from journal pages and other sources.

- Aim for a coherent and visually engaging design.
- Strike a balance between visual and written content.
- Use good-quality images and cite your sources.
- Explain your ideas with clearly legible text.

Tip: Using subheadings that indicate what specific criteria (e.g. 'Critical investigation') you are addressing on each screen will help the examiner to see how you meet the criteria.

A clearly written, legible, uncluttered presentation makes it easier for the reader to understand your process. You can help them further by adding subheadings or subtitles that act as signposts (e.g. 'Initial ideas', 'Experimenting with printmaking techniques', 'Reflecting and refining').

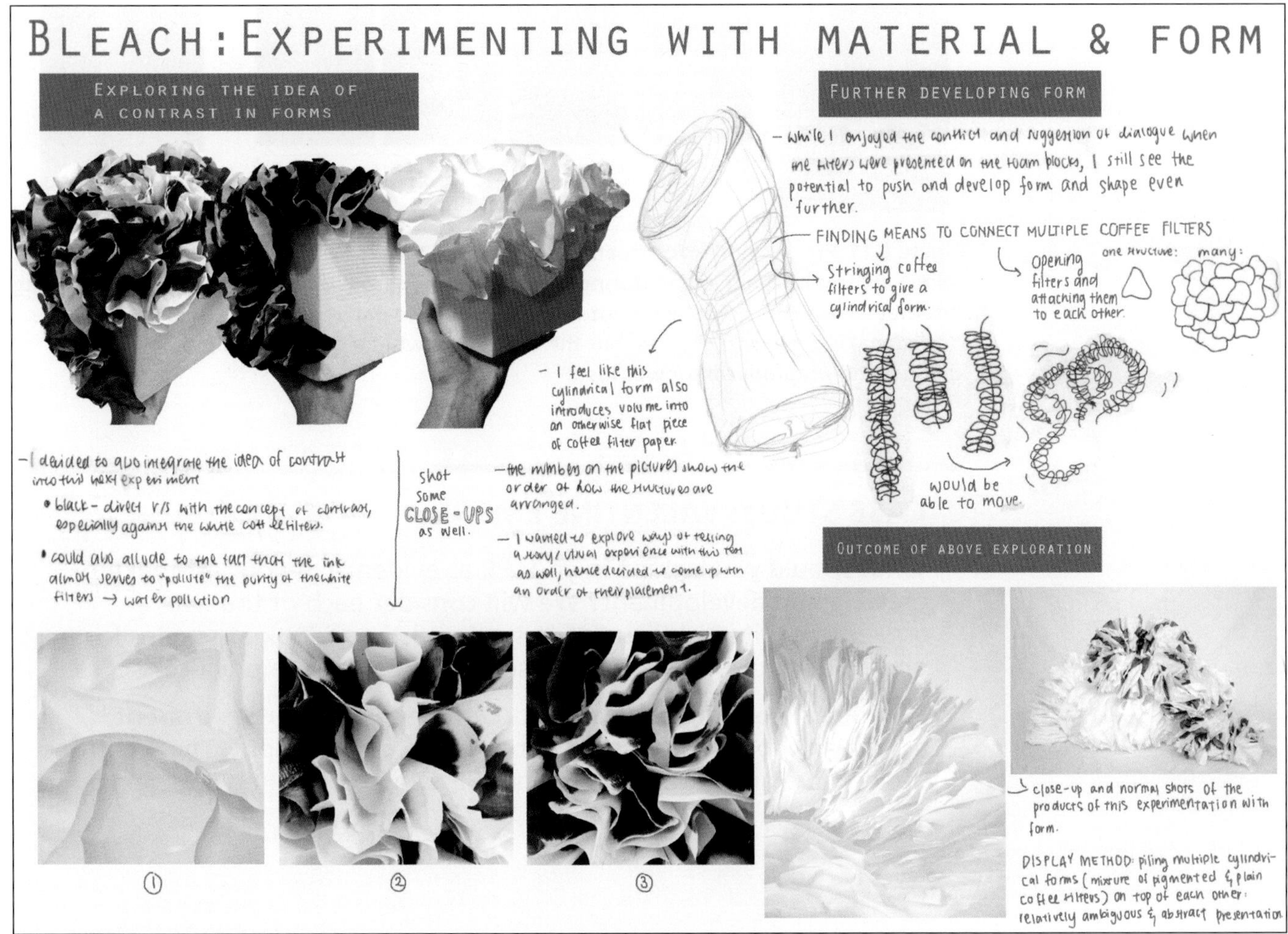

Figure 8.10: Student Natasha Koh, whose process portfolio screen in shown in Figure 8.2, continues her experiments with pigments and materials, taking the work to another developmental stage: stringing multiple coffee filters together to create three-dimensional forms. She is using subheadings to 'signpost' the content on this screen, such as 'Exploring the idea in forms', 'Further development' and 'Outcome of above exploration', helping the reader to understand the stages of her process.

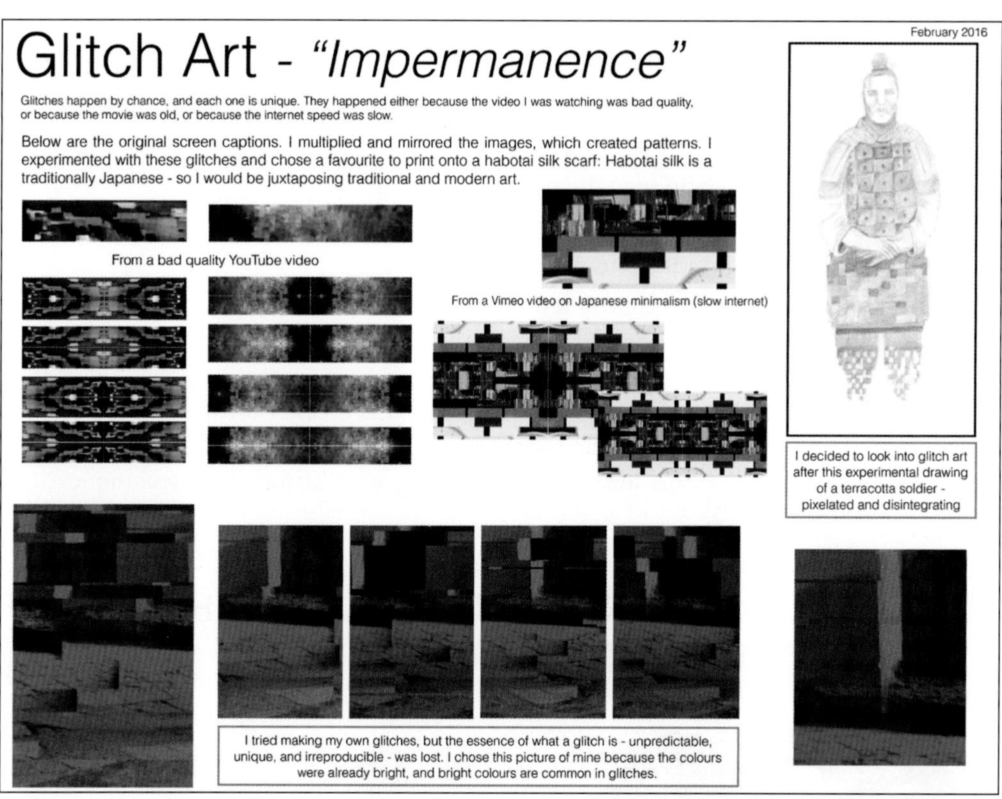

Figure 8.11: Process portfolio screen by student Alexandra Bourget experimenting with 'glitch art', multiplying and mirroring images captured from poor-quality or slow-streaming internet videos (the point being not the image but the pattern created). Alexandra writes: 'I tried making my own glitches, but the essence of what a glitch is – unpredictable, unique, and irreproducible – was lost.'

CASE STUDY: VALENTINE EMENS

What should you include in your PP as evidence of your art-making practice and development? We will consider each of the five assessment criteria (discussed in section 8.1) and look at screens from one student's PP to see how these might manifest in practice.

HL student Valentine Emens's work in the PP is in three different art-making forms: painting, sculpture and photography. The screens shown here are extracted from her PP, which comprised 25 screens.

A: Skills, techniques and processes

In the PP you will give evidence of your experimentation with a range of art-making skills using different techniques, media and processes. You will show how the materials and media that you chose to work with are appropriate to your artistic intentions.

> **GUIDING QUESTIONS**
>
> - What techniques and materials are you experimenting with?
> - Are your choices of media well suited to your ideas and intentions?

Figure 8.12: Process portfolio screen by student Valentine Emens. This screen shows Valentine's process of building a clay monolith. She is exploring ceramic sculpture, a 3D art-making form. The photos show her experiments with textures and surfaces, mixing organic and geometric shapes and trying out different tools and techniques.

B: Critical investigation

In the PP you will give evidence of your critical investigation of artists, artworks, art forms and genres. Through your written and visual investigations, you will make connections and observations about how the artworks, artists and art forms impact your own developing art practice.

GUIDING QUESTIONS

- What artists and artworks have contributed to your development?
- How have your investigations influenced and directed your artwork?

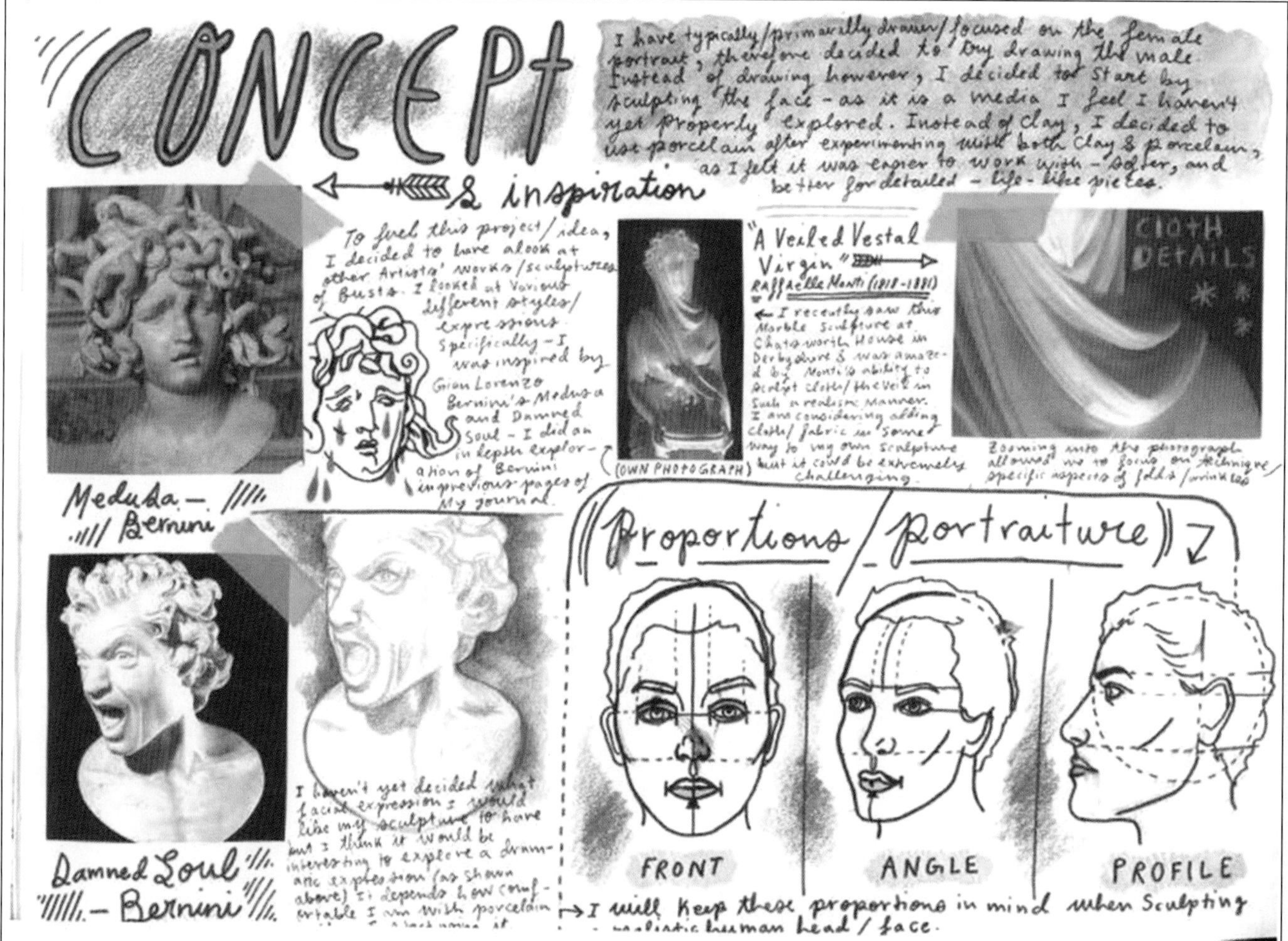

Figure 8.13: Process portfolio screen by student Valentine Emens. In this screen Valentine investigates the marble sculptures of Gian Lorenzo Bernini and Raffaelle Monti, observing how these sculptors use facial expressions and movement to convey emotion, and considering how this could impact on the development of her own portraiture.

Portraiture: The art of making a portrait or artistic representation of a person.

C: Communicating ideas and intentions

In the PP you will communicate your intentions for your work and show how your ideas were formed and developed, how you assimilate skills, choosing and using media and building upon initial ideas. These ideas and intentions can both be communicated visually by example and supported in writing.

> **GUIDING QUESTIONS**
>
> - Can you articulate how your ideas are formed and developed?
> - Can you show how your artistic choices and decisions support your intentions (ideas, goals, visions)?

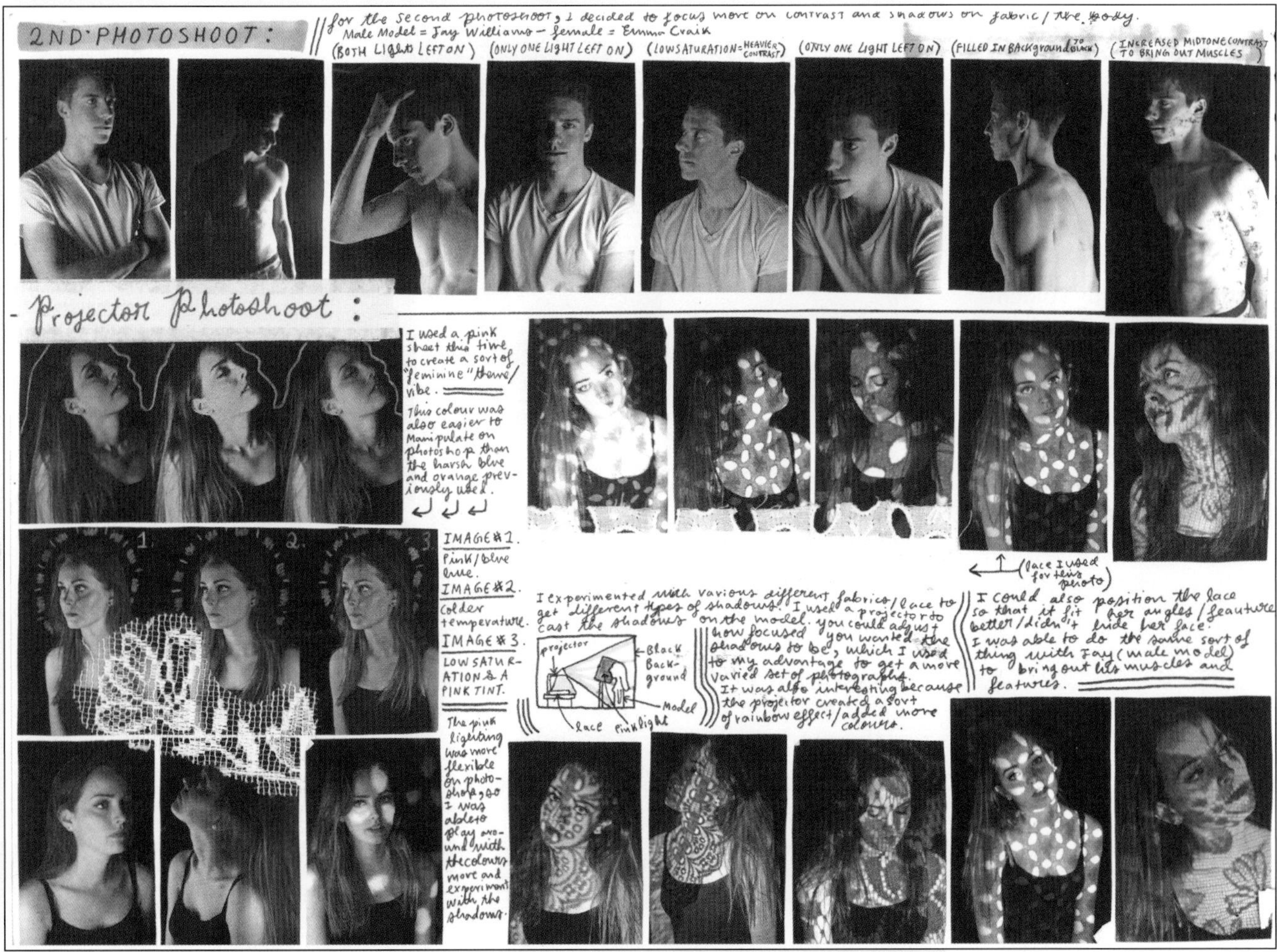

Figure 8.14: Process portfolio screen by student Valentine Emens. In this screen Valentine builds upon her initial photo shoot ideas and focuses on creating effects with projections, filters and fabric. She describes how she made decisions about colours, saturation and textures to achieve the desired results.

D: Reviewing, refining and reflecting

In the PP you will provide evidence of your ability to review and refine your ideas, and reflect on your skills, techniques and processes, as well as on your own development on the whole as an artist.

GUIDING QUESTIONS

Reflecting on your art-making throughout the course:

- What do you think was really successful?
- What has been challenging or difficult?
- What have you changed as a result?
- What have you learned?

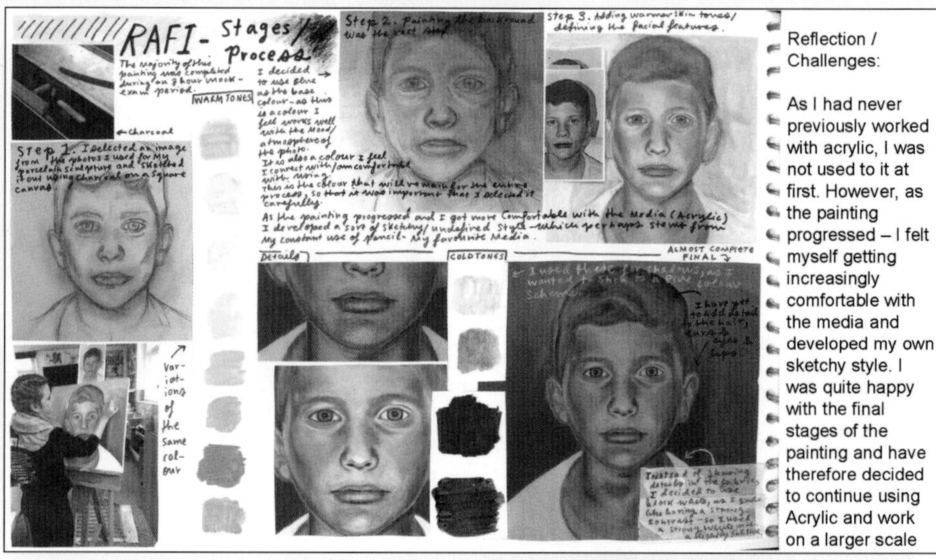

Figure 8.15: Process portfolio screen by student Valentine Emens. In this screen Valentine reflects on the challenges of making her first acrylic painting, the difficulties of the medium and how she progressed in her skills and handling of the technique.

ACTIVITY 8.9: SELF-REFLECTION ON A RESOLVED PIECE

This activity refers to one of your resolved artworks for the exhibition, but don't include the finished piece in your PP if it is in the exhibition, just the process and the reflection.

- How did your original concept evolve?
- What did you discover during the process of making it?
- What did you decide to change along the way?
- What do you feel is successful about the piece?

RESOLVED WORK

Although the resolved artworks presented in your exhibition component (discussed in Chapter 9) should *not* be included in your PP, the *process leading up to the work may be included*. Any work you do not select for your exhibition may be included in your PP.

E: Presentation and subject-specific language

In the PP you will present information clearly and coherently with a visually engaging layout and design. Written content should be easily legible, subject- specific art language used appropriately throughout and all your sources and images clearly cited.

GUIDING QUESTIONS

- Is your writing clear and easy to read?
- Is your layout visually engaging?
- Have you cited your sources for all images and references?

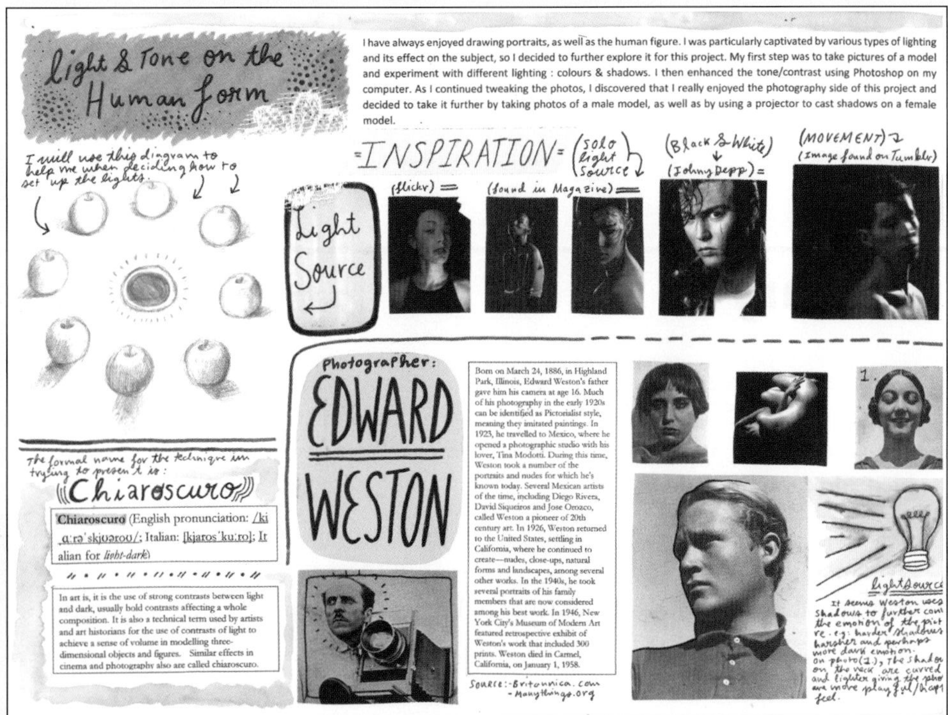

Figure 8.16: Process portfolio screen by student Valentine Emens. In this screen Valentine is looking at the use of light sources in photography and how she can apply this to her own work. Valentine uses subject specific language appropriately, discussing light, tone and *chiaroscuro* with understanding of their meaning. She uses a combination of handwriting and typed text, which are clearly legible, and her page layout is well designed and visually engaging.

Chiaroscuro: From the Italian words for 'light' and 'dark', this term is used to describe the variations in light and shade on an artwork.

Citing sources

The IB policy on academic honesty requires that all images be appropriately referenced to show recognition of the intellectual property of others (Chapter 7 gives more specific guidelines on referencing). You should also identify images of your own work as such ('Label: my work'). When another person's ideas have particularly influenced your thinking but you have not included a direct citation you should include the source as a bibliography reference within your submitted screens.

All images used in the PP should be acknowledged, using your school's preferred referencing style. If in doubt, a good rule of thumb is to label each image with the following information:

- artist
- title
- date
- medium and size
- source (museum collection, website, etc.)

Summary

In this chapter you have seen what constitutes a PP and what is required of you. You have looked at examples of student work and at what kind of content is needed to meet the assessment criteria. You have considered some different ways in which the PP can be assembled and presented.

You have investigated other artists' working methods and looked at ways of documenting your own art-making processes, and engaged in activities to help you design a presentation that appropriately documents and reflects these processes and encounters.

Chapter 9

The exhibition

Introduction

This chapter looks at the requirements of the third assessed component of the course, the exhibition, which constitutes 40% of your final grade. Towards the end of your final year of IB DP Visual Arts you will present a selection of your best work in the form of a curated final show, and justify and articulate your intentions in a written rationale.

Your exhibition is an opportunity to show your artwork to the community in an interesting and engaging way. This chapter guides you through the process of presenting your artwork, with tips on how to successfully set up your exhibition and prepare for assessment. You will explore how to select and present your work for the show, how to compose exhibition texts for each piece, and how to write your curatorial rationale.

LEARNING OBJECTIVES

- Become familiar with the requirements of the exhibition.
- Select and present your work successfully.
- Formulate and articulate personal intentions for your art work.
- Create a coherent and considered exhibition.
- Evaluate how your work communicates to the viewer (HL).

9.1 Selecting a body of work

Body of work: A collection of coherent, unified and related artworks.

Tip: Look for connections between your pieces: remember that your exhibition should be a coherent collection of work. Don't worry if you have pieces that don't 'fit' in your exhibition; they can still be included in your PP.

In your PP you demonstrated your creative process and breadth of investigation. In your exhibition you show a set of rigorously selected artworks that clearly communicate your artistic intentions. This doesn't mean that the all the works need to address the same subject or theme. You can present a **body of work** that is related through exploration of visual qualities or through exploration of ideas and concepts. (Chapter 5 looks at building continuity and developing a body of work.)

Select works that show:

- coherent relationships among the works
- technical skill and appropriate use of materials, techniques, processes
- well-resolved work in line with stated intentions in rationale
- consideration for the overall experience of the viewer.

Figure 9.01: Exhibition by SL student Pauline Peters. All of Pauline's work is related to questions of ethics, injustice and the suppression of women in certain geographical areas of the world. She created clothing from different materials that reflect the content of her work, using tissue paper, stones, maps and fabrics. Her exhibition is coherent and considered, with clear connections between the pieces that she has selected.

ACTIVITY 9.1: PRE-EXHIBITION GROUP CRITIQUE

This activity helps you to prepare for your exhibition and uses the in-class critique as an aid to fine-tuning your selection. Try to schedule this critique well in advance of setting up your show.

- Select the works that you want to display in your exhibition and set up an informal display, or project images of the artworks.
- Explain to your peers what you are trying to communicate through your works.
- Ask your fellow students to tell you which pieces work well together and which ones don't fit.
- Record the critique in your journal.

Coherent and connected: Coherence and connection refer to a sense of continuity and connection among the works. The pieces demonstrate clear connections and work well together to create a unified body of work.

How is my exhibition assessed?

Your exhibition is internally assessed and externally moderated. The assessed criteria are referred to throughout this chapter and you will find detailed descriptors and tables in Chapter 10. There are certain formal requirements of the exhibition task, including a written curatorial rationale and a defined number of artworks per level.

Your curatorial decisions, how you made choices about selecting and presenting your work and why, are explained in your written curatorial rationale and your intentions for each piece are described in a brief exhibition text.

Tip: Remember quality over quantity. Look at the maximum and minimum number of pieces you need in the exhibition. Don't feel that you have to meet the maximum number; you don't get any extra marks for this.

The formal requirements of the exhibition task

- SL students: 4–7 artworks
- HL students: 8–11 artworks
- exhibition texts for each piece
- two exhibition overview photos (mandatory)
- additional supporting photos (optional)
- a written curatorial rationale.

The assessment objectives for the exhibition

A: Coherent body of works

The work forms a coherent collection of works which fulfil stated artistic intentions and communicate clear thematic or stylistic relationships across individual pieces.

B: Technical competence

The work demonstrates an effective application and manipulation of media, materials and formal qualities.

C: Conceptual qualities

The work demonstrates how the imagery, signs and symbols have been successfully resolved to realise the function, meaning and purpose of the art works, as appropriate to stated intentions.

D: Curatorial practice

The curatorial rationale justifies the selection, arrangement and exhibition of a group of artworks within a designated space, as appropriate to stated intentions.

(HL) It also demonstrates a reflection on how the exhibition conveys an understanding of the relationship between the artworks and the viewer.

Although you will prioritise a **coherent body of work** (artworks with a relationship), you also want to show your strongest work, the pieces that show your most skilful manipulation of techniques and processes.

These questions can help you to make a well-rounded selection:

GUIDING QUESTIONS

- Which artworks show my amazing technical skills?
- Which media am I best at using?
- Which artworks are less technically skilful?
- Which artworks are unrelated or 'off topic'?
- Which artworks do I really like but can't justify in my coherent body of works?

Tip: Don't forget!

You can present your work for the exhibition **in any medium, or even just one medium**, as long as you have met the requirements for the PP of working in a range of art-making forms (see Chapter 8).

Figure 9.02 Student Pauline Peters chose to hang these pieces together in her exhibition (shown in Figure 9.01). The individual artworks are clearly related in form and process (sewing, paper, fabric) and are linked conceptually as well (exploring vulnerability and social injustice).

ACTIVITY 9.2: GRADE ANOTHER ARTIST'S SHOW

Visit a gallery with a solo show and assess the artist's work against the exhibition assessment criteria. In your visual journal, write a written justification for the marks you gave and add photos or sketches to support your assessment. Then discuss with your peers what marks you gave this artist and why.

A	Coherent body of work	9 marks
B	Technical competence	9 marks
C	Conceptual qualities	9 marks
D	Curatorial practice	3 marks

When I make a show it's like when you arrive at home and you open your fridge at night and there's two potatoes and one sausage and two eggs, and with all that you make something to eat. I try to make something (art) with what is in my 'fridge'. (Christian Boltanski)

9.2 Communicating your intentions: exhibition texts and curatorial rationale

Your artwork for the exhibition is accompanied by written exhibition texts and a curatorial rationale. These written texts form the evidence of your stated artistic intentions, which are considered by the moderator when viewing and marking your work.

When you talk about your intentions for an artwork, you don't necessarily need to provide an emotional or symbolic reasoning for each piece. Your intentions might be communicating abstract, visual or sensory qualities, or making subtle references to other topics or artists. In other words, your work doesn't have to have to shout out 'I have a message!' You can inform your audience as to your intentions but allow the viewer to form their own response.

Figure 9.03: *Selling Out* by student Kamila Salikhbaeva (photograph, 200 × 100 cm). In her accompanying exhibition text, Kamila clarifies her intentions when making this piece: 'The background is a photograph of a wall which was taken by me on the streets of Tashkent. I decided to print it out as a banner to create an imitation of a wall with ads, which are common in Uzbekistan. Then I added my own ads that say things like "Trading fortune for dignity. Goods cannot be returned" and "We offer Freedom!" which communicate the idea of "selling out" – of emotions, feelings and human qualities. The ads that I made were based on the Seven Deadly Sins described in the Bible, and on life in Uzbekistan.'

Exhibition texts

For each piece you include in your exhibition you must write a brief exhibition text that states the title, medium, size and a brief explanation of your intentions. This is intended to help the moderator, much like a wall text or a caption at a museum explains the context of the artwork to the viewer. This can be a short paragraph or a few lines, a maximum of 500 characters. Examples are shown in Figures 9.04 and 9.05.

Figure 9.04: ***Exquisite Trees*** **by Heather McReynolds.**

Exhibition text:

Title: *Exquisite Trees* (series)

Medium: Sourced photo collage mounted on foam board pieces.

Size: Variable; each piece is approx. 8 × 8 cm.

Intention: A collage made up of movable pieces that can be reassembled to create different combinations. The title, *Exquisite Trees*, refers to the Surrealist game of 'exquisite corpses', drawings of bodies made up of unmatched parts, often made by many hands. This piece plays with similar notions of disparity, whimsy, and creating new meaning from juxtaposition. (490 characters)

Tip: If you are including found or purchased objects, be sure to state this under 'Medium' in your exhibition text.

Tip: When submitting a series or collective piece, state this in the exhibition text: *Title* (series).

Figure 9.05: Film still from *The Last Supper*, exhibition piece by student Enrico Giori.

Exhibition text:

Title: *The Last Supper* (December 2015)

Medium: Short film, black and white, sound (2:21)

Intention: This short film portrays the revenge of a homemaker on her husband. The film draws upon stylistic aspects of Rosler's 1975 *Semiotics of the Kitchen* and Lady GaGa's music video *Telephone*. The presence of the husband is only suggested, and the woman is stripped of all that makes her unique. The sound is from 1950s public domain movie *D.O.A.* and a personal re-adaptation of 1953 instructional film *Marriage is a Partnership*. (488 characters)

Tip: Where relevant, the exhibition text should contain reference to any artists or other sources that have influenced your artwork.

Tip: Although audio components will not be assessed, if you use sound or music in your work make sure you cite your sources or indicate that you have created it yourself.

Tip: Where you are deliberately appropriating another artist's work as a valid part of your art-making intentions, acknowledge the source of the original image in your exhibition text as well.

ACTIVITY 9.3: READING GALLERY TEXTS

When visiting contemporary exhibitions especially, notice how information about the work provided in the exhibition wall texts, or other written material such as press releases, exhibition catalogues or brochures, influence your experience of the art.

- Do you respond to the work visually first, then read the texts?
- How do the texts contribute to your understanding of the work?
- Do you enjoy it more (or less) when equipped with knowledge?

The curatorial rationale

The curatorial rationale is a written statement that explains and supports your exhibition. Writing the rationale is part of the process of self-reflection and of understanding the relationship between the artist and the viewer when showing your work. (You can read an extract from a student's curatorial rationale in Chapter 5, and another in the case study at the end of this chapter.)

Curatorial rationale: SL and HL requirements

SL students: 400 words max

The curatorial rationale fully justifies the selection of the exhibited works, which are presented and arranged clearly, as appropriate to the student's stated intentions in the space made available to the student.

HL students: 700 words max

The curatorial rationale concisely justifies the selection of the exhibited works, which are presented and arranged clearly, as appropriate to the student's stated intentions. The student provides an appropriate and clearly justified reflection on how they attempted to establish a **relationship between the artworks and the viewer** within the space made available to the student.

More details about these criteria can be found in Chapter 10.

Key objectives for your curatorial rationale

- Explain your choices of artworks and the connections among them.
- Describe the context in which the work was made and the challenges or discoveries you encountered along the way.
- Reflect on how you found solutions to issues in the selection, arrangement and presentation of the works in order to connect the work with the viewer.
- HL students: in addition, reflect on the relationship with the viewer and how meaning is communicated through presentation.

Figure 9.06: *Thinking outside the walls . . .* This series of photographs of eyes by Argentinian artist Laura Vinas is displayed hanging between trees. She wanted the viewer to walk among the eyes and feel 'looked at'. Her desire for the audience to have a specific experience of the work was a determining factor in her presentation. The eyes are those of her fellow artists at I-Park Foundation.

Writing your curatorial rationale

Be clear and direct in your language: don't try to appear clever or dress it up with superlatives and grand claims. Accuracy and honesty will make a much better impression! Describe what you see, refer to physical and material qualities of the work as well as conceptual. Stick to the subject and try not to digress into wider philosophical concepts unless they are clearly relevant to your work.

Although there is not a prescribed format for writing the curatorial rationale, it can be helpful to refer to some guiding questions.

GUIDING QUESTIONS

These questions are specifically aimed at addressing the assessed criteria.

- What are the concepts, issues or ideas you have explored here and how are they linked in your work? What experiences have contributed to the making of this work?
- What materials and techniques have you used and why did you choose them? Do the materials have an impact on the meaning of the work?
- How do you explain your selection and the arrangement of the works within the space that you have available?
- How does the way you have exhibited your work contribute to the meanings you are trying to communicate to an audience?

In addition to the above, HL students should also address:

- How does the way the work is displayed, hung or otherwise presented support the relationship between the works?
- What strategies did you use to create a relationship between the artworks and the viewer?
- How do the arrangement and presentation of artworks contribute to the audience's ability to interpret and understand your intentions?
- How would you like your work to be received/perceived by the viewer?
- Do you have an overall vision for presenting this body of work?

Tip: Check for grammar and spelling mistakes.

ACTIVITY 9.4: CURATORIAL WRITING EXERCISE

You may want to use the sentences below as a starting point for writing your curatorial rationale. Complete them and add more of your own.

In my art-making I am investigating . . .
These concepts are linked through . . .
. . . experiences have contributed to this
I have used . . . materials and . . . techniques because they . . .
My work references the work of . . . in that . . .
I have also been inspired by . . .
I have selected . . . in order to convey . . .

The pieces are related through . . .

I have presented this work . . . with the use of (lighting, display, space) . . . in order to communicate . . .

I have placed this piece . . . to communicate . . . to the audience.

This arrangement contributes to the viewers understanding of the work by . . .

I would like my work to be perceived as . . .

Titling artworks

What's in a name? There are as many approaches to titling works of art as there are artists. Giving a title is an opportunity to communicate something else about the work. A title does not need to describe what the viewer is seeing or disclose the hidden meaning of the work – less can also be more. Titling your work can be fun, but if you find yourself searching too hard, your title can just be a number, as in *Drawing #13* or, as a last resort, *Untitled*.

STUDENT EXAMPLE: VALENTINE EMENS

Figure 9.07: *Porcelain sculpture* by Valentine Emens. Valentine (whose PP you have seen in Chapter 8) debated whether to call this piece *Growth* or simply *Raphael*. She has a good reason for either title, as her exhibition text explains:

'The face sculpted is my 13-year-old brother, Raphael. I had never previously attempted to sculpt something detailed, and wanted to sculpt a face. I was inspired by Greek busts as well as the work of Gian Lorenzo Bernini. Considering Raphael's age, he is leaving boyhood and entering maturity, a phase of much change and emotion. I attempted to convey this feeling through his blank expression, as well as use of a rough texture surrounding the face: representing the act of breaking away from the past.'

SPOTLIGHT ON STUDENT: VALENTINE EMENS

Nationality: French and British
Born: Orléans, France

Main artistic interests:

- the relationship between lighting and mood/atmosphere
- the human face and form
- use of certain media to convey global issues.

Influential artists:

- Lucian Freud
- Frida Kahlo
- John William Waterhouse
- Claude Monet.

ACTIVITY 9.5: BRAINSTORMING TITLES

Chose an artwork you would like to put in your show and make up five different titles that:

- describe what you see
- describe what you can't see
- use an associated word or feeling
- express one thing you would like the viewer to know
- incorporate a random phrase you have heard or read.

Ask your classmates to rate them in order of preference and explain why. Choose your title.

TOK and art: Ideas, images and ownership

Figure 9.08: In 1953 Robert Rauschenberg took a drawing by the already famous Willem de Kooning, and, with the artist's consent, he carefully erased it and gave it a title: *Erased de Kooning Drawing*. This wasn't vandalism, he said, but poetry.

- If Rauschenberg erased his own drawing would it have the same effect?
- Is what is **not** there more important than what **is** there?
- How important is the title in this case?
- What is the viewer's role when looking at this?
- Does not knowing what the drawing looked like make us want to see it more?
- Does our imagining make us an active participant in the artwork?

9.3 Curating your exhibition

The way you show your work contributes to communicating meaning. The decisions you make about presentation contribute to the audience's ability to interpret and understand your intentions. You can even guide the viewers' experience of your work by how you display it. (Chapter 6 looks at different methods of display, the role of the audience, and at how presentation of work impacts meaning.)

Some questions to consider when planning your show:

- Do the works you have selected have a clear relationship between them?
- Have you chosen materials and techniques that are suitable to your ideas and to what you wish to communicate?
- Do the works selected correspond to what you have said in your written curatorial rationale?
- Have you considered the exhibition and display in terms of how the viewer might experience it?
- Have you given attention to the presentation, the placement and progression of the work?

Setting up your show

You are your own curator, responsible not only for the selection of your best work to be exhibited but also for choosing how to present and display it. Curating a show can be very rewarding. Careful planning and attention to detail will help you to create a successful exhibit and to have an enjoyable, stress-free experience.

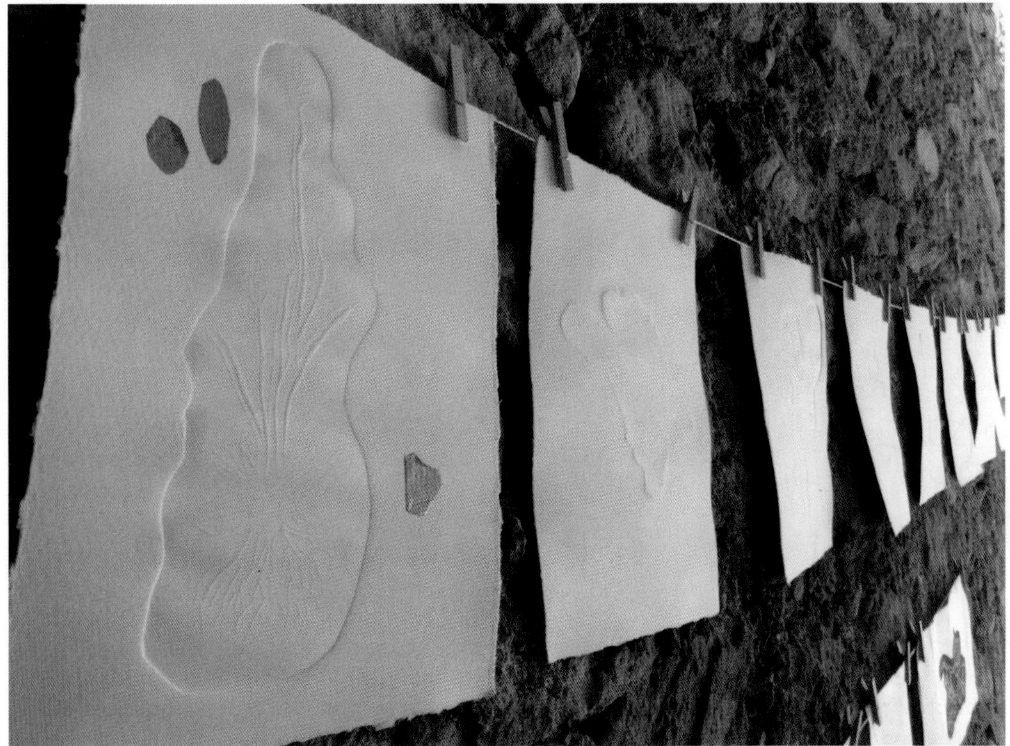

Figure 9.09: Students should consider different solutions to displaying work within a given space, looking for the way most appropriate to the materials and meaning of the work itself. Shown here: embossed prints 'hanging out to dry' at La Vigna Art Studios, Pisa.

Using the space

White cube: A bare, unadorned space that is popular for contemporary art venues. The idea is that without distractions the artwork can command the full attention of the viewer.

Not everyone is fortunate enough to have an empty **white cube** as an exhibition space, especially in schools where space is at a premium. You might have a part of a wall, a corner of a room, a hallway. You will need to work creatively with what you've got.

- Can you use outdoor space too?
- Is working directly on the wall an option?
- What is the best use of the space available?

If you lay all your work out on the floor in the space you are using for the show you can play with sequencing, trying out different solutions until you are satisfied. How you arrange the work and what pieces you place next to each other makes a difference in how the work is perceived, as meaning can be constructed through relationship. Make sure you discuss your reasoning for this in your curatorial rationale!

- How will you sequence the work? By chronology, colour, size, content?
- How does the placement of the work affect its interpretation?

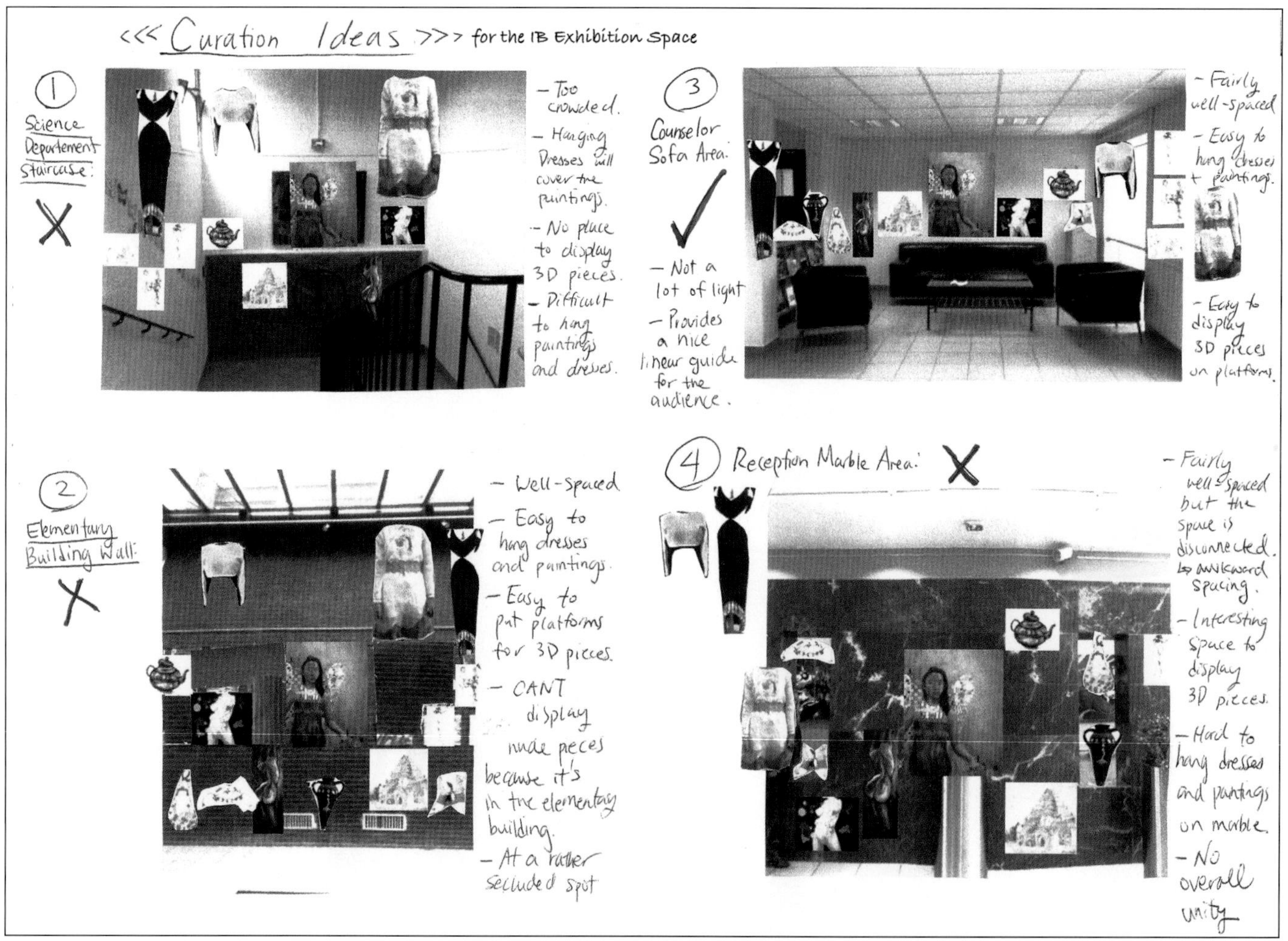

Figure 9.10: Visual journal pages by student Heewon Yun. She looks at four possible exhibition spaces within her school, pasting images of her studio work on photos of the spaces, and lists the pros and cons of each space.

ACTIVITY 9.6: DESIGN YOUR EXHIBITION LAYOUT

In your visual journal, draw your exhibition space or imagined exhibition space from above, working out where each artwork would go.

- Draw a floor plan of the space you have available.
- Try out different placements of artworks, keeping them true to scale.
- Pay careful attention to size and placement of each piece and how they work together.

Tip: Most 2D work does not need a frame, unless the frame is part of the exhibition concept. In fact, framing often places the work firmly in a conventional, old-fashioned context; the work does not photograph well either, due to glare on glass.

Lighting and display

Lighting influences the viewers' experience of the work. Most of the time special lighting is not necessary but in certain instances you might want a specific lighting, such as a darkened space or a spotlight.

Tip: Avoid using superfluous decorations and embellishments; you don't need to strew the floor with flowers **unless** this is part of your installation concept, in which case you will be able to articulate why in your curatorial rationale. Everything displayed in your exhibition should have a clear purpose for being there.

Viewer experience

> Good art should elicit a response of 'Huh? Wow!' as opposed to 'Wow! Huh?'
> (Edward Ruscha)

HL students have the additional challenge of considering the viewers' experience of their show. This means having a sense of how the work will be perceived, and how your presentation contributes to this response.

GUIDING QUESTIONS

- Is there any interactive work that requires viewer participation?
- How do your chosen methods of display, lighting, sequencing, help the work to be seen how you want it to be seen?

You are both the artist creating the work and the curator creating the show.

Figure 9.11: The IB art exhibition is a memorable event in any school community. Although you are curating your own individual show within a larger group show, how your work is shown together in the space will create the experience for the visitors.

ACTIVITY 9.7: VISITOR MAP

Draw a map of how you want the viewer to walk through your exhibition.

- What do you want the viewer to feel when they look at your artwork?
- How can you display, arrange the artwork to help facilitate that feeling (e.g. wow, shock, discovery, careful looking)?

9.4 Documenting your exhibition

Your exhibition is internally assessed by your teacher but you will still need to submit documentation of your work, accompanying texts and curatorial rationale for moderation purposes. (More about the exhibition submission can be found in Chapter 10.)

The quality of your documentation is of utmost importance as this is the only evidence the moderator will see. Take care to photograph your artwork as professionally as possible and make sure the photos accurately reflect the work as shown.

Number of artworks

- SL students: 4–7 artworks
- HL students: 8–11 artworks
- two exhibition overview photos.

Exhibition overview photos (required)

Two photographs that show the overall exhibition are **required** for your exhibition documentation. These photos are not for assessment purposes but to help the moderator better understand the overall layout and viewer experience. Remember that the moderator won't see your actual exhibition.

Figure 9.12: An overview of student Shana Inch's IB DP Visual Arts exhibition. She has curated her exhibition within the space available, with consideration for the viewer's experience. She has used both the wall and the floor to show her photographs, inviting the viewer to walk around the large composite floor piece, which can be viewed from different angles.

Tip: Only include in the overview photos the exhibition artworks that you have submitted for assessment.

Additional supporting photos (optional)

In certain instances you may decide to include up to two additional photographs of each submitted work. These extra photos are not necessary for most studio pieces. The additional photos are intended to provide a sense of scale when showing large works or for pieces that have more than one viewpoint, or to show a detail of a composite piece.

In Figure 9.13, *Gallery of the Subconscious*, an additional supporting photo taken from a different angle is helpful as one viewpoint is not sufficient to take in the whole construction.

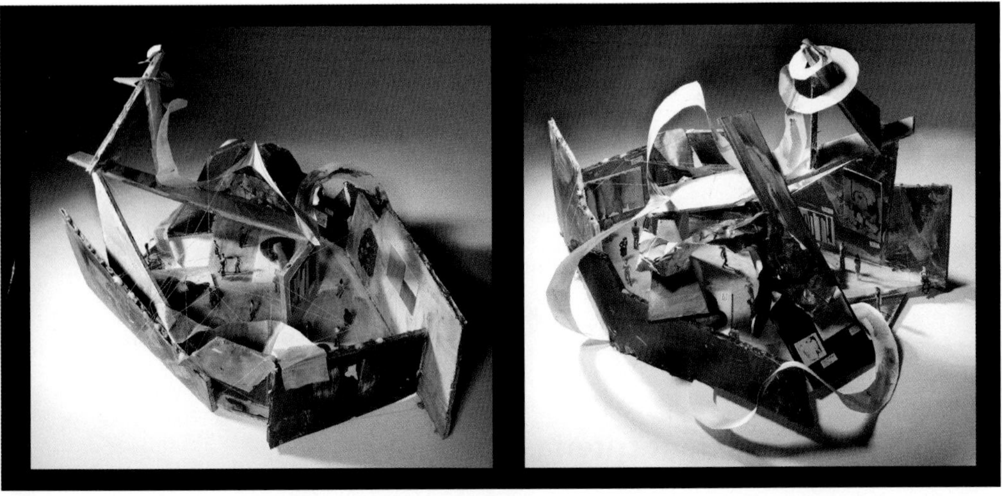

Figure 9.13: *Gallery of the Subconscious* by student So Young Lim: a 3D construction made of wood, acrylic paint, watercolours, string, paper, figurines. The piece (a model of an imaginary art museum) represents a futuristic gallery complete with artwork on the walls, exhibition texts, and of course, the visitors.

Video documentation

You also have the option of submitting a moving image file when this is the most appropriate way to see your artwork. In most cases a good still photo is preferable, but some works will benefit by being documented as a moving image. Video documentation is useful if the art itself is media-based, interactive or involves movement. Keep the documentary footage brief and clear; if possible use natural light and a plain background.

In the case of temporary artworks that are digitally documented, the artwork that you submit for assessment must be consistent with the one that was actually displayed in the exhibition, and the exhibition text should reflect this.

CASE STUDY: GEORGINA HEXTALL

HL student Georgina Hextall's final exhibition was an example of a thoughtfully presented, coherent body of work with clearly articulated intentions. Here we look at several of the artworks from her exhibition and her curatorial rationale, and discuss them with reference to the assessment criteria.

Tip: Take good-quality, sharply focused photos. Blurry photos, background interference or poor lighting will all detract from the viewing of the work.

Tip: Photos should be accurate representations of the work, unaltered except for adjusting exposure and contrast.

Tip: Time-based submissions such as video recordings should not exceed five minutes.

Tip: In your exhibition texts, always label your work to give the format in which it was displayed at your exhibition: for example, live performance is labelled as a performance, a video recording of a performance is labelled as a video.

Figure 9.14: Overview of Georgina Hextall's IB DP Visual Arts exhibition. Georgina has created different viewing solutions within the space allotted: she constructed a black booth in the corner for an installation that required darkness, and placed a laptop inside a beehive on the floor to house a video. The plinth holds a small sculptural object and the rest of the works on paper are arranged sequentially on the wall.

Exhibition assessment criteria at a glance

A	Coherent body of work
B	Technical competence
C	Conceptual qualities
D	Curatorial practice

A: Coherent body of work

Georgina presents a unified and impressively coherent body of work. She explores a thematic content across a wide range of visual approaches. From video installation to beeswax and honey, her selection of media, techniques and imagery is appropriate to her stated intentions.

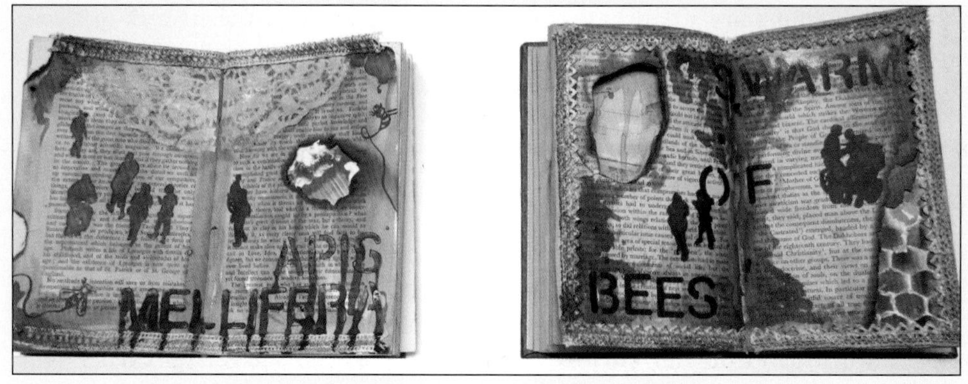

Figure 9.15: Work by student Georgina Hextall. Altered books using beeswax, collage, burning and pigments that feel sticky like honey. The books reference her other work in the show and are displayed on a shelf at eye level, open for consultation.

B: Technical competence

The artworks presented demonstrate an effective level of technical competence. There is manipulation of a range of materials and techniques including drawing, printmaking, **photograms**, collage, graphic design, encaustic, film and sound recordings, some of which are elaborated and refined to a high degree of resolution.

Tip: Working in a range of media is NOT a requirement for the exhibition. You can submit work in a range of media or in only one medium.

Photogram: An image made on light-sensitive paper without a camera. Objects or transparencies are placed on the photosensitive paper in the dark, then exposed to light and processed to fix the image. Where the objects block the light, either partially or fully, a shadow is recorded in reverse (light on dark). Some early artists to use camera-less photography were Henry Fox Talbot, Man Ray (rayographs) and Anna Atkins (cyanotypes).

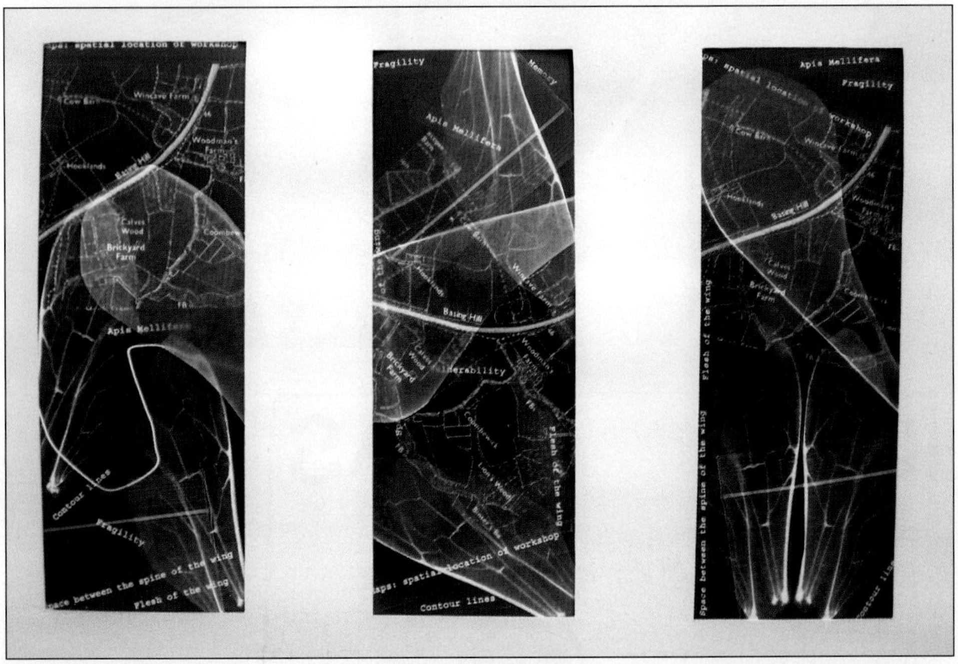

Figure 9.16: Work by student Georgina Hextall. To create this series of photograms, Georgina used maps of the local terrain with text related to the spatial territories of bees. The photograms are made from transparencies of maps, text and photos of wings arranged in overlapping patterns.

C: Conceptual qualities

Georgina has the advantage of an area of focus that clearly fascinates her. She investigates various conceptual qualities across a wide range of sources, exploring cultural and environmental aspects of honeybees as well as her personal experience. She uses sophisticated symbolic imagery, likening the hive to the buzz of the market square in her video piece. In the photograms she investigates flight paths and territories, communicating her stated artistic intentions: to create awareness around the fragility and potential extinction of the honeybee.

Figure 9.17: Georgina's video recording of the market square in Marrakech, embedded deep inside an actual beehive. From a distance the sound of the video is similar to that of a buzzing beehive; it is not until you peer into the hive that you see it is a film of a busy market square full of people.

Figure 9.18: Georgina wants to emphasise the connection between human activity and that of bees. In this visual journal page she brainstorms the logistics of placing her video inside a beehive. The visual arts journal can be used to plan, design and reflect on your exhibition presentation.

D: Curatorial practice

Georgina's written statement (curatorial rationale), shown below, fully justifies the selection of the exhibited works. They are presented and arranged thoughtfully and the relationship among the works selected is evident. Since she is a HL student, she curates her exhibition with attention to and awareness of the viewer's experience. Visitors are engaged in participating actively with some of the work displayed, such as peering into the hive, entering the blackout booth and putting on headphones.

In her rationale, Georgina explains the context of her work, the significant influences on it, and the reasons for her curatorial decisions:

My work in this show centers around the honeybee. The honeybee is a significant contributor to the earth's processes, supplying the world's agricultural systems through pollination, and their global decrease poses grave problems for the planet. I chose this topic because, besides being allergic to bees myself, I'm fascinated by their behaviour and their role in the world's ecosystem. I have explored how different cultures have religious associations with the bee (Egypt and Greece) and compared the gathering of bees and their delicacy to the fragility of society (video piece on Marrakech marketplace).

My initial inspiration arose from my childhood experience of growing up on a farm with swarms of bees, and from my father, an avid beekeeper. I was able to observe the structure of the honeycomb and bee up close, and investigate the significance of bee behavior in pieces such as the waggle dance. My work is also informed and inspired by the artists Francis Alÿs, Tom Phillips, Candy Jernigan, and Graham Sutherland.

The artworks I have selected for this show interpret various aspects of the honeybees' life processes and their significance. Working with the space that I had available, a wall and a corner of a room, I decided to build a booth in the corner with a blackout curtain and create an installation piece that used sound and darkness to heighten the viewer's experience. Entering into the curtained booth the viewer is confronted with a small illuminated square of light on a plinth with a single dead bee. A pair of headphones invites you to listen to the recording of the bees buzzing, in direct contrast to the lifeless bee before you. This private, claustrophobic space allows only one person to experience it at a time; it is my intention to create a sense of the loss of vitality that comes with bee extinction.

A video installation is placed on the floor, inside a beehive. The video is a recording I made of the market square in Marrakech; the sound of the busy square has a buzzing droning quality that resembles a hive. I have embedded the monitor deep inside an actual beehive so that the viewer hears the buzzing sound first and is drawn to look into the hive to see on the screen the human activity of the marketplace.

The other works I selected for the show are mostly two-dimensional works on paper in various media: painting, photography, photograms, and printmaking. Because my intention is to create awareness of concerns around bee extinction, I found that using natural materials from the hive, specifically honey and beeswax, communicates the message most directly. I used beeswax and honey as a medium or mixed with other media in several pieces. Beeswax was an especially exciting medium to work with, because of its smell, its texture and colour, and because of its direct relation to the bees themselves. It is as if I am collaborating with the bees who have provided the raw material for my artworks.

I arranged the works on the wall, paying particular attention to the sequencing to achieve visual balance of colour and size. I choose pieces that are linked by a common colour palette of ochres, browns and yellows, the colours of the honeybee.

My overall vision for presenting this body of work is to create a homage to the beauty and the significance of the honey bee. I hope that the viewer may enjoy the visual and sensual qualities, the golden and amber tones, the scent of beeswax and honey, and at the same time, reflect on the precarious position of the honeybee today.
(615 words)

(Note: Georgina's text was slightly amended to meet the requirements of this book.)

Tip: Examiners are currently instructed not to assess audio components, but when sound is integral to the artwork, students may like to refer to their intentions in the written exhibition text as in figure 9.19.

Figure 9.19: Work by student Georgina Hextall. Inside a darkened booth, Georgina created a simple lighting solution for viewing this piece: a flashlight inside a paper cone shines directly on a dead bee, a pair of tiny headphones (hidden mini iPod) with a recording of a lone buzzing bee invites the viewer to contemplate the threat of extinction for the honeybee in this multi-sensorial experience.

Summary

In this chapter you have seen how to select and present your work in the form of a curated final exhibition and reflected on what a coherent body of work means for you. You have begun to formulate and articulate your intentions for this work (which you will present through the writing of exhibition texts and a curatorial rationale).

You have considered methods of display for your show and how to communicate with the viewer through your presentation and arrangement of your work. You have reviewed the requirements of the exhibition task, including the photographic documentation of your work.

You have seen an example of a student's work that addresses the assessment criteria for the exhibition, and reflects the intentions stated in the student's curatorial rationale.

Chapter 10

The IB DP Visual Arts assessment

Introduction

This chapter provides a general point of reference for the DP Visual Arts course assessment. It includes an overview of the task requirements for the three assessed components: the comparative study (CS), the process portfolio (PP) and the exhibition, along with the assessed criteria and a summary of the assessment objectives. This will help you see the bigger picture of how the assessment components and their individual criteria fit together to form a final grade.

Each of the three assessed components is discussed in greater depth and breadth in individual chapters and supported by activities and examples throughout the book.

Figure 10.01: *Booker T. Washington Legend* by African-American artist William H. Johnson, 1945 (oil painting on plywood), depicting a former slave educating a group of black students. It looks like they are learning about the arts as well as other things. The Obama family borrowed this painting for the White House Art Collection.

10.1 What is assessed?

At the end of the course, you will be assessed on the three components, the CS, the PP, and the exhibition. (Further discussion of each of these can be found in the relevant chapters in this book.) Once you have assembled all your material, and it has been approved by your teacher, you will be instructed to upload the digital files on IBIS, the IB assessment centre.

How is my work assessed?

The assessment objectives for the IB DP Visual Arts address the learning throughout the visual arts course at both standard level (SL) and higher level (HL). They are:

AO1: demonstrate knowledge and understanding of specified content

AO2: demonstrate application and analysis of knowledge and understanding

AO3: demonstrate synthesis and evaluation

AO4: select, use and apply a variety of appropriate skills and techniques.

(The assessment objectives are given in full in the *IB DP Visual Arts Guide*, page 13.)

Each of three components will be viewed by an examiner and marked or moderated against a set of assessment criteria. You will receive an individual mark for each component, the sum of which will then be converted to an overall mark of 1–7. Table 10.1 shows an overview of the three components, the submission requirements and how they fit together to make the final grade.

Table 10.01: IB DP Visual Arts – assessment guide

IB Visual Arts – Assessment Guide

Part 1: Comparative study – 20%				**Part 2: Process portfolio – 40%**				**Part 3: Exhibition – 40%**			
		Max	Can			Max	Can			Max	Can
A	Analysis of formal qualities	**6**		**A**	Skills, techniques and processes	**12**		**A**	Coherent of body works	**9**	
B	Interpretation of function and purpose	**6**		**B**	Critical investigation	**6**		**B**	Technical competence	**9**	
C	Evaluation of cultural significance	**6**		**C**	Communication of ideas and intentions	**6**		**C**	Conceptual qualities, resolution	**9**	
D	Making comparisons and connections	**6**		**D**	Reviewing, refining and reflecting	**6**		**D**	Curatorial practice **(SL/HL different criteria)**	**3**	
E	Presentation and subject specific language	**6**		**E**	Presentation and subject specific language	**4**			**Total**	**30**	
	SL Total	**30**			**Total**	**34**		Important Notes:			
F	HL only - Making connections to own art-making practice	**12**		Important Notes:							
	HL Total	**42**									
	Important Notes:										
	SL/HL - 10–15 screens which examine and compare at least three artworks, objects or artefacts, at least **two** of which need to be by different artists. The works selected for comparison and analysis should come from differing cultural contexts.			**SL students submit 9-18 screens** which show sustained experimentation, exploration, manipulation and refinement of a variety of art-making activities. For SL students the submitted work must be in at least two art-making forms, each from separate columns of the art-making forms table.				**Formal requirements of the task-SL** • SL students submit a curatorial rationale max 400 words • SL students submit 4-7 artworks. • SL students submit exhibition text (stating the title, medium and size of the artwork) for each selected artwork, and a written intention, max 500 characters. SL students submit two photographs of their overall exhibition. There is the possibility of additional supporting photos for each artwork.			
	SL/HL - submit a list of sources used as separate document **HL only - 3–5 screens** which analyse the extent to which their work and practices have been influenced by the art and artists examined. **Submitted as a PDF max 20 MB**			**HL students submit 13-25 screens or pages** which evidence their sustained experimentation, exploration, manipulation and refinement of a variety of art-making activities. For HL students the submitted work must have been created in at least three art-making forms, selected from a minimum of two columns of the art-making forms table. **Submitted as a PDF max 20 MB**				**Formal requirements of the task-HL** • HL students submit a curatorial rationale max 700 words • HL students submit 8-11 artworks. • HL students submit exhibition text (stating the title, medium and size) for each selected artwork and a written intention, max 500 characters. HL students submit two photographs of their overall exhibition. There is the possibility of additional supporting photos for each artwork. **Submitted as separate files.**			
	SL $\frac{\quad}{30}$ x20 = % or *HL* $\frac{\quad}{42}$ x20 = %			$\frac{\quad}{34}$ x40 = %				$\frac{\quad}{30}$ x40 = %			
Part 1 % + Part 2 %+ Part 3 %= /100%											

10.2 Part 1: The comparative study – external assessment (SL and HL)

The CS is an external assessment task in which you analyse and compare artworks from different cultural contexts. (The content and format of the CS are discussed in Chapter 7, where you will also find interpretation of the assessment criteria and examples of student work.) This component is submitted as a PDF and composed of a determined number of screens for each level. The CS constitutes 20% of the final grade.

Comparative study task requirements

Students at both SL and HL select at least three artworks, objects or artefacts, by at least at least two different artists. For the selected works, students will need to:

- conduct research using a range of sources
- analyse cultural context
- identify formal qualities
- interpret function and purpose
- evaluate material, conceptual and cultural significance
- compare selected pieces referring to above analysis
- present a list of sources as a separate document.

HL students will also need to reflect on the relationship between their own art-making practice and the works studied.

SL	10–15 screens
HL	10–15 screens + 3–5 screens that show the relationship of your work to that of the artists you have chosen for the study.

Comparative study: number of screens

Comparative Study: Movement in Art

Louisiana's exhibition of Olafur Eliasson's *Riverbed* in 2014, Denmark, fascinated me, as the apparently static feature of the imitated Icelandic riverbed inside the white walls of the museum still appeared vigorous. Eliasson managed to create this illusion due two aspects of movement, namely the movement of a small spring and the movement of the audience that walked around in the installation. I was inspired and fascinated by the way Eliasson utilised movement to intensify and empower his art piece. Due to this fascination I will throughout this comparative study focus on how movement can be utilised differently to influence the viewers perception of an artwork and how movement is introduced differently in various art medias, such as installation art, film work, sculpture, and painting. I will also focus on how the movement influences the artwork and how the artwork influences the movement. To examine the use of movement in different medias I will be comparing Olafur Eliasson's exhibition *Riverbed* from 2014, Louisiana Copenhagen, *Your Embodied Garden* from 2013 in Berlin produced by Studio Olafur Eliasson, and Gian Lorenzo Bernini's *David* from 1624 Italy.

The role of movement in these works guided me to work with movement and how the movement influences the artwork and how the movement is being influenced in reverse in my own project *Inside Out*, which deals with the complexity of the internal body and mind, as opposed to the simpliyed physical and mental fascade. The meeting between movement and body that these works display intrigued me to work with the living human body and how that through movement can make an artwork more alive and complex.

Figure 10.02: Introductory screen from her comparative study by HL student Alberte Holmø Bojesens. For her CS Alberte chose to investigate movement through artworks by two artists using very different forms of visual expression: site-specific installation, film and Baroque sculpture.

How is the comparative study assessed?

A. Identification and analysis of formal qualities	6 marks
B. Analysis and understanding of function and purpose	6 marks
C. Analysis and evaluation of cultural significance	6 marks
D. Making comparisons and connections	6 marks
E. Presentation and subject language	6 marks
F. **(HL only)** Making connections to own art-making practice	12 marks

The CS assessment criteria at a glance

There are five assessed criteria for the CS, with the addition of one more criterion for HL (criterion F). These criteria address the areas of learning within this component: critical thinking skills and the ability to analyse, evaluate and compare, and to present information clearly and coherently and using subject-specific language.

Table 10.02: Assessment criteria: comparative study

Criterion	Assessment objective	Task details
A. Analysis of formal qualities	An effective discussion of the formal elements of art	Describe what you see when you look at a work of art, analysing the formal elements of design, line, shape, size, space, colour, texture and value, and discussing the materials and media used.
B. Interpreting function and purpose	An informed and appropriate interpretation of the artworks	Discuss the function for which the artwork was made, as well as the artist's intention, and explore possible interpretations of the work.
C. Evaluation of cultural context	An informed understanding of the artworks within a cultural context	Place the work in context: where and when was it made? What is the background from which this artwork emerged – the cultural, social, political, historical and personal influences that shaped it?
D. Making comparisons and connections	Effective and coherent analytical comparisons between the artworks	Compare and contrast the works you have selected. Make connections between the works by analysing the formal, functional and cultural similarities and differences.
E. Presentation and subject language	Clearly, coherently and consistently communicated information	Make the overall presentation visually engaging and appropriate: design a considered layout with clearly legible writing, make sure your sources are cited and images are referenced correctly with use of accurate subject-specific language throughout.
F. (HL only) Making connections to own art-making practice	An analysis and reflection on how the artworks studied influence or otherwise relate to your own art-making	Make meaningful connections between your work and those of the artists in your study, using clear examples. Analyse and reflect on your own development in relation to the work studied.

(For a breakdown of the mark bands in the CS criteria, see the *IB DP Visual Arts Guide*, pages 40–42.)

10.3 Part 2: The process portfolio – external assessment (SL and HL)

The PP is an external assessment task in which you compile into screens carefully selected materials that give evidence of your development as an artist. (The content and format of the PP are discussed in Chapter 8, where you will also find interpretation of the assessment criteria and examples of student work.) This portfolio is submitted as a PDF composed of a determined number of screens for each level. The PP constitutes 40% of your final mark.

SL	9–18 screens
HL	13–25 screens

Process portfolio: number of screens

Process portfolio task requirements

Standard level

SL students submit 9–18 screens that give evidence of their experimentation, exploration, manipulation and refinement of a variety of art-making activities. The submitted work should address at least **two** art-making forms, from separate columns of the art-making forms table (shown in full in the *IB DP Visual Arts Guide*, page 45).

Higher level

HL students submit 13–25 screens that give evidence of their experimentation, exploration, manipulation and refinement of a variety of art-making activities. The submitted work should address at least **three** art-making forms, from at least **two** columns of the IB art-making forms table (shown in full in the *IB DP Visual Arts Guide*, page 45).

Two-dimensional forms	Three–dimensional forms	Lens-based, electronic and screen-based forms
• drawing • painting • printmaking • graphics	• sculpture • designed objects • site specific / ephemeral • textiles	• time-based and sequential art • lens media • Lens-less photography • digital/screen based

(You will find examples of a range of art-making forms in Chapter 4.)

Figure 10.03: PP screen by student Theo Gembler, reflecting on the development and design of a character for a digital artwork. The PP documents the development of your skills and your ideas throughout the visual arts course.

How is the process portfolio assessed?

A	Skills, techniques and processes	12 marks
B	Critical investigation	6 marks
C	Communication of ideas and intentions	6 marks
D	Reviewing, refining and reflecting	6 marks
E	Presentation and subject-specific language	4 marks

The PP assessment criteria at a glance

There are five assessed criteria for the PP. The criteria address the areas of learning within this component: technical accomplishment, understanding and use of materials, the development of ideas and processes through visual and written exploration and reflection.

Table 10.03: Assessment criteria: process portfolio

Criterion	Assessment objective	Task details
A. Skills, techniques and processes	Sustained experimentation and manipulation of a range of art-making skills.	Demonstrate sustained and skilful experimentation with a range of techniques and processes, selecting materials appropriately, meeting the requirements of the art-making forms table.
B. Critical investigation	In-depth critical investigation of artworks with insight and awareness	Demonstrate critical investigation of artists, artworks and art forms, making connections and observations about how these impact your own developing art practice.
C. Communication of ideas and intentions	Articulation of ideas and intentions around art-making and the development of skills and concepts.	Clearly show how your ideas are formed and how you make independent choices about media and techniques that support your intentions. This can be communicated in both visual and written form.
D. Reviewing, refining and reflecting	Effective review and refinement of ideas and art-making skills	Demonstrate the ability to review and refine your ideas, and to reflect on your skills, techniques and processes and your own development on the whole as an artist.
E. Presentation and subject-specific language	Clearly, coherently and consistently communicated information	Present your portfolio in a visually engaging manner, with clear, legible and coherent content. Subject-specific language should be used appropriately throughout and all sources and images should be cited.

(For a breakdown of the mark bands in the PP criteria, see the *IB DP Visual Arts Guide*, pages 46–48.)

10.4 Part 3: The exhibition – internal assessment (SL and HL)

The exhibition is an internal assessment task in which you present a selection of your strongest work in the form of an exhibition, supported by a written rationale and exhibition texts. (The content and requirements of the exhibition and the curatorial rationale are discussed in Chapter 9, where you will also find interpretation of the assessment criteria and examples of student work.) This component is submitted as individual image files with supporting text (as detailed in Chapter 9). The exhibition constitutes 40% of your final mark.

Exhibition task requirements

Both SL and HL students select and present their own original, resolved artworks accompanied by exhibition texts and a written curatorial rationale that supports their curatorial decisions. The requirements are as follows:

- SL students: 4–7 artworks
- HL students: 8–11 artworks
- exhibition texts for each piece
- two exhibition overview photos (mandatory)
- additional supporting photos (optional)
- a written curatorial rationale.

SL	4–7 artworks from your exhibition	written curatorial rationale (400 words max)
HL	8–11 artworks from your exhibition	written curatorial rationale (700 words max)

The exhibition: number of works required

Curatorial rationale: SL and HL requirements

SL: 400 words max

The curatorial rationale fully justifies the selection of the exhibited works, which are presented and arranged clearly, as appropriate to the student's stated intentions in the space made available to the student.

HL: 700 words max

The curatorial rationale concisely justifies the selection of the exhibited works, which are presented and arranged clearly, as appropriate to the student's stated intentions. The student provides an appropriate and clearly justified reflection on how they attempted to establish a **relationship between the artworks and the viewer** within the space made available to the student.

Figure 10.04: HL student Eloise Leibnitz-Armstrong's final exhibition. Curating your final show is one of the highlights of your IB art experience and a chance to show your work to a wider audience.

How is the exhibition assessed?

A	Coherent body of works	9 marks
B	Technical competence	9 marks
C	Conceptual qualities	9 marks
D	Curatorial practice	3 marks

The exhibition assessment criteria at a glance

There are four assessed criteria for the exhibition. The criteria differ for SL and HL in the number of artworks submitted and for criterion D, curatorial practice. (This is further discussed in Chapters 8 and 9.)

The criteria address the areas of learning within this component: selecting and presenting a coherent collection of artworks that show technical competence, understanding of conceptual qualities and intentions, presented to an audience in the form of an exhibition, supported and justified by the curatorial rationale.

Table 10.04: Assessment criteria: exhibition

Criteria	Assessment objective	Task details
A. Coherent body of works	A coherent collection of works which fulfil stated artistic intentions and communicate clear thematic or stylistic relationships across individual pieces	Present a selection of art works with a coherent relationship between them; this might be through exploration of visual qualities or through exploration of ideas and concepts.
B. Technical competence	Application, manipulation and refinement of skills to reach the highest level of technical competency with the selected materials in the chosen media	Present work that shows a skilful manipulation of techniques and media. Less-successful work can be included in the PP.
C. Conceptual qualities	Imagery, signs and symbols that have been successfully resolved to realise the function, meaning and purpose of the art works, as appropriate to stated intentions	Present work that shows an effective elaboration of ideas and concepts, further supported and explained in the curatorial rationale.
D. Curatorial practice (SL ONLY)	A successful selection and exhibition of a group of artworks within a designated space, as appropriate to stated intentions	Justify the selection of the exhibited works in the curatorial rationale. Describe the context in which the work was made; explain your choices of artworks and the connections among them; reflect on how you arrange and present your work.
E. Curatorial practice (HL ONLY)	A successful selection and exhibition of a group of artworks within a designated space, as appropriate to stated intentions. **Reflection on how the exhibition conveys an understanding of the relationship between the artworks and the viewer**	Justify the selection of the exhibited works in the curatorial rationale. Describe the context in which the work was made; explain your choices of artworks and the connections among them; reflect on how you arrange and present your work. **Include a reflection on the relationship with the viewer and how you affect meaning through the way the work is presented.**

(For a breakdown of the mark bands in the exhibition criteria, see the *IB DP Visual Arts Guide*, pages 56–58.) Your final exhibition presentation including images and text will be assessed against the above criteria by your teacher and moderated by an external moderator. It is important that the digital presentation of your exhibition reflects the actual exhibition as closely as possible.

10.5 The extended essay in visual arts

All Diploma Programme students are required to write an essay (maximum 4000 words) on a topic of their choice, chosen from the list of approved DP subjects. This piece of writing is intended to help you learn research and writing skills and encourage intellectual inquiry into an area of special interest to you. For most students, the extended essay is the first experience with a major formal piece of structured writing, and as such it is an invaluable educational experience.

If you have a strong interest in visual arts this could be an appealing subject area for an in-depth research paper. Visual arts topics include fine art, design, architecture, and contemporary forms of visual culture.

Your choice of a research topic might be inspired by your own experiences: an exhibition you have visited, or your interest in a particular artist, style, period or theme. Whenever possible try to engage with primary sources, such as contact with artists and curators, and to see the work you are writing about yourself.

You are encouraged to explore this particular topic or question in visual arts in an independent, imaginative and critical way, with appropriate visuals, and well-documented research.

Choosing a strong research question is fundamental in determining the success of your extended essay. What makes a good research question?

- It is clearly focused.
- It addresses a topic that is genuinely interesting to you.
- It takes an original angle or point of view.
- It provides ample opportunity for research.

If you have a topic that interests you but that is too general or broad in scope, try to narrow it down to a particular aspect or issue that can then become a guiding question for your research:

General topic	Research question
Andy Warhol's pop art	How was Andy Warhol's factory a model for contemporary art production?
Rembrandt's portraits	How did Rembrandt's view of himself change over his lifetime, as demonstrated in five self-portraits between 1628 and 1969?

The extended essay, if you choose to write on a visual arts topic, will enrich your understanding and knowledge of a particular area of interest to you within the visual arts, and may even inform your own art-making practice. Please note that the same piece of work cannot be submitted to meet the requirements of both an assessed component and the extended essay.

Academic honesty

Academic honesty promotes personal integrity and respect for others. You should submit only authentic work, acknowledging the ideas and work of others wherever relevant. Whenever another person's work, ideas or images have influenced your work, include a reference to the source using the referencing style preferred by your school. Specific guidelines regarding academic honesty for each of the components are discussed in the relevant chapters.

Summary

You should now have a clear idea of how your work is assessed, what you must submit for assessment, and the marking criteria for each of the components. Your final grade in IB DP Visual Arts will depend on the sum of the marks for each component.

Your final assessment is the last step of your IB DP Visual Arts journey, but only the beginning of what is hopefully a lifetime of looking at, making and enjoying art!

This is your world. Shape it or someone else will. (Gary Lew)

Figure 10.05: Artist Patrick Jacobs constructs dioramas of miniature worlds that are viewed in exquisite detail through a convex magnifying lens.

Glossary

Annotation: An explanatory note or comment added to a drawing or diagram.

Appropriation: Intentional borrowing. Appropriation in art and art history refers to the practice of artists taking a pre-existing image from another context – art history, advertising, the media, and creating a new image or object by combining or transforming the original.

Artefact: An object intentionally made by human hands, typically of cultural or historical interest.

Assemblage: Three-dimensional collage work produced by the incorporation of everyday objects into the composition.

Avant-garde: This French phrase (literally 'front guard') describes art that puts forward new and innovative ideas, and is generally used in reference to early 20th-century modern art.

Bird's-eye view: An overview, or a general view from above, as seen by a bird.

Body of work: A collection of coherent, unified and related artworks.

***Chiaroscuro*:** From the Italian words for 'light' and 'dark', this term is used to describe the variations in light and shade on an artwork.

Coherence: The quality of forming a unified and consistent whole. (For your final exhibition this means that the artworks are relevant and work together as a unified body of work.)

Coherent and connected: Coherence and connection refer to a sense of continuity and connection among the works. The pieces demonstrate clear connections and work well together to create a unified body of work.

Collage: Collage comes from the French word *coller*, to glue. A collage may include all sorts of paper and other materials, newspaper clippings, coloured or hand-made papers, portions of other artwork or texts, photographs and other found objects, all glued to a support.

Composition: Composition in art refers to the arrangement of visual elements (shapes, lines, colours, forms) and their relationship to each other

Conceptual: Conceptual qualities in art refer to the idea or concept behind the work rather than the actual product.

Constructivism: An art style and movement that originated in Russia in the 1920s and has influenced many aspects of modern architecture and design.

Contemporary art: Work being produced by artists living today or in our times.

Context: The circumstances that surround an event or an idea and help it to be understood.

Cross-hatching: Shading forms by using overlapping parallel lines.

Cubism: Style of modern art in which an object or person is shown as a set of geometric shapes and as it seen from many different angle at the same time.

Curate: From the Latin *curare*, meaning 'take care of'. Curatorial practice is to oversee and care for a collection.

Dada: A 20th-century movement in art and literature based on irrationality and the upending of traditional artistic values.

Diptych: A painting or drawing in two parts, usually the same size. It may be one divided image or two closely related images.

Discerning eye: To discern is to exercise good judgement and understanding, to be discriminating.

Drawing surface: This refers to the paper or any other support – for example, wood, cardboard, a tablet, a wall – on which a drawing is made.

Embossing: A raised pattern or design created by pressure without any ink.

Ephemeral: Existing only for a short time, impermanent, transient.

Ex-voto: An offering given in order to fulfill a vow or to give thanks for a blessing.

Fine art: Drawings, paintings and sculptures that are admired for their beauty and have no practical use.

Formal elements of art: The 'formal' qualities or elements of art do not mean that it is fancy, elegant or conventional. 'Formal' refers to the form, as in the formal elements, such as line, shape, colour, space, size, texture, value, pattern . . .

Found objects: Objects or artefacts not originally intended as art, found and considered to have aesthetic value. Also referred to as *objets trouvés* (French).

Frottage: The technique or process of taking a rubbing from an uneven surface to form the basis of a work of art.

Genre: A category or artistic style that involves a set of characteristics.

Hybrid: A hybrid artwork is made up of elements from different origins, crossing boundaries between art and science, art and social research and so on.

Informed response: In the context of the IB, this is your own individual response to artworks you see, informed by knowledge and experience.

Intaglio print: A print made from ink forced into the recessed lines of a block or plate, like etching or engraving. This technique requires a press.

Linoleum print: A relief print carved into linoleum.

Mark-making: Marks are used to create an image but mark-making can also be explored for its expressive value. The quality of the mark depends on many factors: the tool used, the medium and the surface, as well as the hand making the mark.

Methods of display: How an artwork is put on view, placed, hung, lit, arranged and presented to the viewer.

Modern art: Art from about 1880 (Impressionism) through to the 1970s.

Monotype: A monotype is painted directly on a piece of glass or plastic and printed onto paper. It is usually a one-of-a-kind print, although you can make variations.

Photogram: An image made on light-sensitive paper without a camera. Objects or transparencies are placed on the photosensitive paper in the dark, then exposed to light and processed to fix the image. Where the objects block the light, either partially or fully, a shadow is recorded in reverse (light on dark). Some early artists to use camera-less photography were Henry Fox Talbot, Man Ray (rayographs) and Anna Atkins (cyanotypes).

Plinth: A rectangular block or slab, usually stone, serving as a base for a sculpture.

Pop art: Pop art was an art movement of the 1950s and 1960s in Britain and America. The artists of the pop art movement drew their imagery from popular culture, mass media, advertising and consumerism, often with an ironic or critical undertone.

Portraiture: The art of making a portrait or artistic representation of a person.

Primary source: In the context of art, a primary source is an original document, creative work, artefact or relic, not interpreted by a third party. When you interview an artist or visit an exhibition or studio and experience the work directly, this is considered a primary source.

Ready-made: A 'ready-made' is a commonplace object or combination of objects selected and presented as an artwork. Marcel Duchamp created the first ready-made (*Bicycle Wheel*, 1913) by mounting a bike wheel on a stool. Duchamp and members of the Dada movement challenged the conventional notions of what is art and influenced much of the art that followed – including pop art, which took its subject matter from everyday objects of pop culture, and conceptual art, which values the artist's idea over the actual product.

Relief print: A print which is made from the raised portions of a carved block, like a rubber stamp.

Renaissance: The period of growth of interest and activity in the areas of art, literature and ideas in Europe during the 15th and 16th centuries.

Resolved work: An art piece that has reached a stage of completion where no further changes are necessary.

Scale: Scale and proportion in art are concerned with size. Scale generally refers to the size of an artwork in relation to the world around it (miniature, small scale, full scale (life-size) or large scale).

Sculpture: Three-dimensional art form where objects that represent a person, idea or thing are formed out of material(s) such as clay, stone, wood, metal, metal, styrofoam.

***Sfumato* (Italian):** Shading forms by using subtle and soft gradation of tone.

***Sgraffito*:** A form of wall decoration in which a surface layer of paint is scratched into to reveal the colour beneath. The wall is prepared with lime plaster using the same materials and techniques as fresco painting.

Site-specific art: A work of art designed for a specific location that has a meaningful relationship with that place.

Still life: A still life is an arrangement of inanimate objects.

Thumbnail sketch: A small, rough sketch that records only the essential information. Making thumbnail sketches is a good way of working out ideas and trying compositional variations.

Tokenistic: Doing something only to show that you are following rules or doing what is expected or seen to be fair, and not because you really believe it is the right thing to do

Tonal values: This refers to the degree of light or dark on a grey scale (from white to black).

White cube: A bare, unadorned space that is popular for contemporary art venues. The idea is that without distractions the artwork can command the full attention of the viewer.

YBA: The Young British Artists were a group of art students who graduated from Goldsmiths, University of London, in the late 1980s and became influential in shaping an entrepreneurial approach to art marketing and branding in the 1990s. (Notorious YBAs include Damien Hirst, whose work showed dead animals preserved in formaldehyde, and Tracey Emin, who presented her own unmade bed in an artwork.)

Index

本书凡涉及Hong Kong, Taiwan, Macau (Macao), Tibet等地区的表述应为：Hong Kong, China; Taiwan, China; Macau (Macao), China; Tibet, China。

Index

Index

Index

Acknowledgements

The authors and publishers acknowledge the following sources of copyright material and are grateful for the permissions granted. While every effort has been made, it has not always been possible to identify the sources of all the material used, or to trace all copyright holders. If any omissions are brought to our notice, we will be happy to include the appropriate acknowledgements on reprinting.

Cover image: Günay Mutlu/E+/Getty Images

Fig 1.2 Bronze, c. 1960-1, Johns, Jasper (b.1930) / © Jasper Johns / VAGA, New York / Mayor Gallery, London, UK / Bridgeman Images / DACS, London 2016; Fig 1.3 Bullshead 1942, Pablo Picasso © Succession Picasso / Granger Historical Picture Archve / Alamy / DACS, London 2016; Fig 1.6 The Betrayal of Images: 'Ceci n'est pas une pipe', 1929 (oil on canvas), Magritte, Rene (1898-1967) / Los Angeles County Museum of Art, CA, USA / Bridgeman Images / © ADAGP, Paris and DACS, London 2016; Fig 1.8 Still Life (oil on canvas) (detail of 209896), Zurbaran, Francisco de (1598-1664) / Norton Simon Collection, Pasadena, CA, USA / Bridgeman Images; Fig 1.9 Oppenheim, Meret (1913-1985): Object (Le dejeuner en fourrure), 1936, New York, Museum of Modern Art (MoMA). Fur-covered cup, saucer and spoon; cup 4 3/8' (10.9cm) diameter: saucer 9 3/8' (23.7 cm) diameter; spoon, 8' (20.2 cam) long; overall height 2 7/8' (7.3 cm). Purchase, Acc. n.: 130.1946. a-c.© 2016. Digital image, The Museum of Modern Art, New York/Scala, Florence / DACS, London 2016; Fig 1.10 'There's some wonderful things in the world' by Maurice Citron, cable drum and exercise balls, 1.25 x 1.25 x 2.25m.; Fig 1.11 Miro', Joan (1893-1083): The Beautiful Bird Revealing the Unknown to a Pair of Lovers, 1941. © Successió Miró New York, Museum of Modern Art (MoMA). Gouache and oil wash on paper, 18 x 15' (45.7 x 38.1 cm). Acquired through the Lillie P. Bliss Bequest. 1945© 2016. Digital image, The Museum of Modern Art, New York/Scala, Florence / DACS, London; Fig 1.13 Cadavre exquis (Exquisite Corpse) by André Breton, Jacqueline Lamba, Yves Tanguy / © ADAGP, Paris / ARS, NY and DACS, London 2015 Bequeathed by Gabrielle Keiller 1995 / National Gallery of Scotland; Fig 1.14 © Susan Hiller; Courtesy Lisson Gallery; Fig 2.2 Londono, Jose Antonio Suarez (b.1955): Sketchbook: From January 1 to December 31, 2008. New York, Museum of Modern Art (MoMA). Mixed media, 81/4 x 2". Latin American and Caribbean Fund. Acc no: 1155.2009 © 2016 Digital image Mies van der Rohe/Gift of the Arch./MoMA/Scala Florence; Fig 2.3 © Banco de México Diego Rivera Frida Kahlo Museums Trust, Mexico, D.F. Kahlo, Frida (1907-1954): LAS DOS FRIDAS/THE TWO FRIDAS. Page 79 from the Frida Kahlo diaries, 1944-1954. Mexico City, Frida Kahlo Museum. © 2016 Photo Shalkwijk/Art Resource/Scala, Florence / DACS, London 2016; Fig 3.2 Dinodia Photos / Getty Images; Fig 3.3 Print Collector / Getty Images; Fig 3.4 Maliheh Afnan, 'Veiled threats', ink on paper overlaid with gauze, 2006 © / The Trustees of the British Museum, all rights reserved, and used with permission from Lawrie Shabibi and Rose Issa; Dynamism of a Dog on a Lead, 1912, Balla, Giacomo (1871-1958) / Albright Knox Art Gallery, Buffalo, New York, USA / Bridgeman Images / DACS, London 2016 Fig 3.5 The Art Archive / Alamy; Fig 3.7 © Malekeh Nayiny; Fig 3.9 © Luigi Ghirri/Aperture Foundation; Fig 3.10 Where Do We Come From? Where Are We? Where Are We Going? 1897, (left side detail) (oil on canvas) (see 207297, 207299), Gauguin, Paul (1848-1903) / Museum of Fine Arts, Boston, Massachusetts, USA / Tompkins Collection / Bridgeman Images; Fig 3.13 Invisible Ink, 1947 (collage), Schwitters, Kurt (1887-1948) / Private Collection / Bridgeman Images / DACS, London 2016; Fig 3.14 © Victoria and Albert Museum, London; Fig 3.15 Kathy Prendergast City Drawings Series: London, 1997, pencil on paper Image courtesy of the artist and Kerlin Gallery, Dublin; Fig 3.18 Rajiv Chopra / EyeEm / Getty

Images; Fig 3.19 CHRISTO AND JEANNE -CLAUDE: SURROUNDED ISLANDS, BISCAYNE BAY, GREATER MIAMI, FLORIDA 1980-83, COPYRIGHT: WOLFGANG VOLZ / LAIF, CAMERA PRESS; Fig 3.20 Christo, Surrounded Islands, Project for Biscayne Bay, Greater Miami, Florida, collage 1983, ball-point pen, colored pencil, graphite, enamel paint, photograph by Wolfgang Volz, and tape, on paper, 31.8 x 33 (12 1/2 x 13).

National Gallery of Art, Washington, The Dorothy and Herbert Vogel Collection, Gift of Dorothy and Herbert Vogel, Trustees 2001.9.6 © Christo 1983; Fig 3.22 Nimbus d'aspremont by Berndnaut Smilde Courtesy of Berndnaut Smilde and the Ronchini Gallery; Fig 3.23 Memorial to 418 Palestinian Villages whith were Destroyed, Depopulated and Occupied by Israel in 1948, 2001, refugee tent and embroidery thread, 8x10x12 feet, photo: Stefen Rohner, © Emily Jacir Fig 4.2 Detail from Map of an Englishman, 2004 © Grayson Perry, Paragon Press & Victoria Miro, London; Fig 4.25 Imran Qureshi/Corvi Mora Gallery; Fig 5.3 Tiffany Chung UNHCR/ REUTERS Syrian Refugee Crisis- refugees as of 02 Sept 2012: 235,368-IDPs as of Jan 2012: 988,275, 2014 oil and ink on vellum and paper Courtesy of the artist and Tyler Rollins Fine Art; Fig 5.4 The Natural History Museum / Alamy; Fig 5.9 Mark DION Mandrillus Sphinx 2012 wood, glass, plastic, tar, metal, ceramic paper, cork, ribbon and string overall installed dimensions: 69 x 26 1/2 x 50 1/2 inches; 175.3 x 67.3 x 128.3 cm © Mark Dion. Photo courtesy of the artist and Tanya Bonakdar Gallery, New York; Fig 5.10 Les Demoiselles D'Avignon by Pablo Picasso, 1907 / Stan Honda / AFP / Getty Images / © Succession Picasso / DACS, London 2016; Fig 5.14 Cindy Sherman "Untitled (#224)," 1990, Courtesy of the artist and Metro Pictures, New York; Fig 6.2 & Fig 6.3 Thanks to Tim de Christopher; Fig 6.5 Caption: Joseph Cornell, Untitled (Forgotten Game), c. 1949, box construction, 21 1/8 x 15 1/2 x 3 7/8 in., Lindy and Edwin Bergman Joseph Cornell Collection, 1982.1852, The Art Institute of Chicago. Photography © The Art Institute of Chicago / © The Joseph and Robert Cornell Memorial Foundation /VAGA, NY DACS, London 2016; Fig 6.8 Pitt Rivers Museum, University of Oxford, Acc No 1985.52.275; Fig 6.11 Hassan Massoudy - I believe in the religion of love, whatever direction its caravans may take, for love is my religion and my faith. Ibn Arabi 13th c. ink and pigments on paper 75x55cm - 2005 calligraphy © Hassan Massoudy, image courtesy October Gallery, London; Fig 6.14 © Song Dong, courtesy BTAP / Tokyo Gallery; Fig 6.15 © Romare Bearden Foundation / DACS, London / VAGA, New York 2016; Fig 6.16 Photo by George Tatge for Alinari / Alinari Archives, Florence / Alinari via Getty Images; Fig 6.17 Fountain, 1917/64 (ceramic), Duchamp, Marcel (1887-1968) / The Israel Museum, Jerusalem, Israel /Vera & Arturo Schwarz Collection of Dada and Surrealist Art / Bridgeman Images/ © Succession Marcel Duchamp/ADAGP, Paris and DACS, London 2016; Fig 6.18 Popeye, 2009-2011mirror-polished stainless steel with transparent color coating 78 x 51 3/4 x 28 1/2 inches 198.1 x 131.4 x 72.4 cm © Jeff Koons; Fig 6.19 PAINTING / Alamy; Fig 6.20 Details of Renaissance Paintings: Leonardo da Vinci, the Annunciation, 1472, 1984 (silkscreen inks on paper), Warhol, Andy (1928-87) / Private Collection / Bridgeman Images / © 2016 The Andy Warhol Foundation for the Visual Arts, Inc. / Artists Rights Society (ARS), New York and DACS, London 2016; Fig 6.21 Goldfish, 1911, oil on canvas, by Matisse, Henri (1869-1954). Artwork © Succession H. Matisse/ DACS, London 2016. Digital image: Archives Henri Matisse; Fig 6.22 Still life with goldfish and golf ball, 1972 (oil & acrylic on canvas), Lichtenstein, Roy (1923-97) / Private Collection / De Agostini Picture Library / A. Dagli Orti / Bridgeman Images / © Estate of Roy Lichtenstein / DACS London 2016; Fig 7.2 Ian Goodrick / Alamy / DACS,

London 2016; Fig 7.4 © Trustees of the British Museum, all rights reserved; Fig 7.5 Rikki Wemega-Kwawu LIBERTY LIBERTY, 2007; Fig 7.6 Las Meninas or The Family of Philip IV, c.1656 (oil on canvas), Velazquez, Diego Rodriguez de Silva y (1599-1660) / Prado, Madrid, Spain / Bridgeman Images mixed media, used phone cards on canvas, 152 x 152 cm Courtesy ARTCO Gallery, Photograph: Jutta Melchers; Fig 7.13 © Banco de México Diego Rivera Frida Kahlo Museums Trust, Mexico, D.F. / The Artchives / Alamy / DACS, London 2016; Fig 7.17 The Perfect Home II, 2003, translucent nylon, © Do Ho Suh, Courtesy of the Artist and Lehmann Maupin, New York and Hong Kong; Fig 7.18 Giacometti, Alberto (1901-1966): The Palace at 4 a.m., 1932-33. New York, Museum of Modern Art (MoMA). Construction in wood, glass, wire, and string, 25 x 28 1/4 x 15 3/4' (63.5 x 71.8 x 40cm). Purchase. 90.1936 © 2016. Digital image, The Museum of Modern Art, New York / Scala, Florence / © The Estate of Alberto Giacometti (Fondation Giacometti, Paris and ADAGP, Paris), licensed in the UK by ACS and DACS, London 2016; Fig 8.3 © Nicholas Calcott; Fig 8.5 Edward Hopper 'Room in New York', 1932, oil on canvas, 37 x 44 1/2 x 4 inches (93.98 x 113.03 x 10.16 cm), Sheldon Museum of Art, of Nebraska-Lincoln, Anna R. and Frank M. Hall Charitable Trust, H-166.1936. Photo © Sheldon Museum of Art; Fig 8.6 Fiona Hall, 'Tender', 2003-2005 US dollars, wire, vitrines, vinyl lettering, reproduced by permission of Queensland Art Gallery/Roslyn Noxley9 Gallery; Fig. 8.7 'Retrospectre' by Mat Collishaw, courtesy the artist and Blain / Sorthern, and Mat Collishaw interview transcript is used by permission of the artist and Tate; Fig 9.8 Robert Rauschenberg, Erased de Kooning Drawing, 1953 traces of drawing media on paper with label and gilded frame25 1/4 x 21 3/4 x 1/2 in. (64.14 x 55.25 x 1.27 cm) San Francisco Museum of Modern Art, purchased through a gift of Phyllis C. Wattis © Robert Rauschenberg Foundation / Licensed by VAGA, New York, NY photo: Ben Blackwell / DACS, London 2016; Fig 10.1 Johnson, William H (1901-1970): Booker T. Washington Legend, c. 1944-45., Washington DC, Smithsonian American Art Museum. © 2016 Photo Smithsonian American Art Museum/Art Resource/Scala, Florence; Fig 10.5 © 2015 Patrick Jacobs.

Text excerpt from *Surrealist Art: The Lindy and Adwin Bergman Collection at the Art Institute of Chicago*, by Dawn Ades. © 1997 Thames & Hudson Ltd., London. Reprinted by kind permission of Thames & Hudson

The author and publisher would like to thank the following students for their contributions to this book: Sage Dever, Julia Granillo Tostado, Ewa Nizalowska, Polina Zakharova, Eleanor Wells, Daryl Baclig, Anastasia Leonovich, Anabel Poh, Elisabeth Lauer, Enrico Giori, Beverly Chew, Edoardo Modenese, Shinichiro Yoshii, Karen Laanem, James McGoldrick, Mahshad Rezaei, So Young Lim, Ksenia Klimova, Jacob Elias Meyers Jing Long, Markus Karl Friedrich Specht, Alyssa Spaeth, Shihaam Adams Wonhee Lee, Alberte Holmo Bojesens, Meiqi Liu, Garance Courbon, Sara Sashar, Yasmin Baratova, Ida Karaszy, Roberta Shreyer, AnaGrace Rose, Lavinia Fasano, Isobel Glover, Erika Murakawa, Talia Stern, Sari Imai, Daimei Wu, Mila Gajic, Natasha Koh, Alexandra Bourget, Valentine Emens, Pauline Peters, Kamila Salikhbaeva, Hee Won Yun, Shana Inch, Georgina Hextall, Theo Gembler, Eloise Leibnitz-Armstrong

And thanks to the following teachers and schools for their collaboration on this project: Nicola Shears, St Louis School of Milan; Jeff Seaberg and John Smalley, TASIS England; Alistair Boyd, International School of Geneva; James Chedburn, Brian McCrosson, Emma Cooch , International School of Paris; Vladimir Mickovic, United World College in Mostar; John Parnham, Marlborough College; Siwei Fang and Wee Lit Tan,

School of Budapest; Ronald Kleijer, Tashkent International School; Carla Meisel, Collège Alpin Beau Soleil; Susan Applegate, St Edmunds College; Barbara Rexmann, Felix-Klein-Gymnasium Göttingen; Cora Enard, American School of Paris; Jo Tilton, Bonn International School; Stinne Bo Schmidt, Norre Gymnasium; Lorella Veglia, United World College of the Adriatic; Helena Staufenberg, Munich International School; Irene Winkel, Southbank International School; Deborah Ivey and Andrew Gray, International School of Zug and Luzern; Anita Guerra, St Stephen's School, Rome